Through Indian Eyes

COLIN HENFREY

Through Indian Eyes

A JOURNEY AMONG THE INDIAN TRIBES

OF GUIANA

HOLT, RINEHART AND WINSTON

NEW YORK CHICAGO SAN FRANCISCO

Published in Great Britain under the title of
The Gentle People

Library of Congress Catalog Card Number: 65 – 14455

First published in the United States, April, 1965

First Edition

83572 – 0115

Printed in the United States of America

For my mother and father

Acknowledgments

Grateful thanks to R. T. Smith and the Oxford University Press (under the auspices of the Royal Institute of International Affairs) to quote from *British Guiana* and V. S. Naipaul and André Deutsch Limited to quote from *The Middle Passage*; and Laurence Pollinger Limited and the Estate of the late Mrs. Frieda Lawrence to quote from D. H. Lawrence's *The Plumed Serpent*.

Contents

Illustrations

Illustrations

between pages 208 and 209

Blood tests being taken among the Macusi by a member of the Guianese anti-malaria squad

Agricultural training at the Nappi resettlement project in the Northern Rupununi

Macusi children learning English in the new school at Moka-Moka village

Four sets of Indian homes which symbolize the different ways in which their inmates' lives are changing:

1. A traditional round-house

2. The last traditional house being abandoned in a Seventh Adventist Day mission

3. Modernized Indian houses built under missionary influence

4. The ideal Indian home, combining traditional methods with modern standards

'Auntie Bella' Atkinson of the Moruca district, in traditional Catholic head-dress

ACKNOWLEDGMENT

The photograph of Aibilibing was lent by Dr. Audrey Butt of the Pitt-Rivers Museum, Oxford. The rest of the photographs were taken by the author.

MAPS

Author's Note

THE traveller is the world's guest, and this book could not have been written but for the kindness of numerous friends both in England and British Guiana. My thanks are especially due to Sir Ralph Grey, for his advice, and to Mr. Bamford, Mr. Cassou and all the members of the Interior Department for their considerable help. Also to Tom and Pamela Wheating, who provided me with a base camp in Georgetown, and to the many school-teachers in the interior who welcomed me to their villages. Above all I shall remember the help given to me by all the Indians, old friends and new, who fed, housed, guided, entertained and instructed me during my travels.

When I came to rewrite my diaries Mrs. Hemsley, Mrs. Edwards, Mrs. Tettersall, Annabell Scotland and Nikki Gordon helped me with their diligent typing. Graham Nicol, of Hutchinsons, advised and encouraged me throughout. I should like to thank Nicholas Guppy, John Amos, Dr. Audrey Butt and my mother and sister for reading my manuscript, and also my wife, June, for helping me with the proofs.

In describing a current situation, one is bound to be critical at certain points. The views expressed are entirely my own; but my main concern has been with particular attitudes, policies and systems, rather than the individuals concerned in implementing them. Also, the period described is from July to October 1962, when the Interior Department of British Guiana had only just come under the control of a Guianese minister; the Indian situation at the time was mainly the legacy of the phase of British administration which ended in the previous year.

I should perhaps draw the reader's attention to Appendices A and B, which are partly introductory and describe the background history of Guiana and its Indian tribes, and also to Appendix E, which summarizes Guianese politics through late 1964.

Ithaca, N.Y., 1965   C.H.

It is not really even the beginnings
of a nation . . . Yet it is a people. There
is some Indian quality which pervades the
whole . . . Unbroken, eternally resistant, it
was a people that lived without hope,
and without care. Gay even, and laughing with
indifferent carelessness . . .

D. H. LAWRENCE. *The Plumed Serpent*

BRITISH GUIANA

Prelude

Antigua, July 3rd, 1962

Slow clouds adrift on the hills of Antigua, an argument against time. Our flight across the West Indies, destined for Trinidad, Guiana and Venezuela, was delayed by engine trouble. Meanwhile we had been taken to an hotel on the far side of the island. The passengers lounged on a wooden verandah, sapped by the heat of an afternoon that was measured out in rum punches and the murmur of calypso.

Palm trees below us, and a glistening beach that swung back into a broken inlet. The deep, translucent blue of the sea was furrowed by a lone water-skier. Dark blotches of seaweed beneath it and then the shoulder of the hills, enclosing the sun-swept bay. Disconsolate little heaps of baggage dozed in every corner. An unclaimed baby hunted the sunshine that patterned the coconut matting floor. Beside me sat an East Indian[1] woman, a Guianese, with dark brown eyes and a sari of blue silk. Taxi-drivers lay outside, half asleep in the speckled shadow of a scarlet flowered flamboyant-tree. One of the hotel boys was watching me; an imperturbable, timeless expression, peculiar to the West Indies, melting into a lazy grin each time I looked up.

A taxi-driver and a Barbadian had cornered a young Englishman at one of the nearby tables. They were using him as a virgin foil for the old West Indian argument, carried on in endless banter, about the merits of the different islands.

'So is what you going do in this West Indies?' asked the taxi-driver laconically.

---

1. A term used in Guiana to distinguish immigrants from India from the indigenous Amerindians. This second name is a contracted form of 'American Indians', but, for the sake of convenience, I have simply used the term 'Indians', by which most of the Guianese refer to them.

17

'I'm working in sugar,' said the Englishman. His complexion, already mottled by the sun, deepened slightly.

'Listen,' said the taxi-driver, pushing back from his forehead a shapeless combination of straw which served as a hat. 'You see this man sitting here?' He pointed at the Barbadian tourist. 'That is only a kind of a man, 'cause he come from an island they call Barbados. They only got one beach there, and that is one they thief from Antigua when we eyes was shut. You ain't hear about this 'Bados, man?' He pointed down at the limpid blue bay. 'When they want some blue water they got to fetch it from Antigua.'

The Barbadian leant forward, unperturbed. 'Yes,' he said, 'this salty water is all they got in Antigua—just that and a few people who does gaff all day. I ain't see a nice girl yet. But I ain't so surprised about that.' He appealed to the pink-faced Englishman. 'You remember what happen when we come here this morning? This place so small, the pilot can't find it. I hear him say the sea must have swallow it up.'

Suddenly I was jerked out of my dreams, as the stray baby pounced on my shoe-lace with a gurgle of triumph. The clouds were moving out to sea—the sea between us and British Guiana, still eight hundred miles away, on the northern coast of South America.

It was two years since I had left Guiana, after spending twelve months there before going up to Oxford. I had been sent out by Voluntary Service Overseas to encourage community development in a village called Orealla, perched on a hill by the Corentyne River, which forms the boundary with Dutch Guiana. Its inhabitants are Amerindians, the indigenous people of the country. Known in Guiana simply as 'Indians', they are a short, stocky, coffee-coloured race, with straight, dark hair, sensitive faces and Mongolian features. Ethnically they are thought to be an offshoot of the Behring Strait migrations, which also produced the Aztecs and Incas. Passing through North America, they crossed to the Caribbean islands and the coast of South America. The first Europeans to meet them, during the fifteenth and sixteenth centuries, distinguished between the warlike Caribs and the more friendly Arawaks. But despite their different temperaments, they both suffered the same fate. In the islands they were slowly exterminated by the European settlers. A few Caribs still survive in Trinidad and Dominica, while others fled through the Orinoco to join their relatives in Guiana. Another Indian tribe, the Warraus, had already given the country its name, more correctly spelt Guyana, meaning 'Land of Many Waters'. For a while its forest protected them; then the Europeans followed and set up the three colonies of British, Dutch and French Guiana, often known in their early days as

Demerara, Surinam and Cayenne. The Indians' numbers dwindled again. In British Guiana they now amount to some twenty-five thousand people, in a country whose total population is over half a million.[1]

Living scattered throughout the interior, among the forests, creeks and savannas, the Indians are completely detached from the narrow coastal strip where the rest of Guiana's mixed population live. But during the past fifty years their contacts with the coast have increased. Missionaries, traders and cattle-ranchers, and occasional gold and diamond prospectors have started to penetrate their world. Under these new influences their way of life has begun to change from the primitive level of the past. Tradition has almost died. The Indians are now a drifting people, faced with the prospect of being absorbed by the motley society of modern Guiana. This was always inevitable, and yet there was no preparation for it. As the Indians played no part in the mainstream of Guianese affairs, they were virtually ignored. Towards the end of the nineteenth century British officials expressed the view that this minor problem would soon be solved by their extermination. It is only during the past few years that this widespread indifference has changed. A few attempts have now been made to provide for the Indians' future. But the gulf created by the past has prevented any immediate success, and their own baffled feelings are still discredited and, for the greater part, unknown.

I arrived among them late in 1959 with all the well-meaning assumptions of an English eighteen year old. I had been sent to contribute something to the lives of a people who had been described to me as the most backward in Guiana. But within a short time the world I had entered began to reorientate me. For three months I worked with the Arawaks of the Moruca River, in the north-west of Guiana. Then, early in 1960, I moved on to Orealla. Apart from a school-teacher from the coast, I was the only non-Indian there. We worked on a variety of schemes— starting a local council and a boys' club, building houses and a wharf and introducing new crops. I was soon treated as a member of the village. In a world so completely Indian, external values lose their meaning. Eventually I found that my own, a bundle of now remote preconceptions, had drifted away on the lazy-brown waters of the Corentyne.

Sometimes I was still discouraged by the gulf of European status, which history has taught the Indians to regard as privileged. But in the end they grew accustomed to having me work beside them. They lost the feeling that I came 'from outside', and as their spontaneity grew, I realized how

1. Their historical background is more fully discussed in Appendix B.

acute they were. The Western concepts of profit and progress have no real place in their world, where material needs are satisfied simply by hunting, fishing and shifting agriculture. Instead, personal relationships, within the family and the village, are still the engrossing part of their lives. Hence their immediate intuition. A newcomer's motives and character are rapidly assessed, and amongst themselves they are always conscious of each other's feelings. This awareness is so inbred that even the children share it. Somehow they communicate by their very silence.

Yet even at Orealla the old way of life was declining. For over a generation the Indians had been in touch with the coastal society at the mouth of the river, some fifty miles away. Beneath the security of a close-knit community and a traditional way of life, rifts were already appearing; the dollar, calypsoes, rum and bright shirts had all found their way in, along with the distrust which permeates a competitive society. The old songs and dances were dying out, while their animistic beliefs had long since been suppressed by the missionaries. Even their language was almost forgotten in favour of pidgin English. The village consisted of three generations who belonged to different worlds—the old people living as they always had done and the middle-aged caught between them and their children, who were rapidly acquiring all the most superficial aspects of coastal life.

I remember the moment when this first struck me. We were in an Indian house, little more than a leaf roof on four posts, where a birthday party was being held. The setting was typical—a band of home-made violins, banjoes and drums, dancing that promised to last all night, and large jars of paiwari, their traditional cassava drink. For much of the afternoon they had been performing Indian dances which, like most things in their lives, are largely communal and almost indiscriminate of age and sex. Later in the evening the young men took over with their guitars. Preferring the music they hear from the coast, they started to play a calypso. The old man who owned the house lurched up to them, somewhat tipsy. It promised to be a revealing moment, as paiwari releases the shyness which often obscures their real feelings.

He pointed at them indignantly. 'Boy,' he said, 'that is what kind stupidness you fingers got? If you going to play that thing me ain't want all these people here in me house, 'cause they going to dance one-one, each man by heself, and then me must dance alone. Me ain't want no white-man story, no black-man story in me house, me does want we people story, that is Indian story. Play the mari-mari, man.'

The calypso gave way to the tumbling rhythm of the communal

20

mari-mari, an old Indian dance. Then came a précis of their whole situation. The old people danced on, backwards and forwards, arm-in-arm. The younger ones joined in satirically, stamping, jostling and pushing each other. It reflected the death of a world. The old people were dancing proudly, true to a timeless way of life, while their children stamped on its shreds, their feet confused, ashamed to belong to it.

Once I realized what was happening I wondered what I was doing there. My own work was part of a process which I no longer accepted. The Indian is a refugee from his own culture, a displaced person around whom a new house is being built with little regard to his personality; somehow I had got involved in laying the bricks. But the outsider's romantic conception of a primitive way of life can easily prove harmful. Any attempt to seclude the Indians would be unrealistic. My work seemed to be justified by the fact that change was inevitable. The problem is not that the Indians are changing but simply the way in which it is happening. There has been a clash, but no compromise. Their own way of life is dying out, but no real substitute has been offered. The Indian is caught in a vacuum, a semi-citizen of two worlds—one which he no longer respects and another that he barely understands.

Because of the tension which this creates—this sense of disinheritance, without any apparent solution—the Indian withdraws into himself. The visitor's first impression is one of apathy and suspicion. V. S. Naipaul, the West Indian writer, conveys this vividly: 'I had tried hard to feel interest in the Amerindians as a whole but had failed. I couldn't read their faces; I couldn't understand their language, I could never quite gauge at what level communication was possible.'[1] This defensive mask has almost become their identity. Superficially it was common to all the Indians at Orealla. It seems to be caused largely by the way in which people approach them. The first thing they always learn is a sense of shame at their own way of life. The Wai-Wai, for instance, the most remote tribe, are controlled by a small evangelical sect which has even published an Indian's 'confession' of the evil of his own beliefs.[2] A few communities are recovering, through schools and development schemes, but elsewhere their collapse goes on. In the more advanced districts the Indian is not only a soul for the missionary and easy game for the trader; he is also a vote for the politician, who has no scruples about adding to his confusion.

The only people who recognize the Indians' critical situation are a

1. V. S. Naipaul, *The Middle Passage* (see Selected Bibliography).
2. *The Winning of a Wai-Wai Witch Doctor* (published by the Hawkins family through Bible Fellowship Inc., Dallas, Texas).

small minority of the missionaries and officials dealing with them; but even their efforts are hamstrung by poor communications, meagre resources and, above all, the distrust and apathy caused by previous contacts with the coast. A few tribes have been vaguely secluded by a reservation system. But this has retarded rather than protected them, and is likely to be abolished once Guiana is independent. Impressions like those of Naipaul are widespread, and the Indians may receive little sympathy when they finally confront their new situation. They are seen as a race without hope, the lowest class in Guianese society, parasites on its fringe, who can take no part in it. Yet from their own point of view it is the outside world which is either unable or unwilling to provide for them. If only they were known from behind this mask of defeat communication would be easier. They might be recognized as a people who could still have a positive future.

I left Orealla laden with presents after a day and a night of farewell celebrations. The sound of the local band still echoed down the river long after the village had disappeared from sight. Many of the Indians reproached me for leaving and made me promise to return. But although I promised, I had little idea of when it would actually be.

I had heard that their feelings were short-lived, but during the next two years their letters reached me regularly. They still talked quite spontaneously about their everyday concerns. Uncle Charlie would tell me about the new basket he was making, the fish he had caught or an old song he had remembered. Albert wrote to me about his two children, Nelly and Henry, who had spent so much time in my shack at Orealla. 'Captain', the local headman, told me how the village schemes were progressing. One of my closest friends there was Vin, an Indian of my own age, who had helped with the speed-boat which the Government lent me. He also wrote to me about the boys' club and his family. Their letters were a constant reminder of the day to day feeling of life in the village. But I thought it would be unwise to go back, as if searching for something that was over. Then, quite suddenly one spring, during my second year at Oxford, I grew restless again. There was work, of course— but also a promise. And why should I delay keeping it?

Once I had made the decision it seemed quite simple. There were five months before the summer vacation. I immediately wrote off to Guiana for permission to arrange two community projects, one in a coastal village and the other in an Indian settlement. With a group combining people of my own age from both these backgrounds, I hoped to create a meeting-point of a kind which had scarcely existed before. A voluntary scheme with a single objective might give each group a new awareness of the other's character and situation—an awareness which is vitally needed now that their backgrounds are starting to blend. Also it might contribute something to the uneasy relations between the Africans and East Indians, who form the two largest racial groups on the coast.

Ten days later, however, Guiana leapt into the headlines for the first time since the suspension of the constitution in 1953. The road towards Independence had been full of tension for several years. The austerity of Premier Cheddi Jagan's budget was followed by the riots of Friday, February 16th, when the centre of Georgetown was burnt and looted. Racial feelings were running high. After 'Black Friday', as it came to be known, the crisis on the coast offered a new challenge. The potential value of the scheme was heightened, despite its obvious risks; but in view of the lasting tension I was advised to drop my plans.

Although it was too late to argue, I could still go back. I decided to avoid the troubled atmosphere of the coast and return to the Indians, who had not been affected by the disturbances. I had always wanted to see the other tribes and areas, and the later I left it, the more they would change. If possible I would get Vin to come with me. I knew he would be a good travelling companion. In three and a half months we could cover almost every district, by a combination of plane, foot and canoe. Starting with the more remote tribes and moving on to those nearer the coast, I hoped to follow the complete pattern of their haphazard transition.

Even when I had made my plans it was hard to believe that I was returning. But a few days before I left England I had some letters from Orealla. One of them was from Vin. 'We preparing paiwari,' he wrote. At last I knew I was on my way back.

And now, with an Antiguan sunset burning on the rim of the sea, Guiana was just a few hours away, and Orealla a day or two further. Dusk was edging over the bay, and with it a sudden breeze which set the palm trees dancing below us. The afternoon's reverie was over. A voice echoed round the verandah, rousing the huddle of passengers. It was time to board the plane.

I

A Troubled Guiana

A BURST of sunlight piercing the clouds that hung over the coast of Guiana. Its rays were stacked in long, pale sheaves on the heavy green of the forest. Trinidad had slipped away in a veil of grey skies, but now there was only a faint rainbow, suspended beneath the wing of the plane. A moment later the mouth of the huge Essequibo River came in sight, over twenty miles wide, spawning a handful of islands into the mud-brown sea. Two hundred miles to the south, beyond the unbroken carpet of forest, lay the Rupununi savannas, home of the Macusi and Wapisiana Indians. Beyond them, near the Brazilian border, were the Wai-Wai, Guiana's smallest and most remote tribe.

The Indian world was far away from the coastal villages and sugar estates which were passing below us; the trim pattern of cane fields, surrounding the neat staff compounds, each with a cluster of red roofs. Then, as we came down to land, the forest rose up to meet us. Purple, brown, orange and yellow scattered amongst the different tones of green. The cactus-like figures of ité palms and a lone silk-cotton tree, towering over its neighbours. Occasional patches of low scrub and signs of rough cultivation on the banks of the Demerara. Slowly the airport swung into view, a flock of buildings in a wide-flung clearing, scooped out of the forest. We skimmed over the tops of the trees, bounced along the tarmac airstrip and taxied to a halt.

The makeshift airport, Atkinson Field, is a relic of a war-time American base. There was hardly a sign of political tension; instead, the jaunty atmosphere, coloured shirts and expectant faces, of two years ago.

'So you're back again, Mr. Henfrey?' said a genial African[1] official, glancing at my passport.

1. The Guianese of negro descent prefer to be known as Africans. The term 'negro' is unpopular, as it echoes the days of slavery on the sugar estates.

'Yes,' I said, 'for a couple of months.'

'I heard on the radio that you was coming. You must have had labba and creek water.'

He laughed. The Guianese have a saying that anyone who drinks water from the creeks of the interior and eats labba, a forest rodent, is bound to return to their country. I had almost forgotten the official's face. But his greeting was a warm reminder of the friendly Guianese character—one which could still bridge the gulf bred by the politics of the last ten years.

As we sped along the road to Georgetown, still twenty miles away, all its familiar details came back with vivid force—children on their way to school, in blue and white uniforms; cattle asleep in the dust-dry road, the splintered shadows of coconut fronds, and the heavy, sweet scent of molasses drifting over the pale green cane fields. But already the signs of change were conspicuous. 'Vote P.P.P.' was scrawled on a bridge, proclaiming the cause of the People's Progressive Party, led by Dr. Cheddi Jagan, the East Indian Premier of Guiana. The same slogan was repeated by almost every wall and hoarding. At each corner the advertisements for Banks Beer and D'Aguiar's Rum, both manufactured by companies directed by the leader of the mainly Portuguese right wing party, the United Force, had been shattered by an impoverished political hatred.

The honky-tonky rhythm of a steel band, as we turned into the open vista of Georgetown's High Street. A trickle of scarlet flame down the centre, where the flamboyant-trees had bloomed. A thousand images of contrast, with wealth and poverty rubbing shoulders. Transport ranging from donkey-carts to Chevrolets, neither the least abashed by the other, and the Georgetowners from smartly dressed lawyers to the hideously crippled beggars crouching in the shadows. Behind their crabbed, outstretched hands, the placid facade of old wooden buildings, blending the elegant Dutch colonial and squat Victorian styles. Along the clatter of Water Street, with its dark warehouses and Chinese groceries, a milling hucksters' paradise, alive with the haggling of the pedlars whose bare knees line the pavement. Their wares are cried to a heedless world, to a sea of features and complexions which echo a motley past—East Indians, Africans, Chinese and Portuguese, with every degree of mixture. A heavy, sweet scent lingers up and down, its timeless quality drifting across the bustling atmosphere—a blend of sugar, rice and rum, borne along by the chattering crowds. Only two of Guiana's six races are missing from this typical scene—the British, in their offices, and the Indians, away in the forest.

Beyond, in the outlying districts of Albouystown, Ruimveldt and Kitty, the wooden houses huddle closer. They have a wan, dejected air, relieved only by children's laughter. Every corner is a rum shop, a dim grotto lacing the sunlit street with a steady murmur of voices. In front of the city the old sea-wall still rests on Dutch foundations, facing the mudflats, whose stagnant silence is broken by the cry of egrets, wheeling overhead. And then the sea, a low-swooping horizon, dun-brown cut by a splash of white, the sail of a single clipper.

A colourful, easy-natured setting. But its sleepy rhythm barely concealed the tension mounting beneath the surface. Even in Water Street the events of the past few months had left their scars. Two years ago its wealthier section had consisted of smart new stores and office buildings. Now only their charred skeletons and twisted girders remained, as a bitter reminder of Black Friday and a hint of future dangers. The impulsive anger of the mob had taken its toll from the waterfront, on one side, to the High Street, three blocks away, on the other. Even faces had changed. I remembered the crowds at political corners as noisy and volatile; now they were watchful and sullen. The sound of the steel bands was less frequent, and when I heard them, their rhythm had quickened, reaching a higher, apprehensive pitch. The once relaxed strings of the Guianese atmosphere seemed to be tuned to breaking-point.

The next few days confirmed these impressions. Georgetown smouldered with distrust. Everywhere politics were being discussed in anxious undertones. There was a new feeling of insecurity which threatened to destroy any hope of a single national outlook. Guiana's political structure is simple, due to its isolated development; but its internal complexities are endless, sustained by conflicting personalities, day to day events and unlikely rumours which easily sway the minds of a people thrown suddenly into a state of political consciousness. Almost every conversation led to an explanation of the riots. Yet each one attributed them to the malice or misguidance of a different section of the community.

Ten years ago racial feeling scarcely existed. But this situation has changed rapidly. Dr. Jagan's party, the P.P.P.,[1] draws its followers mainly from the East Indian peasantry. As descendants of the indentured labourers who came to work on the sugar estates, most of them live in the country districts. In August 1961, when Guiana acquired internal self-government, the P.P.P. won the elections. Apart from the British Governor's emergency powers, the status of Dr. Jagan's Government is

1. The People's Progressive Party. As the Guianese always refer to all three political parties by their initials, I have done the same throughout.

similar to that of an independent country. The main opposition party, the People's National Congress, led by Mr. Forbes Burnham, depends largely on the Africans, many of whom are in Georgetown. A small third party, the United Force, is supported by the Portuguese and Chinese, who have only recently begun to take part in politics.

The reasons for this pattern are mainly historical,[1] but every crisis emphasizes its dangerous racial nature. The riots had been no exception. The Commission of Enquiry which followed them had produced few conclusive results, apart from Dr. Jagan's being badgered into an admission of Communist sympathies. Although this was later qualified and adapted to 'Marxist Socialism', fear had immediately deepened. Political meetings were being held every night. The crowds on Bourda Green were growing and the speakers' voices had a note of violence. Accusations of racialism were being bandied backwards and forwards. Speculation was still spreading. Did the pattern of the riots, which victimized mainly East Indian stores, suggest that they were a planned attempt to unseat the P.P.P. Government? It was even rumoured that the loss of a bullet which had killed a police officer suggested the complicity of a leading politician. It was hard to develop a clear picture of what had really happened.

The trouble had been sparked off by Dr. Jagan's austerity budget, which embodied his radically left wing ideals. The large companies, most of them British or Portuguese owned, were hard hit by several of its measures. The most controversial of these was a Compulsory Savings Bill, enforcing the purchase of Government bonds by all Guianese whose incomes were above a certain level. This alarmed the lower middle class, which is centred in Georgetown and opposed to the Government. The Public Service, which is mainly African, was already on strike. Unemployment had been mounting and the budget led to demonstrations. In a moment of panic, the police used tear gas, and a child was thought to have been killed. At the same time, a stone was hurled, breaking a shop window. A false rumour and a tiny incident; but in a flash the riots and looting began. Like any Guianese occasion, Black Friday had a touch of comedy. Young men were seen bicycling down the streets with refrigerators on their handlebars, and petticoats fluttering behind them. But the results were out of all proportion to the incidents which provoked them. Although the trouble was confined to Georgetown, some eleven million dollars'[2] worth of damage occurred within a few hours.

1. They are discussed in Appendix A, along with the social, economic and political background of Guiana.
2. The British West Indian dollar is equivalent to 4s. 2d. sterling.

Even those who took part seemed bewildered at what had happened. It was neither planned nor intentionally racial. Under the pressure of circumstances, including British and American policy, Dr. Jagan had adopted radical measures at the least opportune time. His opponents in business and politics had fanned the discontent. Excited by rumour and opportunity, the largely unemployed mob had suddenly turned to violence. For a country as small and poor as Guiana, it meant a setback of several years in terms of unity and economy.

It was disturbing to have returned to a country where old friends were often afraid to talk openly to each other. The world of coastal politics was not the one I had come to see. At the same time, I had once known it well, and, despite their remoteness, the Indians' future lay in coastal hands. Two years before, their problem had simply been one of integration with Guianese society. Now, if integration succeeded, even the Indians would be involved in these new conflicts.

Before leaving Georgetown I went round to see Jimmy Bamford, the Commissioner of the Interior, who was in charge of Indian affairs. For the last twelve years they had been administered by the Interior Department, with the Commissioner at its head. Until recently he was responsible, through the Chief Secretary, to the British Government; but in August 1961 the Department was incorporated in the Guianese Ministry of Home Affairs. This means that the Indian problem has now passed into Guianese hands. Jimmy Bamford is a short, round, jovial figure, a Guianese of English descent, with a roisterous sense of humour. His life-long experience of the Indians had introduced me to my work at Orealla. In two minutes he was the same as ever, telling his endless tales of bush life. He seemed to have almost forgotten that I had been away. Our conversation gradually turned to details of the Indian situation.

'Have there been many changes?' I asked him.

'No, not really,' he said. 'We're still so short of money that there's precious little we can do. Things are much the same as they were when you left.'

'Is anything new being planned?' I asked.

'I believe they've got some high level talks coming off soon,' he said. 'The ministers are going to discuss Indian policy and the development of the interior, but I don't know what will come of it.'

I wondered what the result would be. In the days of British administration, similar reports were drawn up; but most of their better proposals did little more than gather dust in the archives of the Colonial Office. The Indians' decline was too remote to disturb the colonial conscience into more than a few murmurs of sympathy. This is not the fault of local administrators like Jimmy Bamford, who have always been faced with a shortage of funds and personnel. It is due to higher policy, which has hardly looked beyond the coast. The transfer of their problems to the Guianese Government is a critical stage for the Indians. It could lead to effective help; but with the tradition of neglect and the pressure of coastal issues, the policy of the next few years still remains to be settled.

As we chatted on in his heat-laden office, Jimmy reduced my plans to reality. He was pessimistic about my chances of seeing the Wai-Wai. The rainy season had been prolonged, and there was still extensive flooding in the south. The journey to Wai-Wai country would be long and expensive. In any case, he said, it was hardly worthwhile, as the tribe was now under mission discipline, thanks to a small unorthodox sect who had moved in among them some ten years before. Their customs were already changing. There was probably little about them which I would not see elsewhere.

There was another disappointment in store. Vin, with whom I had hoped to travel, was unable to come with me. He was now permanently employed by the Interior Department. But Jimmy had found me a substitute, a young Macusi called Andrew Macdonald, from the cattle-ranching Rupununi savannas. Three-quarters Indian, he had acquired his name from a Scottish grandfather, who settled in the Rupununi and married a Macusi girl. He sounded an exotic mixture of several different worlds. Living near the border, he spoke Brazilian Portuguese, as well as Macusi, Patamona and English. He was said to know all the trails I hoped to follow, from the mountainous Patamona country down to his home in the south.

At last my plans were settled. First, back to Orealla, and then a visit to the Akawaio tribe, in the Pakaraima Mountains. From there I would go to the Patamona, after meeting Andrew in Georgetown; together we would follow the trail down the Brazilian border to the Rupununi. After this there would be the Moruca, near the north-west coast of Guiana, where the Indians had reached a point of development similar to that of Orealla. Here I hoped to see the outcome of the changes which were just beginning amongst the more remote tribes.

Plans rarely survive in Guiana; but at least I had a pattern in mind. The new face of Georgetown had few attractions. I was not sorry to be leaving on the following morning.

I had long since evoked a picture of the day when I would set out for Orealla. A sunlit dawn, an early departure, and with luck on my side I would be in the village by dusk. I felt a trifle injured when I was woken by a furious cloudburst that only the peak of the Guianese rains could have mustered. I peered out into the grey half-light of dawn. The road was awash in a mud-brown swirl still peppered by the storm. The flamboyant-trees bowed and dripped in resignation. I cursed my luck. The weather would be dull, the roads flooded and the river rough and miserable. But a few minutes later Providence smiled. The rain gave way to a watery sun, spilling over the rooftops and plashing on to the road, which steamed contentedly. There was still a chance of reaching the village that evening.

There was just one problem, a trunk to collect. It had arrived two days before, and I was assured that it would be off the boat by seven o'clock, in time for me to catch the morning train. But fortune intervened once more, this time in the form of bureaucracy. There was a slight delay, I was told; I would have to wait until nine. Nine o'clock came and ten was mentioned, and at ten it became eleven. In a fit of spleen I hurried off, bought a shirt and a pair of trousers, borrowed a hammock and abandoned any hope of seeing my trunk in the near future. A camera and a notebook filled the last gap. There was still time to catch the midday train.

The sun soon dispelled my petulance. In its place there was something I had almost forgotten, something only felt when one is setting out alone. It was the mood of sunlit mornings in Mediterranean harbours, as you wait for a boat to the islands; of dawn by South American rivers as the mist begins to clear—a lyrical feeling I had sometimes tried to recapture in Oxford, by donning a pair of moth-eaten sandals that had slipped across the cobbles of a Greek summer. An old yen for a vagabond freedom, now briefly restored.

The little train was puffing impatiently by the time I reached the station. A single ticket to Rosignol, on the banks of the Berbice River; from there another sixty miles by road to Springlands, at the mouth of the Corentyne, where I would now have to spend the night. Porters ambled here and there, weaving their way through the luggage that lay in a heap on the platform. The day to day temperament of the Guianese inspires every moment of their lives with a sense of the dramatic. Their travel is full of departures with an echo of scenes in old war films, when a train is leaving for the front—a similarity reinforced by the hazards which often lie ahead. Passengers were indistinguishable from the people saying goodbye, while their clamour and gesticulations matched the chaos of colour schemes in their West Indian shirts.

An African porter seized my bag and carried it on to the train before I had a chance to protest. I fumbled for a tip, but he shook his head with a smile of rebuke. Fascinated by the colour and banter of the Guianese crowds, I had always travelled on decks and in third class carriages, not often frequented by Europeans. I had never been made conscious of any distinction, except by friendly incidents like this. Perhaps it would have been different ten years ago, when local politics first became anti-British; but I myself had never met with a trace of hostility. It made it seem strange that the Guianese were now embittered amongst themselves.

The rough wooden seats were crammed to every corner. Blue-capped schoolboys monkeyed on the railings round the little open platforms between the carriages. A typical crowd of fellow passengers—young East Indian girls, in their silken dresses and white lace, and their wrinkled, sari-swathed mothers beside them, viewing the world with detachment from eyes darker than hazel-brown, which seem to deepen with age. Africans in threadbare suits and open-necked shirts, and a brown baby squawling in protest at their intrusion on its sleep.

Suddenly the train gave a warning lurch. I imagined that we were off. The platform became a mêlée of human figures who gave the impression that those intending to board the train were being pushed steadily away, while those who wanted to stay behind seemed to have been pulled irrevocably on to it. After a moment, the wooden carriages clattered to a halt. The engine puffed sulkily and shunted back again. Order was rapidly restored. The abandoned passengers jumped on board, and once more the little train pooped and chumbled its way out of the station, past the freshly painted face of Georgetown, which soon gave way to the backyards of the slum quarters.

I found myself in the company of a bizarre political trio—a bearded East Indian called James, hiding behind a large pair of sun-glasses, which lent him an air of mystery as he muttered about Mexico and Cuba, an African, who soon fell asleep after nodding his assent to James's doubtful observations, and a swarthy, good-looking East Indian boy, apparently known to all who passed. James and I were soon talking. The Guianese always treat a foreigner with insatiable curiosity.

'What are you doing in B.G.?' he asked.

'Writing about the Indians,' I told him.

'Yes, I heard about them,' he said. 'I seen one or two in town, but I never spoke to them. We scarcely see them down on the coast. I hear they're nice people—quiet though.'

'Yes, they're quiet,' I replied. 'And what do you do?'

He turned his head slowly to see if anyone was listening. Almost everyone was. He raised his hand in a way that suggested the infinite delicacy of the situation, and winked mysteriously. A moment later he pulled out a cigarette packet, scribbled on it furtively, and passed it to me. 'Pollitical sicurety', it read. I nodded gravely, fulfilling my role in the obviously intended mystery.

'Politics,' he hissed suddenly, repeating the word slowly and rolling it round his tongue, as if to give a varied impression of his alleged occupation. He leant forward and offered me a cigarette. 'And what do you think of the riots?' he asked, in a whisper that echoed up and down the carriage.

A newspaper moved slowly in the far corner, revealing a watchful eye. I lit my cigarette, playing for time.

'A big set-back,' I replied non-committally. 'But I don't think it would have happened if the British Government had given Cheddi better loans. He had to draw up that kind of budget, to get the money he needed.'

He paused, taken aback by my answer. Then he nodded. 'Big business,' he said. 'Big business behind it. They frightened of Cheddi. That's why they call he Communist.'

I nodded. His comments were not unjustified.

'And what about this Independence?' he asked.

'I think it should have come long ago. Then this trouble wouldn't have started.'

'And why we didn't get it?' he said.

'It's not just a political problem—it's an economic one. The British Government just toed the line of big business until a few years ago.'

'Yes,' he hissed, 'big business, capitalists!' He spat conclusively out of the window. Suddenly he slapped me on the knee. He grinned. 'You know what is my hobby?'

A dozen possibilities flitted through my mind. I refrained from suggesting any of them.

'Writing love songs,' he said triumphantly. 'I been in Mexico and Cuba, man, and I meet so many lovely girls that since that time I been a great writer of love songs. At home they does call me Calypso King. You would like to hear one of my songs?'

It seemed safer than politics. I nodded, and he broke into a calypso of indisputable originality, which would have brought a blush even to the cheeks of the girl it described. A ripple of interest ran through the passengers. One or two of them laughed at his bawdy humour, and shouted encouragement as he came to the end. A few of the women looked mildly indignant. His talents were on the point of being publicly debated when another East Indian, neatly dressed, came and sat down

33

beside us. He was older than James, perhaps in his fifties. He looked at me for a moment.

'Sir,' he said, 'do you believe in the Lord God above?'

This threatened to be harder than politics. 'I'm not an atheist,' I replied.

'Man, do you believe the Lord God made we people for singing and lechery?' he asked.

The whole carriage pricked up its ears. James put on a dead-pan expression. I began to feel caught between two fires.

'Not lechery, perhaps,' I said. 'But I'm sure He doesn't mind a song now and then.'

'Calypso,' said James breaking in suddenly. 'The Lord God is very partial to calypso.' He offered me a cigarette.

'Did you know, sir,' said our new companion, 'that the Bible says that smoking is ungodly?'

James pulled out a cigarette-lighter, flicked it casually and held it forward. There was no going back now. I lit my cigarette with an unconcerned air.

'I don't remember the passage,' I said.

'Yes, sir,' he said firmly, 'smoking is the Devil at work in man.' James puffed vigorously, watching the newcomer with an inscrutable air. The counterblast to tobacco went on, supported by a string of quotations of doubtful relevance.

'And may I have your address?' he said, when at last he had finished. I fumbled for a piece of paper. James suddenly came to life, and handed him a biro, and then, still with a dead-pan face, an empty cigarette packet to write on. They exchanged looks.

'The day is nigh,' said the stranger. James blew a defiant smoke ring, as if to declare his intention of smoking before the seat of judgement.

The little train whistled in triumph. The countryside was speeding by at almost twenty miles an hour, amidst a medley of creaks and groans which blended with the sound of laughter and the clamour of boys who passed up and down selling sweet drinks. Outside, the fields of muddy water were speckled with young paddy shoots, which would soon burst into a carpet of whispering green. Here and there a stilted house, standing marooned in the floods. The cattle lumbered about dejectedly, up to their haunches in water. The haphazard network of dams and sluices told of an age-old struggle against sea and rain, carried on for over three centuries, since the days of the first Dutch settlers. A large sum of money had just been spent on an irrigation scheme for a limited number of rice farmers; but, for others, the struggle was still going on, divided alternately between threats of drought and flooding.

Guiana has an ambiguity which is common to most West Indian and South American countries; each of them is a paradise concealing abject poverty. This paradox is expressed in the two radically different schools of literature which the Caribbean has produced. The one, mainly European, is built on the sunset-and-palm-tree theme. The other, essentially West Indian, cries out against this complacent idealism, voicing a human situation and searching for a culture of its own.[1] The country on either side of us, vivid and yet cruel, echoed this ambiguity.

The long, low horizon was broken by an occasional grove of coconut palms, with a few roughly thatched houses crouching beneath them. Far away inland, the dark smoke of a sugar factory drifted slowly across a steel-blue sky. The sheep and cattle raised their heads in wonder at the Berbice train. A flock of yellow and black kiskadees dipped over the water, perching on the stems of the moka-moka reeds which lined the railway. White egrets scrambled and fluttered amongst the vegetation. Dapper little spurwings, pale green and brown, stepped across the water-lilies, picking their way through the pink blooms and rising panic-stricken in front of us. I glimpsed a group of East Indian boys, bathing in the corner of a paddy field. They danced up and down with obscene gestures, while the passengers leant out of the windows, shouting at them with good-natured and equally obscene reproof. Every now and then we ground to a halt at a little wooden station. The school-children tumbled on and off, while women walked by with trays on their heads, laden with mangoes, nuts and bananas, oranges and yellow pawpaw. James had lapsed into silence, allowing me to observe our surroundings in peace; everywhere, colour and cruel beauty, and expressive faces caught between them.

The sun was stooping slightly by the time we reached Rosignol, on the banks of the Berbice. The white roofs of New Amsterdam, Guiana's second largest town, came slowly into sight as the ferry turned across the dark stretch of the river, laced with a patter of rain. James was still with me, chatting on and soliciting my approval for another song, when I felt a hand on my shoulder. I turned round to find Justice, one of the boys from Orealla, standing beside me. Suddenly, out of the blue, the first Indian face I had seen for two years. Short and unusually slight, with high cheekbones and dark watchful eyes, he had been teaching in the primary school when I left the village. He smiled as we shook hands, with his eyes lowered slightly in shyness at my long absence.

'The people been waiting on you,' he said, in a quiet tone of

1. The works of St. John Perse and Aimé Césaire, both poets of the French West Indies, are typical of this contrast.

voice, which was very different from the clamour around us. 'Since a few days back they been making paiwari for the day when you reach Orealla. They say is a long time they didn't see you, and they wondering what happen.' He was silent for a moment. 'We were sad when you gone,' he added.

'Yes, I was sad too. But what are you doing here?' I asked.

'I'm trying for the police force now,' he said. 'I just started my training in Georgetown. Alan is there too.'

So both of them had left the village—Alan had also been teaching at the school. In all Indian settlements within easy reach of the coast, many of the young people are attracted to Georgetown. But few of them settle down there. They soon feel oppressed by the abrupt manners of the coast and the discipline of regular work. Usually they just disappear one day and return to the carefree life they have left. But when they get back to their homes, they are rarely content again. Their brief glimpse of city life destroys their faith in their own traditions. Justice and Alan were two of the brightest of Orealla's young generation. I wondered what would become of them.

Justice was staying in New Amsterdam. We said goodbye on the crowded stelling[1] and I joined a taxi for Springlands. It had an empty, rattling tone, tinny and heat-laden, which every car soon acquires on the pot-holed roads of Guiana. Most of the local taxis run a shuttle service of closely packed human cargoes between the neighbouring villages. We soon had at least ten people aboard. Once or twice a sleepy-eyed policeman raised a protesting hand, only to meet with hoots and jeers and a burst of acceleration from the driver. Every few minutes we stopped to disgorge an inextricable passenger or deliver a string of messages. They reminded me of the family ties, especially among the East Indians, which link all the coastal villages into one long, straggling community.

Once a group of children gathered round, peering into the car. 'Look, a white man inside,' exclaimed a rag-tag and barefoot little East Indian boy, with an angelic face and a mischievous glint in his eye. It was not the first time I had played the rôle of a travelling zoo. They pressed forward for a closer look.

'You got to pay five cents to see me,' I said. I winked at the ragged mischief-maker, producing a wave of imitations and giggles.

'You no worth five cents,' he said, pulling a monkey-like face.

The taxi driver leapt out. 'Hi, boy, where your manners?' he exclaimed,

1. Wharf. All local terms and their origins are explained in the index and glossary on page 280.

as the children scattered to points of safety. 'That man got a big gun in the car. Which one of you boys want he shoot him?'

A chorus of voices. 'Me, me.'

'Shoot me, man,' said the first little boy, pulling another face.

'I got no time to shoot monkey,' I said, removing a flustered chicken from my lap. 'When I come back I going to try.'

They laughed and shouted and waved goodbye as we set off again, weaving our way through the sheep and cattle which lay half asleep in the road. Overhead, the sun slanted down through a sky still hazy in memory of the morning's rain. On our left a moment's glimpse of the surly-brown face of the sea. All along the Guiana coast it is darkened by the silt bellied out by the huge rivers. Beside each village the quilt-work of cane fields reaching green hands to the sky. Coconut palms lining the road, with their slim trunks bowing slightly and stretching back in a criss-cross, abstract pattern. The high-pitched wail of East Indian songs rode over the back of the afternoon, from the home-made combinations of a musical box and deep freeze, which the ice-cream sellers pedalled up and down. The multi-coloured local buses rattled their way past, pursued by a cloud of dust, with doors aflap and passengers clinging on to the sides. Each one had a name of its own painted across its brow— Diamond Queen, Luxury Liner and Calypso Boy—echoes of the comic, improvising genius of the Guianese imagination.

As the afternoon sun faded, the rum shops were coming to life. The jaunty rhythm of calypso stirred the first hint of dusk. Even here, fashions were changing. East Indian women, in their saris and coloured head-cloths, mingled barefoot with the younger people in European dress. Occasionally I heard a snatch of Hindi, still spoken by the older generation, swallowed up in a chatter of pidgin English. Once we stopped by a group of men, lounging at a corner. One of the passengers delivered a message. A brief, hurried conversation, while the others eyed us in silence. Lean faces, with a trace of suspicion, watching non-committally, ready to curse or laugh in a moment—a typical village gathering, passing the evening with casual talk, centred on the rice crop.

In the country districts the subject of rice is always being discussed. During the past few years its cultivation has transformed the lives of many East Indian families. Most of them now have a field of their own, whose annual harvest has a guaranteed market. The stranglehold of the sugar economy, the father of Guianese poverty, was broken by Dr. Jagan's early political campaigns. Until then the unused land on the sugar estates was hardly ever released for private cultivation. This secured King Sugar's monopoly of employment and so enabled wages to be kept down. But now resettlement schemes are under way, providing small-holdings for new rice farmers. The Guianese people are slowly reaping the profits formerly reserved for distant shareholders in the sugar companies. Everywhere there were signs of this change—in the conversation in the taxi, the tractors and combines in the backyards, and the contrast between the old tumbledown hovels and the newly built houses in almost every village.

There were exceptions to this trend. The first time I passed through the coastal villages, I noticed that some stood out from the rest; they still seemed crushed by the poverty of a generation ago. Often flooded and scarcely rebuilt, with few signs of cultivation, most of them belonged to the Africans. The East Indians had gained far more from the changes of the past few years. Their villages were quite different—full of street-corner politics and the new houses and machinery which lent them a tidy, almost prosperous air.

The separatism of the two races is not based on prejudice; their characters are as radically different as their villages. It is here that Guiana's problems lie—in the fact that her people have little in common, apart from having been thrown together by sugar's rapacious demand for cheap labour in the same remote corner of the world. As soon as the Africans' slavery ended, the East Indians took their place as indentured labourers. Their descendants have hardly mixed. In so far as one can generalise, the African tends to be good-natured, with an open, uncalculating charm. He is generous and thinks in day to day terms, and with little inclination to save, he lives as well as his income allows. The East Indian is less easy-going—a born politician, always planning. His standards of living are sacrificed to the purchase of land and his children's careers. Otherwise his income is saved or invested in jewelry. He is ambitious and consistent, while the African is spontaneous and flexible. The one exploits his situation; the other accepts it with a grin.

Perhaps these distinctions are too precise; but they seem to be the starting-point of Guianese politics. History has reinforced them. Most of the Africans live in the towns, with white-collar jobs as their ambition; with little African culture left, they have less solidarity than the East Indians. The latter are still bound together by their ambitious character and peasant background, and the survival of their religion and many of their customs. Ten years ago, the two groups were political allies in the cause of anti-colonialism. But in 1955 the Africans, led by Mr. Forbes Burnham, broke away from the P.P.P. to form the P.N.C. Since then the group-consciousness of the East Indians, along with their increasing numbers, has kept the P.P.P. in power.

The problem of the minority groups has been left behind in the wake of these larger issues. The Portuguese and Chinese, who also came as indentured labourers, keep very much to themselves. They are mainly business men and shopkeepers. Outside Georgetown, they are unobtrusive—a lone face in a darkened rum shop, or the name of Wong Yow over a grocery. It was only in 1961 that they formed their own party, the United Force. For the Indians, hitherto unnoticed by the others, this was an introduction to the whirlpool of coastal politics. Their fatherfigure, Stephen Campbell, the only Indian member of the Legislative Council, joined up with the U.F.; seventy-five per cent of them voted the same way. This is their latest point of contact with Guianese society —another step, perhaps the last, towards the end of their waning independence.

Justice's face had stayed with me, as we passed through the coastal villages. Two hours later we reached Springlands. Familiar shadows crept out of the dusk; the squat silhouette of the administration office, and the dusty little petrol station. Behind it lay the Corentyne River, with the blanket of a starless night slung over its back; then the dark coastline of neighbouring Dutch Guiana.

A greeting at the corner. It was Johnny, a young Guianese of mixed East Indian and Portuguese parentage, whose father owned a shop nearby. He too had just come from Georgetown, where he had been making his final arrangements for taking up a scholarship abroad.

'Where are you going?' I asked.

'Cuba.'

'And what are you going to study?'

'I don't know yet,' he said with a laugh. 'It might be agriculture. There are one or two others going from here. I'm just going to see what it's all about. I want to see something outside B.G. We stay in Cuba for a couple of years and then they send us on to Moscow to have a look around.'

His expectations seemed ingenuous. He was one of many young Guianese who are being sent to Havana and beyond for mainly political purposes. I suspected that his spirit of adventure would soon be reduced to a harsh reality. The Guianese need technical training and a great deal can be learnt from Cuba. But over these opportunities there hangs the price of subjection to big power politics, which, coming either from East or West, are likely to damage Guiana's future.

The dim light of the Indian depôt, where the people from Orealla sling their hammocks when they come down river to shop, struggled through the darkness on the far side of the road. I said goodbye to Johnny and walked across. A pair of figures sitting on the steps—Alan and William, two boys from the village. They greeted me without surprise. They had recognized my voice when I was talking to Johnny. I wondered how much they knew of the world we had been discussing, which had suddenly come so close to their lives. They had just sold a batch of logs, they explained, and come down to buy food and clothes for their families. The light flickered on Alan's copper-brown features. I remembered a faraway dawn when I had brought him down river with suspected tetanus.

'We never believed you coming back,' he said suddenly, with a shy smile.

'And how's Orealla?' I asked.

'Everything just the same,' he replied. 'And the people waiting on you.'

'When are you going back up?' I asked, still uncertain of how I was going to travel.

'We waiting on a boat,' said William.

I promised to try and borrow a speed-boat from one of the local saw-millers; if all was well we would leave together in the morning. We said good-night quietly. The thought of the other world of tomorrow had suddenly grown closer.

2

The Gentle People

I T W A S midday before we finally secured a boat from an East Indian called Debbie, who lived at Crabwood Creek, the last of the coastal villages. I remembered his face, as some of the men from Orealla had worked on his timber grant, some two hundred miles up river, beyond Wanatoba Falls; a barefooted, alert little man, clad in a vest and a ragged pair of shorts, with a crowd of children milling round him. How much should I pay for the boat? I asked him. I would need it for about ten days. I should have known better. He brushed my offer lightly aside, as if I had questioned the unwritten code of the river-man's hospitality. Guianese generosity had become almost a penance. It was another two hours before I had escaped from the rum and jovial company that went with the gasoline which I bought from the filling-station in front of the brightly painted Hindu mosque. Then came a lunch of chicken curry with Basil, an old friend who drove one of the local taxis. I began to see set travelling plans in a light I had long since forgotten.

By the time I had found Alan and William and taken our belongings to Debbie's house, the river was flurried by a strong breeze. A swarm of East Indian boys followed us down to the inlet where the boat was moored. It turned out to be a corial, an Indian canoe, long and slim, designed for an outboard motor. It looked fast. We would take about three hours to reach Orealla. We clamped the outboard motor on to the stern and piled our baggage inside. As we edged our way out, curious little fish, shaped like miniature landing craft, scimpered off the mudflats and plopped into the water. On either side, the mangrove roots arched upwards in a sinister pattern, while the branches snatched at our heads as we passed underneath. A moment later we were out on the river, and I lowered the engine. Debbie had done us well; a single pull of the cord and we were away, leaving the troop of East Indian boys laughing and splashing behind us.

The river was soon growing choppy. The corial skipped and bounced as we cut our way through the water at half throttle. There were still some three hours of daylight left.

'What time we going to reach Orealla?' I shouted to Alan, who was sitting at the bow.

He glanced at the river bank, to gauge how fast it was slipping by, and then up at the sun.

'After this first point,[1] we going get smooth water,' he said, 'and then we going travel more fast. But we getting plenty rain top-side,[2] and water running down hard. That going humbug we a little. I believe we going meet before night.'

All this from a single glance at the sun, the tide and the river bank. Although there was little in Alan's appearance, apart from his features and shy manner, to distinguish him from boys on the coast, he was still in touch with his Indian environment. He had made no mistake; as soon as we rounded the first bend, the water was calm again. I turned the throttle full out. The spray leaped up on either side of us, catching the sun in its hands. I suddenly felt an old exultation, limitless water flung wide beneath a clean, sky-washed horizon. An urbanized eye becomes strangely cramped in a setting where space and distance are always challenged by vertical lines and shortened perspectives. Here, in the unbroken stretch of the river, the world's dimensions were free again.

On either side stood the dark curtain of the forest, with the water lapping at its ankles. As we drew closer its details emerged—a green monotone, flecked with purple-brown, where the young shoots of the mora trees were bursting into life. Once or twice we heard the chitter of a flock of tiny sakawinki monkeys, playing up in the branches. Then a splash of russet-brown, as a large howler monkey looked down at us. Each morning their call echoes out of the forest, a fearsome roar which carries for miles and dies away in the distance. The river stretched on for several miles before the next bend. Enormous islands lay in our path, blending with the dark line of the bank. It seemed only a day or two since I had last swung the handle and turned towards the short cut on the far side. Into the channel and past Baboon Island, with its menacing sandbanks. It was here that Vin and I had once hit a manatee, or water-cow, in the speed-boat. A strangely ugly creature, with a shapeless body and tiny, deep-set eyes, it is credited by the Indians with mischievous supernatural powers. At the time we had simply earned a rather injured, lugubrious look from our unintended victim; but within the next few days I was to learn that it might have had strange effects.

1. Bend.   2. Up river.

42

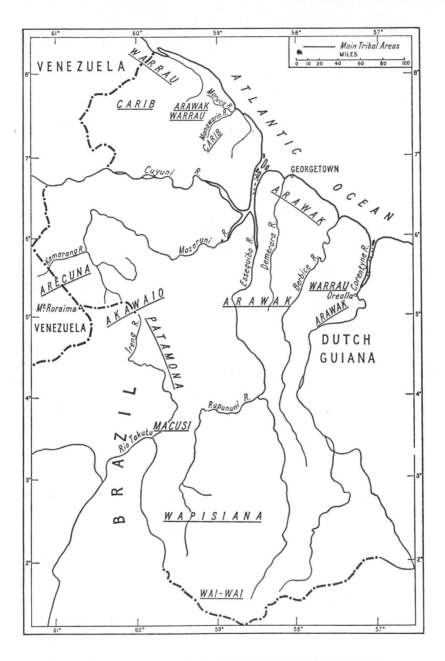

THE DISTRIBUTION OF THE INDIAN TRIBES

By now we were keeping close to the side, to avoid the powerful current. The dark brown fruit of the wild cocoa plants whisked by, and then a purple-flowering vine, dipping its fingers in the water. The skeletons of dead branches and trees reached out of the mud in a vain appeal against being slowly submerged. The forest was broken by occasional clearings, with steps leading down to the waterside, where pioneering East Indian families had moved up river to farm. The fifty miles that lay between Springlands and the Indian reservation at Orealla were gradually being reduced.

This process began long ago. British vessels were trading with the Corentyne Indians in the late sixteenth century, when the population consisted mainly of the Carib tribe. The account, by Raleigh's lieutenant Berry, of a voyage in 1597, suggests that the site of Orealla, which he called Warawalle, was already occupied. But the Indians' contacts remained casual until the middle of the eighteenth century, when the Dutch Government[1] allowed the Moravian Church to found a mission at a point named Semira, opposite Orealla. For several years a priest called Daehne survived the ravages of malaria and the hostility of the Caribs, until he finally won them over. But his efforts were short-lived; by the turn of the century, smallpox had decimated the Indians and the mission was abandoned. Thirty years later, when the Anglican Bishop Austin visited the Corentyne, the only trace of Christianity was a blind old man who still remembered a few Moravian hymns. The Caribs had almost disappeared, giving way to the Arawaks and Warraus, whom they had once dominated. Then, near the end of the nineteenth century, the Anglicans founded a mission at Epira, some thirty miles above Orealla. This time it was a 'flu epidemic which almost destroyed the Indians. The mission was moved to Orealla, a natural site for occupation, with a view for several miles down river, and a wide savanna behind it. Eventually it proved a success. The outside world had penetrated the lives of the Corentyne Indians.

With the amenities of the Church and the protection of a reservation which only the Indians were allowed to enter, Orealla grew rapidly. But no one was ever stationed there, except for a school-teacher from the coast. When I arrived, early in 1960, it was the largest Indian village in the country, with a population of nearly a thousand people, consisting of Arawaks and Warraus. They are still aware of their tribal distinctions. The Arawaks are adaptable and easy to approach, but the Warraus are much more independent, clinging to their old customs

1. Apart from a brief phase of French rule, from 1782 to 1783, what is now British Guiana was Dutch territory until 1796 (see Appendix A).

and resenting change. There is little intermarriage; while the Arawaks live beside the river, the Warraus are up on the hill, close to the forest and savanna which lie behind the village. There is just one exception to this tribal pattern—a childless Carib, called David John, who is blind and half deaf, and thought to be eighty-six years old. Apart from his unnoticed figure, the past has almost vanished. Settlers, engines and outboard motors have brought the Indians nearer the coast. The reservation and the size of the village have helped to preserve their independence, but traders, the Church and the timber industry have led to many changes. Although they accept the fact of change, the Indians have never been equipped to deal with its different aspects, such as a cash economy. Apart from Christianity and a primary education, there has been no substitute for their own traditions. This has created a wide gulf between the young and old people and a sense of inferiority to the coastal population. This was the confused setting in which I had worked for a year. I was followed by another volunteer, and a Government station was then established, with a permanent officer. I wondered how these three years would have affected the Indians.

Over two hours had passed, with Alan and William gazing endlessly at the tangled forest. Already the afternoon light was quailing, leaving a silver-grey etching on the horizon. Above us, the chatter of a flock of parrots, beating their short, stubby wings hurriedly, to escape the approaching darkness. Behind them, a single pair of macaws, with their long red tail feathers trailing against the light. As we passed Jumbi Island, the last before Orealla, the white hillside came into view, still several miles away. The cliffs were laid bare, so the Indians say, by an enormous snake which glides out periodically to drink the waters of the Corentyne. My impatience seemed to be slowing the boat down. Alan and William saw my expression and smiled quietly. Dusk was edging over the river, with the night close at its heels. Way ahead in the darkness a single light winked its way into being below the hill.

As we neared the village, a child bathing at the water's edge glanced up and waved.

'Look! Mr. Henty,' she cried, as we slowed down and passed along the bank.

The silhouette of a corial and a murmur of greeting. I glimpsed a group of men at the corner, under the cluster of bamboos.

'Mr. Colin, you back again.' I recognized Albert's voice. 'The paiwari waiting on you,' he shouted.

A flock of children scampered along the path, as we reached the far end of the village and the little shack where I had lived. I turned the handle and we came to rest on the mud. The children tumbled down the bank and splashed into the water beside us. They crowded round the corial. A moment of hushed silence.

'Look, he hair long,' said a little girl's voice. A ripple of laughter ran through them. They pressed forward nudging each other and whispering timidly. I began recognizing their faces—eyes gleaming shyly in the half darkness, and ebony hair falling carelessly over bare shoulders. A hand reached out and touched my arm. It was Henry, Albert's little son, with the widest grin in the village.

'Uncle, you come back,' he said. 'You no going away again?'

'I staying a little time,' I replied. My answer was passed round in a whisper.

They jumped into the corial, seized my bag and scrambled up the bank. By now a little crowd had gathered. A figure came forward with a lamp in his hand. It was Captain, the headman of the village, a short Arawak, with striking looks, who had often written to me.

'Is a long time we did expect you,' he said. 'Since the day when you left us we waiting on you. The old people glad to see you too. They been making paiwari for you.'

I laughed. At least this was unchanged. Hospitality and paiwari were still two of their first thoughts. One by one the others came forward, murmuring a shy good night and melting back into the crowd. Last of all came Lillian, the little old Warrau with twinkling eyes, who had always been so maternal towards me.

'You no bring no wife with you, Sonny Boy?' she asked, using the nickname which she had coined for me.

'How can a small boy like me get a wife?' I joked, as the other women giggled shyly at Lillian's boldness.

Henry was still clutching my hand, as we filed up the fallen tree which served as a step-ladder on to the bank.

'You see the new officer house?' said Captain, pointing to a large white building, just beyond the wooden shack.

I paused for a moment. The house was unlit, as the District Officer was away. It had an air of remote authority which seemed out of place in the village. Albert must have sensed my feelings. He pointed at the house.

'The thing so big that when a man inside he can't see we poor buck[1] people at all,' he said.

---

1. A derisive term applied to the Indians by other Guianese. With typically good humour, they have removed the sting from its tail by using it amongst themselves in their everyday banter.

The others murmured in agreement. His remark confirmed something which I had already suspected. The earliest link we had established, when I first arrived, was the shack which the Indians built for me. We had worked on it together, and when it was finished it was similar to their own homes. This was invaluable, in that there was no gulf to be crossed when they wanted to come and see me. Once their first shyness had disappeared, they would drop in quite casually. Living in different circumstances, it might have been hard to win their trust. It was difficult to envisage any relationship between the barefoot lives of the Indians and the large white house, which had been planned some time ago, in the days of British administration. Incidental though it may have been, it was symptomatic. The official policy of the past had never found a real level of communication with the Indians.

'You no going stay in the big house?' Albert asked tentatively.

'No,' I replied, 'I going stay in the old one, just like before.'

He laughed and opened the wooden door. We filed inside and Captain hung his lamp on a nail. The shack was just as I had left it, with the trim pattern of rafters laid in criss-cross Indian fashion, beneath a neatly plaited leaf roof. A trace of cobwebs and a slight gap in the leaves were the only signs of the time that had passed since I last slung my hammock there. Outside the lamplight glittered on the surface of the river to which I had listened every night.

The others paused at the door. A circle of upturned faces peeping shyly inside—impassive faces, save for their eyes, which are always speaking to each other. A moment later they came up the steps and pressed into the little room. The familiar patter of bare feet on the dusty wooden floor, and gasps of wonder as my bag was unpacked.

'Look how it big,' said a woman's voice, as I produced the Brazilian hammock which I had borrowed in Georgetown.

'And the colours nice,' said another.

'And look he new bag,' said Lennox, Vin's impish little brother, as the children crowded round. 'Me going jump inside and let he put me in corial. Then me going to England with he.'

'He got no corial,' said another. 'He does go in aeroplane, silly.'

'Then me going fly,' said Lennox firmly.

A moment later Vin appeared, broad-shouldered and smiling. He had an air of assurance which few of the young people shared. Perhaps it was lent by his permanent job, in looking after the speed-boat. His brother Winston had left school now, he said, and gone to work on the Demerara River. Like Vin, he had been one of the most able boys in the village; but his independent, wandering spirit must have lured him away. By now he would be just eighteen. I wondered if he would come back.

Familiar figures were still appearing—Eric, the village musician, whose curly hair suggested a trace of Portuguese blood in his ancestry, and one-eyed Adolphus, a lovable old rogue, who had once made it his ambition to see me married to an Orealla girl. Then came the presidential George, the most ambitious farmer in the village, a stolid Arawak who, like the others, was little more than five feet high. He looked up at me and grinned broadly.

'We hear you was coming back,' he said. 'And to how you was the first man here, we say we got to get present for you.'

He handed me a gnarled, beautifully polished walking stick. The others clapped and crowded round to see his offering. Suddenly they were quiet again, as an old man appeared in the doorway. It was Uncle Charlie, the wisest head in the village. He was one of the last people who still knew the Indian legends and the traditional basket-work. I remembered the letter he had written to me just after I left, with its quaint, elegant style, reminding me of all the evenings we had spent together. He had aged since I last saw him. His frail figure was slightly bent and the carefully engraved lines on his face had grown more distinct. He gazed at me for a moment, with his head tilted to one side. The others waited eagerly to hear what he would say.

He laid a wrinkled hand on my arm. 'You come from far again,' he said. 'When you gone, you got we in tears. Me see yourself did get a little water in you eye.' He smiled as he remembered it all. 'That same afternoon we had paiwari, but the people say they ain't want to drink, because you gone away. They say look how far he gone, to England side, he going forget we forest people. But I tell them he promise he coming back, and so he surely going come. Ain't so?' he asked, turning to the others, who murmured their assent. 'Is so me said,' he went on. 'But when I got your letter from England I start feeling sad. I am an old man now, coming in seventy years. I say peradventure is only in Heaven we going drink together again, because I getting near to the grave. But we got good luck today, because you come back to this place.'

The little crowd clapped in delight.

'But, Chief,' he said, 'how you come from England? I hear you come in a flying machine.' And he tilted his head to one side again, never too old for a new story.

The brief ceremony was over. The Indians melted slowly away, fading into a few quiet whispers in the darkness outside. A handful of children still played in the corner, absorbed in a *Geographical Magazine* which I had

48

brought for them. Vin stayed behind and we chatted for a while. Though confident, he was still quiet-spoken. Yes, his work was going well, he said, but—and he looked at me for a moment—it was different now, not quite the same as before.

I realized how lucky I had been, with my undefined status in the village. It had been easy to make friends. Personal contact of this kind is always difficult for an official, as the Indians are shy of authority. Although it is vital in working with them, past systems have prevented it. Somewhere there has been a gap which still seems to survive.

As we were talking, Captain returned. The people had some paiwari at a nearby house. They wanted me to 'take a sip' with them—a happy understatement, with which the Indians always refer to their drinking sprees. We wandered out into a starlit night and down the sand-white path, still moist with rain. A murmur of voices from each house and figures caught in the dancing firelight; past the mango tree on the corner and the silhouette of the new school, built since I had left. As we climbed the steps of the house where the party was being held, a little boy stroked my arm shyly. The Indians are a smooth-skinned people. One of the children's favourite entertainments was to touch the hairs on my arms and legs in uninhibited wonder.

The house was one of the best in the village. The leaf roof stretched high overhead and the raised wooden floor was walled in to about waist height. Inside there were almost a hundred people, men on one side and women on the other, a custom which is still practised on every occasion in their lives. Here and there a few Warrau faces, with slighter features than those of the Arawaks; high cheekbones and long, dark hair, catching the dim light of a lantern which sputtered in one corner. As soon as we were seated, one of the girls came forward with a calabash-full of paiwari in each hand. Memories of the aftermath of long, sun-beaten days came back as I tasted its bitter, refreshing tang. I swallowed it at the single draught which custom demanded. According to an Indian tradition, if you have only one drink in a house, your next child will be one-eyed. The calabash was soon replenished.

'Another eye for the pikaninny,' I said, as I drank once more. They laughed in delight at my having remembered the legend.

Every now and then another couple appeared, parting company as they entered, the men to sit on one side and the women on the other. Some of them brought their own drink. Whenever a new jar was opened, the owner came forward to Captain and myself with a calabash in her hand, full of paiwari or cane juice, a strong, sweet liquid, brewed from sugar-cane. In the past I had found a balance between sobriety and tact,

49

which makes it hard to refuse a drink, by sharing each one with a willing neighbour. As the calabash went round Captain rose to his feet. The others listened as he welcomed me back. By the time I replied, the paiwari had lifted the last of their shyness. I told them how glad I was to be there and about the faraway myth that was England, my family and the snow, which they always enjoyed.

'But you no get cold over there, Chief?' said Adolphus, whose sense of humour was always aroused by paiwari. 'Me hear say the sun never open he eye that side.'

'And what about Sonny Boy's wife?' asked Lillian, remembering the hammock she had made for me. 'Me no make a two-people hammock?' she said, turning to the other women, who were giggling in the background. 'Up to now he got no wife and half of the hammock wasting.'

The slow rhythm of the evening, disturbed for a moment by my arrival, had returned to normal. The women moved patiently round the house, refilling the calabash as it passed from hand to hand. The men were discussing the day to day topics that still made up their lives —the fish they had caught, the price of logs, or who was making the best paiwari.

As Captain and I sat down again, Henry and his sister Nelly came over to us. The other children followed them.

'Tell we about the snow,' they asked.

As I talked, they listened quietly. I could feel their imagination building a fairy world.

'Is a bigness of whiteness,' said Nelly suddenly, almost to herself.

An hour or two later Albert and I were walking back to the end of the village. Nelly and Henry were close behind us. The night chorus rose through the darkness—the whoop of an owl over the hill, piercing the chicker and scratch of the crickets, and the deep-bellied croaking of the frogs, that challenged the waiting stillness. Already two years had slipped away. I gazed at the river for a while, almost out of habit. Fingers of moonlight played on its ripples, conjuring up the myriad sounds of its restless way to the sea. The last thing I saw, as I fell asleep, was a distant twinge of summer lightning, stabbing the darkened forest.

In every Indian village life begins at dawn. The distant call of the howler monkeys, a jagged roar from the heart of the forest, that dwindles to a whisper. The lonely cry of a flock of parrots, winging their way overhead. Children's laughter, caught on the chill air; a splash by the water's edge. The hunters will have left already, to watch for the shadows of the deer that browse beside the savanna. A moment later, the wooden beaters, a slow thud echoing up and down, as the women turn to their washing. A handful of sounds that drift together, pause, and then begin to unfurl, as another day is born.

Over the river a touch of sunlight, glimmering on the water. There was hardly a tremor on its surface; just a hint of a lone corial, that hung adrift like a stray note of music caught in the mist. Two boys in the crook of a fallen tree, with its branches framing the distant bank like a piece of wild sculpture. Their backs were turned as they gazed at the water, watching for a tell-tale gleam where a fish leapt up towards the light.

A little girl, who was bathing nearby, turned round and saw me watching. She bent down and dipped her hands in the water, throwing it up in the air to catch the fragments of sunlight. She laughed as it fell on her bare shoulders. The two boys sprang up and leapt into the river, tumbling, rolling like a pair of brown fishes and scattering the morning stillness.

A moment later Alan arrived, with a bunch of bananas which his mother had sent as a present. Then a familiar patter of feet and Nelly and Henry peeped round the corner, carrying a large stick of sugar-cane between them. Another little girl appeared and thrust a package into my hand, wrapped in a banana leaf. 'Kukreit,' she said, shyly—the fruit of a wild palm tree which bears during the rainy season. The children shared them out gleefully. As I peeled off the skin and tasted the rich, caramel-like flavour of its orange flesh, they watched me in curiosity and laughed at my approval.

Suddenly the school-bell rang. Seizing their slates and exercise books, they tumbled down the steps. A flash of bare feet on the glistening white sand, and they were gone. I followed them out and felt the first warm breath of the sun on my back. A hint of smoke rose slowly from the house at the end of the path, where the women were baking cassava bread. Already two or three of the flat, round loaves were laid out on the roof to dry, in a pattern that would spread from home to home as the morning ebbed on.

I stopped for a while to watch them at their age-old task. A little girl sat in a corner, scraping the ungainly cassava roots and grating their white flesh into a pulp. This was passed on to her elder sister, who packed it into a matapee, a long straw container, hanging from one of the beams; when it was full, she leant on a stick passed through a loop at the end. The matapee lengthened, squeezing the cassava until the pale juice welled out into a calabash. Their mother was squatting in front of the fire, fanning the low flames and spreading the flour lightly over a round

51

baking-pan. As soon as it began to harden, a quick, deft flick of the hand, and the new loaf was turned over; then she smoothed the edges down carefully with her neatly woven fan. Despite the simplicity of her work, her movements suggested a quiet pride, as she brushed the loose crumbs off the surface.

I had often wondered how the Indians discovered the use of cassava, which forms the staple diet of many South American tribes. The juice is highly poisonous. I once saw a fully grown ox die within a matter of minutes from drinking a bowl of it. But even this, when boiled down, produces starch and casareep, a rich brown Indian sauce. There are several other by-products. Some of the savanna tribes bake the flour into a hard, loose cereal, known as farine, which is popular in Brazil. The bread is used to make paiwari and its many variations. First the loaves are burnt slightly, to give the drink its bitter quality. Then they are broken up and boiled in the large cauldrons which have almost replaced the Indians' earthenware pottery. If they want to make cassiri, which has a sweeter, more mild taste, they omit to burn the bread. Finally the water is strained and left to ferment for two or three days.

The women worked on steadily, without exchanging a word. The harder aspects of family life are almost entirely their duty. The men are expected to hunt and fish, clear the trees for cassava farms and gather forest materials for a new house or a hammock. They also do all the straw-work, making fans, baskets and matapees. At Orealla, with saw-mills nearby, most of them leave the village each year to cut logs for sale. But they still have plenty of time for paiwari and their wives do the bulk of the work—looking after the farm, caring for the children, making cassava bread and weaving new hammocks. Until recently this was accepted as a part of tradition. But now a conflict is setting in. The children, especially the girls, are divided between their family duties and the demands of school hours. Their Westernized primary education makes them ashamed of their rôle in the home and hence the rift between old and young is felt even on a family level. This had been one of the main problems when I was working at Orealla. It was evident, in different ways, on most occasions. But it would have taken them several years to regain their self-respect, and now the problem hardly seemed to be noticed.

I walked on past the scattered houses. Most of them were simply built, just a leaf roof on wooden posts, sometimes half enclosed. The smoke from their fires drifted out into neatly swept yards, dotted with mango and citrus trees. Round the next corner, a low hum of voices.

It was 'mission day', held once a week, when they used their system of communal work, known as a masromani, to keep the village tidy. Most of their tasks are done in this way. When a family has a field to be cut or leaves to be gathered for a new roof, they make paiwari and call their friends, who come along to help. After the work they return to the village and spend the afternoon drinking.

I was greeted by Adolphus, whose sense of humour always made him the leader of the chatting and drinking side of a masromani. With a bright yellow kerchief over his blind eye, his face had a piratical air.

'Take a little sip, Chief,' he said, offering me a calabash of paiwari. As I drank, he bantered on, aware that the others were listening.

'Me really work hard today,' he said. 'Sun up high and me belly holler. Even if paiwari coming just now, me forget he when me belly so, 'cause me is a belly-study man.'

All the Indians, especially Adolphus, loved this game of improvised word-play. The others laughed and sucked their teeth.

'This old man is pure gaffing,' said Cecil, a middle-aged Warrau standing next to Adolphus. 'Is only by how you got so much mouth that you belly holler 'pon you. Pure gaff does make you hungry, 'cause me ain't see you work at all.'

Adolphus started with feigned indignation.

'What!' he exclaimed. 'Adolphus no work!' He turned and looked at me. 'Chief,' he said, 'this Cecil is a scampy young buck-man, don't worry with what he say.' Suddenly his expression grew serious. 'But you know what really happen?' he added. 'The young people don't like this work. They ain't worry with masromani, they say is old people story. When they come home they getting pure sport. They does drink beer, buy shirts and so, get a little fight and they gone again. They ain't worry with the village at all. So what we old people going do?'

Being an effective part of tradition, we had often used masromani in our village schemes. But Adolphus was right. It was dying out. Few of the young people were helping. Unlike their parents, they had learnt to expect a cash return for their work. Adolphus shrugged and looked resigned. But his sense of fun was not easily suppressed.

'If young man ain't want to work,' he said, 'then this old man got to work alone—but he going drink all the paiwari.'

Captain joined me as I walked on. The swish of cutlasses died away as we climbed up the path. The sand was scuffed with the flight of bare feet, a pattern that still echoed with laughter, where the children had tumbled and played on their way to school. At the crest of the hill, the first Warrau house, surrounded by coconut palms. A shy, scarcely audible greeting from an old woman sitting inside. She raised her head to look at us. She was one of the last people in the village who still wore a frayed karasuna, the first type of shawl introduced by the missionaries, joined at the shoulders and falling diagonally across the chest. Her deep face was crinkled with age and a dark lock of hair fell carefully over her temple. She bowed her head and went on with her work. She was rolling dry strands of silk-grass over her bare knee and twisting them neatly together into a hammock rope. As we watched, she seemed to forget us. She still had a silent dignity, grave and withdrawn, that was lost to the rest of her tribe.

Among the Warraus, up on the hill, the old way of life had changed much less than in the Arawak part of the village. Their houses were as simple as ever and their old skills had declined very little. Most of the men had gone out to work, but the slow-drifting tang of cassava bread confirmed that the women were at home. One of them was weaving a hammock on a rough wooden frame, passing a shuttle up and down through the long strands of wool which is carefully picked and sorted before the work begins. Beside her sat a little girl, plaiting a basket of tibisiri, a raffia-like reed which grows in the swamps. The floor of the house was simply bare sand. The sunlit glare from outside was fractured by a curved pattern of hammocks, slung criss-cross from the beams and draped with rough mosquito-nets. Overhead, on the rafters, lay a collection of bows and arrows and a rusty shotgun. Paddles and matapees stood in one corner, next to a battered suitcase and a jumble of clothes. The Warraus' concept of property is still superficial. Anything they acquire is short-lived, the victim of a day to day outlook in which their old independence survives.

We continued along the narrow path that walked the brow of the hill. The sun throbbed down from a one-cloud heaven. The endless, high-pitched note of the sunbee was stretched against the vapid heat, so much a part of the day's very texture that, if it stopped, the world would pause. Below us, the village was almost hidden by a sea of coconut palms. Their slight fronds wavered in the breeze, giving way to the tangled colours of the forest, which faded into a toneless green. An occasional leaf roof, tucked away, as shy as the Indians themselves; the white splash of the village church and a glint of sunlight on the school. A vast, sprawling bend in the river, almost half a mile broad, and beyond it the endless forest again, this time in Surinam—a stronghold even less explored than the interior of Guiana.

Captain pointed at the river. 'Look there,' he said. I followed his gaze. At first I was dazzled by the sun and then I saw the flash of a porpoise, leaving a touch of foam on the surface. 'You want to go to the back?' he asked. 'I believe the women is working there.'

We turned through a grove of ité palms and past the last houses. As we emerged again into the savage eye of the sun, the savanna lay in front of us, a broken sea of scrub and grass, patched here and there with an island of trees and webbed by Indian trails. The women murmured as they worked, but unlike the men they hardly paused, even when they laughed quietly. The colours of their shapeless dresses were splashed against the green and blue backcloth of the forest and open sky. A wave from Lillian as we appeared, and whispered comments among the others. Here, too, there were mainly old people working. They were cutting the grass on the burial ground, a little patch of mounds and crosses, crumbling away in the sun. As we turned back, something caught my eye—a handful of flowers on a freshly cut grave. A rough notice clung rakishly to the wooden cross at its head. 'In memory of Marius Linguard.' He had died a few months ago—an old man with a watery smile, who was strangely loved by the children.

Late that afternoon I saw Uncle Charlie sitting in the shadow of a mango tree by his house. He paused at the basket he was weaving and beckoned to me to come and join him. He was always good company. As a boy, he had learnt every detail of the Indian crafts and legends. Then, during a wandering life, his knowledge had been supplemented by a motley collection of books, borrowed from itinerant priests. But despite this and his seventy years, he still had the primitive powers of memory which are usually destroyed by literacy.

'Tortoise-shell,' he said proudly, pointing at the pattern on his basket. 'The old people teach me that one. But the others can scarcely do it now—only me and this old man.' He raised a hand to Jeremiah, an old Warrau who was just passing.

He came and sat down beside us, glancing at Uncle Charlie's work with a critical eye. 'Tortoise-shell. That is Arawak style. We Warraus got different ones.'

'Yes,' said Uncle Charlie. 'We saying how people forget them now.'

Jeremiah nodded. 'Is true. They forgetting everything—this kind of work and the dances and stories. The Warraus had some fine stories. The old people used to say that one time we was living up so, on the clouds, in sky-land. That was before they got Indians in this Corentyne River. We was living nice up there, eating pure birds. That time was no corial, no house, just bow and arrow. Then one day a young man gone hunting, he name Okonote or something so. He seen a big bird, and when he shoot it, the thing make a hole in the clouds and come tumbling down below. Up to now the Warrau people never seen this earth. But when he was looking through the hole, this Okonote seen a nice place. So he take bush-rope and tie it from the cloud and then he climb down to earth. When night come, he gone back to sky-land.' He smiled. 'Yes, is a fancy story. When this Okonote reach back, he telling the other people about it. He say, "Man, I find a nice place down there, tomorrow let we all take a walk." So the next day the people go down to shoot some deer and so. They take bush-rope and they climbing down, man, woman, children, all. But the last was a lady who was getting baby. She so big she can't pass through the hole. A man underneath, he push and pull, but the lady just can't move. When they want to come back, she was still in the hole. So the Warrau people stay on earth and make corial and so. An' up to now this lady still there. When you see the morning star that is the very same Warrau lady. Is so we come to be in this place —to how the old people say.'

Uncle Charlie nodded in approval. 'Yes,' he said, 'different tribes got different story. We Arawak people used to say that God come down and sit in a big silk-cotton tree. He pull off the branches and throw them all down. Some turn to birds, some to fishes and some to snake. The finest branches that fall on the ground is we the Arawak people.' He laughed for a moment at this mild conceit. 'But everybody got he own story. I hear a thing about these Caribs. An Indian woman was living with a camoudi.[1] That is how the first Carib was born. Is that make them so fierce, you know.'

'Is so I heard,' agreed Jeremiah. 'They got different stories about it.'

'These Caribs is a very warlike nation,' Uncle Charlie added. 'Before the white man come here they was fighting the other tribes, Arawak and Warrau and so, making war upon them. Eating them too—I heard a story about how this fighting begin. An Arawak man gone to hunt one day and there in the forest he meet with two Carib people, a lady and she son. The boy was climbing a big tree, to catch the fruit. But the lady was a piai, a sorceress, and she telling the boy he must climb with his back to the tree, in a magic way. When the Arawak man come and see this thing he say: "This is semichihi.[2] These people going do me wrong. Let me put arrow 'pon this boy one time and make he dead." So he shoot the boy, and when he dead he chop up the body piece by piece and throw it about in the bush. Now the lady vexed bad and she find all the pieces and make

1. Anaconda, the largest of South America's non-poisonous snakes, which sometimes reaches thirty feet in length. It plays a leading role in Indian mythology, usually of a sexual nature and often with anthropomorphic qualities.
2. Magic (Arawak).

the boy come alive again. When he there good she tell him, "Boy, to how this Arawak man troubling you, and you is a Carib, you must always fight with his people." Since that time they been enemies.'

'And when did they stop fighting?' I asked.

'Well,' said Uncle Charlie, 'they finish now. When the white people come the Caribs was selling other Indians to them. The white people give them guns, axe, beads and all kind of thing. Then the white men stop buying slaves and the Arawak people defeat the Caribs and drive them far away. And up to now they feeling hostile. One time when I was a boy the Carib people in Surinam send a challenge to the Arawak nation, saying, "Come, and we going fight you." That was fifty years back. But the Surinam Government stop them. They say they going give the Arawak people guns, and by how the Caribs only got bow and arrow, the Arawaks going kill them. So they leave off and the whole thing finish. And now the Caribs left this place.'

A realm of half-forgotten history lay behind the old man's story. Little over a century ago the Caribs were the warriors of the Indian world. Raleigh described them as 'a naked people, but valiant as any under the sky'.[1] When Captain Berry travelled up the Corentyne in 1597, they ruled the upper reaches of the river, menacing the other tribes. Laurence Keymis, another of Raleigh's lieutenants, who sailed the Guiana coast in the same year, reckoned the Indian population at nearly two hundred thousand, with the Caribs outnumbering the Arawaks by more than three to one. During the days of Dutch rule they acted as a virtual police force, capturing runaway African slaves. The latter were terrified of them, regarding them as cannibals. This is no longer thought to be true. The rumour probably arose from their custom of making flutes from their enemies' thigh-bones. Only their hearts were actually eaten, in a dried, pulverized form, as a means of gaining a part of their spirit.

The Caribs' reputation lasted well into the nineteenth century. In 1810 Mahanarva, a Carib chief from the Essequibo, threatened the British Governor with war unless he were granted tribute. It was promptly given to him. Twenty years later, when Schomburgk, the famous explorer, came up the Corentyne River, they were still powerful. Striking up river over the falls, they made their way to the Rupununi, where they plundered the peaceful Macusi, a tribe on the Brazilian border. Their victims were brought down river and sold to the Dutch planters as slaves. When Schomburgk reached Tomatai, a Carib village above Orealla, his Arawak

1. Sir Walter Raleigh. *The Discoverie of the Large and Bewtiful Empyre of Guiana* (see Selected Bibliography).

helpers refused to go any farther. A few days later their fears were justified when a large war canoe arrived on the scene, laden with Caribs on their way south to conduct another raid.

An Anglican priest called Bernau has left a vivid description of them in the last of their conquering days:

'These are a fine-looking race of men; their demeanour is friendly, but their war-like appearance threatening, as they are always found armed with a gun and bows and arrows, or with a club and long knife. Their bodies are painted with the arnotto dye, their faces tattooed; and strange to say, their hair is more like that of the coloured people, and curling. Their beards and eyebrows are plucked out when beginning to grow; all, without exception, live in a state of nudity. . . .'[1]

This was as late as the 1840s. But their death-knell had already been sounded, with the abolition of slavery. Deprived of their brief livelihood, they melted away into the forest. During the next few decades their numbers declined rapidly through contact with European diseases. When Veness, another priest, visited the Corentyne in 1866 there were only twenty-nine Caribs left, and most of these were of mixed blood. Within a generation, they had almost disappeared from the river which they once terrorized. The former highway of the Indian slave trade was left to the Arawaks and Warraus, whose numbers have increased ever since.

Old Charlie seemed to have guessed my thoughts. 'Long time back,' he said, 'this Corentyne River was pure Carib people. That was before my father born. Now they all die or they fled away. Some gone into the forest in Surinam, and back to Essequibo. Only one living here now. Look him there.' He pointed to a tattered figure which had appeared from the waterside—it was David John, over eighty years old, the last of the Corentyne Caribs. He came slowly down the path towards us, feeling his way with a stick. As he passed the mango tree, with a gourd of water in his hand, Uncle Charlie called out to him.

'Where you going, Grandpa?' he asked him in Arawak.

David muttered a reply.

'Washiati, let we drink,' said Uncle Charlie, who seemed almost sprightly beside the old man. He beckoned to his wife, who brought a bowl of paiwari. David felt for a seat beside us.

'The white man come back again,' said Uncle Charlie, still speaking Arawak. 'He's asking about the old times. You remember?'

The old man paused, with the bowl in his hands. A few white hairs on his firmly drawn chin, sunken cheeks and a parchment-like skin that was lined and blotched with age. Intricate wrinkles gathered up beneath a

1. The Rev. J. H. Bernau, *Missionary Labours in British Guiana* (see Selected Bibliography).

dim pair of eyes, whose blindness lent them an almost prophetic distance. His peaceful, faraway expression made it hard to believe that he was the last, in the Corentyne, of a tribe who had ruled and plundered the Indian world. He licked his weathered lips and muttered a few sentences in Carib, broken here and there with a word of English.

'Old people fighting . . . priest come. Old lady dead. . . . People gone now'—words that fell like bits of a distant dream.

'He getting old,' said Uncle Charlie, 'forgetting the old time days. They say he got eighty-six years now. His wife was a Carib too, but she dead. Is only this awa[1] left.'

David sat quite motionless, gazing into space. I lit a cigarette and placed it in his hand. He puffed gratefully, nodding his head, and finished it without a word. Then he stood up, raised a hand and disappeared down the path.

Dusk was creeping over the river, strangling the last glow of light on the hill. Jeremiah went on his way. Below us, the movement of corials, as the men returned from their farms up river, their baskets laden with bananas, green maize and pawpaw. A little crowd at the water's edge, where someone had caught an enormous lau-lau, a curiously flat-faced, bewhiskered fish, which must have weighed some sixty pounds. He was cleaning it with a cutlass and handing pieces round to the others—food for almost every family that night. Suddenly a little boy appeared, with a piece for Uncle Charlie and another for me. He had a message—we must eat it tonight, while it still had the taste of the river.

Uncle Charlie and I wandered over to Julius's shop at the foot of the hill to buy a beer. A sturdy, ambitious little Warrau, Julius was quite different from anyone else in the village. A few years ago he had been like the others, happy-go-lucky and improvident. Then he suddenly began to save. A heap of boards arrived from the saw-mill and Julius converted his home into a neat little wooden shop. Already he was growing plump. A jump ahead of the rest of his people, he was the only man in the village who had learnt to deal with change. The others viewed him with mixed feelings. Success in such new, alien terms had set him slightly apart from them.

Uncle Charlie leant on the counter; his grave head was silhouetted against the rows of tinned food and stacks of brightly coloured cloth on the shelves behind him. Somewhere in the background a radio was playing. His bent old figure seemed to belong to another world—one of remote legends and beliefs, and a wisdom that was dying with him.

1. Old man, grandpa.

3

The Face of Change

EVENINGS spent with Uncle Charlie, rounds of paiwari and children's laughter gave Orealla a lotus-eaters' atmosphere. But beneath the surface changes were still going on. Three years ago the local primary school had been run by the Anglican Church. It had since been taken over by the Government, which had put up a new building. I stopped outside it early one morning. The slow chanting of children's voices floated out on to the sunlight that glittered on its zinc roof. It had a cold, rather functional look, compared with the old mission school, which had stood in the shadow of the mango trees, tumbledown and informal.

There were almost two hundred children inside, of every age from five to fifteen. I stood and watched them for a moment, as they bowed over their slates and glanced up at the blackboard. Their bare feet and hushed voices were the only signs of their Indian past. The head-teacher came from the coast, but all his assistants were local people. In one corner sat Ellen, a girl of nineteen, who was typical of the new and yet insecure generation. She was neatly dressed, with her hair up and her face intent on the girls round her. I had often wondered what went on behind her thoughtful, reserved expression. The life she led as a teacher was utterly different from that of her parents. Apart from her quiet personality, she was similar to girls on the coast. In terms of the standards set from outside, she was intelligent and successful, and yet she had an air of detachment which made her seem alone in the village. The distant world whose ways she followed had never really come close enough to penetrate the community. It was as if her ability had set her apart from all that she belonged to.

The girls were learning embroidery, a new art form for the Indians. It showed how easily their skill with their hands can be adapted to fresh techniques. If only it were more emphasized, this type of subject could provide a real basis for their education; it would give their natural ability some valuable new outlets. But the next class explained the disruptive way in which the school syllabus has often affected the Indians. They were reciting poems under the watchful eye of Clifton, a boy of about eighteen, who had still been a pupil when I left the village. The choice of the moment was 'The Owl and the Pussycat'. Their parrot-like, monotonous tone echoed the Indians' reactions to so many aspects of change—the passive acceptance of new fashions which were still remote from their lives. They needed something more than this—something which they could call their own, while relating it to their future.

I slipped out of the school, thinking about the young people I knew who had taught there. Ellen, who seemed so isolated, and Clifton, who, despite his intelligence, was unsure of himself; Justice, the Indian I met on the ferry, who had now left the village, and Dennis, the brightest of them all, who had taught for a while, then grown restless and gone to work as a log-cutter. Why had their intelligence apparently unsettled them? It seemed to be due to their new horizons. Their Westernized primary education had given them a set of ideals which had no real place in their lives. Had they been taught subjects with some local value, such as agriculture and home industries, this confusion would not have arisen. Their ability could have stabilized the changes taking place in the village. As it was, they had two alternatives—either to imitate all they learnt or else to withdraw from it.

Albert agreed with me when we talked about it later that afternoon. 'Yes,' he said, 'these young people, they scarcely know what they going to do when they finish school. They ain't like to work in the forest, like we older ones.' Suddenly he raised his head, as if listening for something. 'A boat coming from below,' he said. 'An outboard. It sounding like Mahood.'

Although my hearing was fairly sharp, it was some time before I caught the hum of the engine, still a good distance away. A few minutes later a battered launch rounded the distant point. Albert was right. It was Mahood, an enormously plump East Indian, who lived down at Springlands. He had made most of his money by selling cheap clothes and trinkets to the Indians, along with rum, which often accounts for a month's hard won earnings overnight. Uncrowned king of the river rogues, he had always been wary, but genial, towards me. The last time I had seen him, some two years ago, he was fast asleep on the floor of Julius's shop, having drunk, so I was told, some thirty bottles of stout since landing at dawn.

The little boat drew into the bank. Mahood gave me a roar of welcome, followed by a friendly pat on the back, which almost sent me spinning into the river.

'Oh lord, Chief, we been missing you,' he said, with tears of good fellowship in his eyes. 'And since dawn I been upon watertop and never a taste the whole way here. Let we go and get a drop over at Julius' place.'

I could, quite literally, smell a lie, but it seemed a good-natured one. We walked over to the shop together.

'Things getting bad since you gone,' he said. 'Jagan giving we punishment. I'm a poor, hard working fellow, but look at this P.P.P. story—they taxing every cent we got.'

I sighed in sympathy, as was expected—knowing quite well that he was a staunch P.P.P. member, and he no doubt fully aware that I knew. It was an old game that we had often played. He assumed a melancholy air, but by the time we reached the shop he was himself once more. A non-committal greeting from Julius. Mahood ordered a round of beer for the two or three men at the counter. A moment later he was talking to Egbert, a quiet, rather cautious Arawak. He launched into politics again, but this time on a different level. Either he must have forgotten me or else he thought that I was no longer listening.

'Look,' he said to the passive Egbert, 'me is a man got no worries with politics, got no worries at all, I tell you. But next time the election come this Jagan surely going to win. So is better you all vote for him. Because if you vote for a next man he going come and torture you right here.'

Egbert's face hardly flickered. The others were silent for a moment. I could see what was going on in his mind. Just who was deceiving him now? Vote for Jagan, someone had said, and he voted for his own destruction; but now he was told, in threatening terms, that this was his only chance of survival. Since the last elections, a year ago, politics had invaded the Indian world. The U.F. had seen them as a new political weapon and gone all out to win their support. Faced on every side with conflicting threats and promises, most of the Indians had voted for them. This alignment with the mainly Portuguese party reflects their trust of the Europeans, who have patronized them for over two centuries. But it can be of little avail. They are hoping for some form of protection which is no longer possible. Their loyalty to the U.F. adds to the mutual suspicion between them and the mass of the Guianese. Politics have simply been another source of confusion. The Indians' anxiety has increased and now, with nothing to show for their votes, they feel that they have been exploited.

I had guessed that this would happen; but Egbert's obvious bewilderment was the first sign I had seen of it. I told Mahood what I thought of his methods and left him to his beer.

For the past few days the Indians had been drifting back from their camp-grounds, where the wood is cut to be sold to the saw-millers. During the rains, when the creeks are in flood, the timber can easily be floated out. Now that they were nearly over, the rush to finish each batch of logs was drawing to a close.

A few men were still working at Aribi Creek, not far from Orealla. Alan suggested our going to see them. By the time we left in his corial the sun was gleaming on the back of the river. Large rafts of timber were moored by the bank, bound together with creepers, ready for the saw-millers who would come up river to buy them. An hour later we reached Aribi, where we were joined by William and an impish boy of about fourteen called Austin. We edged our way through the rafts that clogged the mouth of the creek, and slipped into the shadowed stillness beyond them. The water was still running down fiercely, with the force of the flooded swamps behind it. The heavy silence of the creek was broken by the plash of our paddles. Enormous satin-blue butterflies flopped drunkenly through the sunlight that pierced the green canopy overhead. The swamp birds whistled enquiringly and once a fish leapt up at the bow.

Suddenly a patter of rain broke the still surface of the water. At first a hesitant warning, sounding strangely hollow on the leaves around us. Then it turned rapidly into a torrent, cascading down every leaf and branch. We drew into the side and Austin scurried off and returned with a bundle of enormous leaves, which he solemnly held over my head. I glanced upwards for a moment; the rain seemed to gather speed, as it spiralled its way through the corridors of dark green vegetation. Soon the mosquitoes had discovered us. The dank forest echoed with slaps, each one leaving a smear of blood behind it.

Within a few minutes the storm had passed. The forest began to steam gently. Its heavy scent had a fresh tang, as we set off again. The creek narrowed rapidly, until we could hardly see its direction amongst the flooded swamps in front of us. Suddenly we heard a shout. A timber raft came into view, poled slowly round the corner by one of the men from Orealla. Even now his work was not over; transporting logs was a slow, lonely task, guiding them round the continual bends and over the grave-yard of fallen trees that lurked beneath the surface.

'You bring some paiwari?' he asked with a laugh. He smiled cheerfully —the smile of a man intent on his job, after weeks of slender rations and

63

mosquito-bitten solitude. Away from the easy tempo of the village, the face of the Indian changes quickly. He fades into the forest around him, working hard, with scarcely a pause. His mind is always set on the day when he can return to the happy-go-lucky life of his home.

We soon reached the working-ground, a rough camp on a patch of dry land, with a cluster of hammocks slung close together and the bare utensils of bush life stacked in one corner—cutlasses, guns, bows and arrows and some fishing lines. A pair of short-haired hunting dogs jumped up eagerly to greet us. Most of the men had already left, but a few were still there, trimming their logs and binding them into rafts. The sound of their axes rang through the forest, as they worked with a seemingly effortless rhythm that could last from dawn till dusk. Once more I noticed how their faces differed from those I knew in the village, still cheerful and ready for a word of banter, yet hardened and serious. In a day or two their work would be over, until the rains began again. There would be money from the sale of their logs and paiwari to drink. Their spirits lifted as we ate together—the flesh of a wild hog, killed that morning, and cassava bread, dipped in pepperpot, a stew of fishes steeped in red peppers. A rugged life, but one they were used to, which left them as their own masters, the only terms on which they could work. As they sat there, eating quietly, they had a pride and isolation which they seemed to share with the forest, brooding heavily round us.

By late afternoon we were back at Orealla. Someone was waiting to see me. It was David, a Warrau from up the hill.

'You been waiting long?' I asked.

'No,' he said, 'a little time only.' His face was drawn. He looked at me. 'I got worries with the work,' he added.

I let him go on, without interrupting. At first he was shy, but as he talked his whole story emerged. For the past four months he and his cousin had been employed by a man from the coast. He had sent them to work on his timber grant, farther up river. Their wages were to be paid when they finished. Eventually the two of them earned over a thousand dollars. While they were there, some equipment was stolen from a Dutch grant owner on the far side of the river. When they left, soon afterwards, their employer promised to pay them within a few days. He then told the Dutch police that David and his cousin had stolen the equipment. This earned him a bribe from the actual thief and helped him to withhold their wages. The Dutch police were now looking for them. If they left the village to claim their wages, they would probably be arrested. I knew that his story was genuine—otherwise he would not have come to me. Had the accusation been true, he simply would have vanished.

Political demonstrations are an everyday scene in Georgetown. This one, demanding Independence, is taking place in Water Street, the scene of the February riots

The Indians live in a different world. With its hammocks, gourds, baskets and cooking pots, this is a typical Patamona home in the village of Kaibarupai. The man in the foreground is weaving a wareshi, or Indian carrier. (Flash)

An Akawaio child grating cassava. The pulp is later squeezed and dried before being baked into the cassava loaves which form the Indians' staple diet

A Warrau woman weaving a hammock rope at Orealla. Made from silk grass, or wild hemp, it can hardly be distinguished from the machine-made product

David John, the last survivor, in the Corentyne River, of the once dominant Carib tribe

'I been to the officer,' he added, 'and he say he can't help. I got to see the police down river.'

'And you been to see them yet?' I asked.

'No,' he said, 'I get afraid, because maybe the Dutch people going catch me. And if I go to the police, sometime they going shout and stamp they foot. We Indians don't like that. We is not a rowdy people. So what I going do now? My family starving, I got no money and I can't go out to work.'

There was little that I could do for him, not having any authority. Like others with similar problems, he found it hard to understand that this time I was just a visitor. But I promised to take him down to Springlands and try to arrange something there. He thanked me and left silently.

Problems like this were always occurring. Because of their shyness, the Indians rarely complained. A few days later I met Dennis, the boy who had left his teaching post for a freer, if harder, life in the forest. He had strained his back and looked sick and feverish. He hardly smiled as we talked. He had little of his youthful eagerness of two years ago. Like the others, he felt exploited. His unusual intelligence had simply made him more aware of it. And when he received his meagre wages, they were usually spent in a day or two, on drink and clothes that would hardly last until the next time he went out to work.

All this could have been prevented. With some form of logging society, they could have acquired their own timber grants, with equipment, fixed markets and saving schemes. Similar plans had been tried elsewhere and most of them had failed. It was said that the Indians could never grasp the long-term horizons involved. But the real reasons seemed to be deeper. Schemes of this kind are rarely adapted to the Indians' understanding and particular needs. Given the requisite time and money the problem could easily be solved. But certainly it would be difficult, if only for psychological reasons—the Indians are so used to exploitation that they often seem resigned to it.

I had almost forgotten the thought of continuing my travels. But two or three thousand miles lay ahead of me. In a few days a plane was due to leave Georgetown for the Kamarang airstrip. From there I could visit the Akawaio, who live near the Venezuelan border.

A party was planned for the evening before I left—to wish me happy travels, said Albert. Captain called on me in the morning. Would I have lunch with them first? he asked. I was surprised at his request. Meals are shared, in Indian homes, with anyone who happens to be there. But a formal invitation is unusual. I wondered what it could mean.

We stopped on the way for a round of paiwari, which his wife had prepared. He showed me proudly round his house, the first to be finished under a scheme we had started two years before.[1] In planning it we had tried to keep as close to traditional lines as possible. We had aimed to improve, rather than change, the old building methods. This meant that the houses would still be in keeping with their way of life. To create the feeling of working as a group, we used the masromani system. Each day one of the men would call his friends out to help, in return for an after-noon of paiwari. At first the scheme had gone well, with methods and aims which they understood; but now, for some reason, it had come to a standstill. I had not yet discovered why this was, but our plans had clearly been forgotten. Captain's house was fully enclosed, with a roof of corrugated iron. He had probably tried to imitate the newly built officer's quarters. It stood out almost garishly from the modest Indian homes nearby. The old style had been rejected in favour of the prestige symbol of something more Westernized. They hardly seemed to be using it. The children were playing on the ground underneath, while Captain's wife still baked her cassava bread in the rough little camp she had always used.

We walked on to the house where the meal was arranged for us. Inside was a table, neatly laid for half a dozen people. The others were already there—Albert, Vin and two other boys, called Clarence and Lionel. I could see at a glance what was intended; they would entertain me in the new fashion before the party began. One of the girls had prepared a curry. Needless to say there was still paiwari, but never before had I drunk it from a glass. The atmosphere was restrained and self-conscious. There was little talk as we sat round the table, eating gingerly with knives and forks. I was almost tempted to use my fingers, an Indian custom I had always followed when sharing meals with them.

Once this well-meant ritual was over, the ice was easily broken. We sat on the steps and chatted quietly. Someone mentioned the elections, held in the previous year. Already they were disillusioned with their brief taste of politics. They had heard nothing more of the promises which had won their votes. Meanwhile there had been a price for their loyalty to the U.F.

'Some of us had no chance to vote,' said one of them, with a shrug. 'Plenty of names were left off the register. I hear they did know we was voting U.F., so they never put them down.'

'I myself had worries,' said one of the others. 'The people at Spring-

1. Schemes of this kind are run on a self-help basis; materials are provided by the Government, up to the value of the work done by the people themselves.

66

lands heard how we voting. So they threaten me, saying they going to beat me. I couldn't leave the village at all. At the time I had some logs to sell. The saw-millers are P.P.P., so they all refuse to buy them. They say I must sell to Mr. Peter.[1] I had to leave them and one night somebody thief them all. Two months' work gone to waste with this politics.'

'But you made any complaint?' I asked.

'Is no good we complain,' he said. 'Those people just call we buck-man. If they hear we voice they only shout and try to punish us. So we saying is better we keep to weselves. Is only you we telling.'

'They scarcely worry with us,' said Vin.

'Is so,' said Captain. 'Look at this housing scheme. When you was here it was going nice. The people think the scheme was good, because you was working beside us. But afterwards nobody give us advice. They only telling us we must try fast, or else they going stop the scheme. So the other men was getting suspicious. They say, sometime if they build new houses, the outside people going take them away. Is that make them leave off the work. Is only me and Harry finish, and Uncle George still trying. Since then they tell us the scheme closing down. I hear they say we Indians is lazy. And now they take the wood away, so we can't do any more.'

'What did you do when the wood was taken?' I asked.

'We ain't say nothing,' said Captain. 'Since then we ain't worry with the houses. To how we getting no advice, we say is better we leave it.'

It was easy to see what had happened. Their traditional pace of work was slow and a sudden rumour had discouraged them. The authorities were too remote to diagnose the trouble. It was simply put down to laziness, which puzzled and embittered the Indians. This gulf was a product of the past, but it threatened to survive. Schemes like this would never succeed without a completely new approach, based on personal understanding.

Dusk was closing over the village. The Indians were drifting into the house, and by now it was almost full. The bowl began passing from hand to hand, while jars of cane juice and paiwari were rolled ceremoniously up the steps.

I found myself next to Uncle Charlie, who was watching the proceedings quietly.

'You know about the Oriyu?' he said. 'They is a people living in the water. Sometimes they look like manatee. Proper mischievous people too. You remember the time your boat knock a manatee, couple years back, near Baboon Island?'

1. Peter D'Aguiar, leader of the U.F.

I smiled. The old man never missed a piece of news.

'That was the water spirit,' he said. 'When you knock she so, she get proper vexed. Since that time the boat scarcely working and that is because she troubling it. She put a kind of spell upon it.'

He paused for a sip of paiwari.

'How you know about this Oriyu?' I asked.

'The old people used to tell me,' he said, 'and I myself seen it. Water-mamma we sometimes call it. If they like a young man, they does take him to live with them. When they carry him down below the water, he never come up again. This Corentyne River got plenty. When I was a young man, fishing by night, this water spirit used to chase me. A time I heard one calling to me, koo, koo'—he gave a soft, drawn-out whistle —'then she pick up the corial and bang it down till I nearly sink. At the time I get so frighten my hair stand up in a perpendicular.'

He laughed in delight at his own quaint rhetoric, gleaned, no doubt, from some obscure volume which he had happened to read.

'Yes,' he said, 'they does often trouble us. One day I been fishing with my brother and we hear them calling again. They start to shake the corial. My brother say we must put rum on the water and then they going leave us. So we throw some rum and they drink it up. Then they ain't worry us no more.' He nodded thoughtfully to himself. 'Yes, they proper mischievous. But they looking beautiful. One day I left the village soon morning, around six o'clock.' He glanced up to where the sun would have been, a gesture instinctively used by the Indians when-ever they mention the time of day. 'When I reach the hill-foot I seen a lady, a water spirit with long hair down to her waist. I stop the corial to watch her. She come out of the water and walk on the sand. All she was wearing is high-heel shoes. By the time I follow, she disappear. All I see is the mark of her shoes, to the size of number six.'

He chuckled and looked at me quizzically. Was it paiwari, I wondered, or had he got his tongue in his cheek? Perhaps it was just the artist in him, combining anything new that he heard with his own traditional stories. A party of American surveyors had been to the village recently. Perhaps he had added his impressions from one of their paperbacks. So many different worlds met in his vivid imagination that Indian mythology and American fiction might easily have blended.

He took a long draught of paiwari and sat back in contemplation. It was not the first time he had told me stories of the water people. They were similar to other Indian folk tales, which usually involve animals and spirits, often in comic rôles. Together they have a definite purpose, acting as a substitute for scientific knowledge. Each one explains some

68

phenomenon in the world around the Indians—the behaviour of animals, the origin of tribes and the properties of plants and trees. The Oriyu tales help to account for unusual incidents on the river—freak tides and currents, or an upturned canoe. This is why there is so much emphasis on the Oriyus' mischievous nature. Although they can be of either sex, they are usually described as female. They are often seen combing their hair by the water's edge. Sometimes they adopt young Indians as their lovers, luring them away to their homes beneath the water, where the alligators are used as benches. An affaire of this kind must be kept secret. Celibate Indians are often thought to have an Oriyu lover.

'Since I was a boy,' said Uncle Charlie, 'they troubling me and my brother. For a long time they was chasing him and then they put a spell on him, make him proper sick.'

'What happened to him?' I asked.

'Well,' he said, 'he get a bad fever. We had to visit an old witch-doctor, what we call a piai-man. When night come this piai-man start to smoke his wina.[1] He sitting on a special bench, with an alligator head carved on one side. Then he shake his shak-shak[2] and call the tobacco spirit. He ask him who troubling my brother so. The tobacco spirit say is the water spirit. So the piai-man call the water spirit and ask why she do this thing. She say is because she like my brother, so she did wink an eye at him. He ask if she sorry. She say no. So the piai-man say he going punish her, by putting pepper in she eye. Is only then the spirit get frightened and promise to leave my brother alone.'

'Did he get better after that?' I asked.

'Yes, he get better right away.'

'And the piai-man made him better?'

'Well,' he said, 'perhaps, yes. The piai-man and the mercy of God.'

The two worlds of pagan and Christian, both of which he clearly believed in, hardly conflicted in his mind. But already one of them was dying.

'The young people laugh when you tell them about water spirits,' he said. 'But they is here up to now and the young boys got to be careful. Same thing happen with this piai. They ain't believe in it any more and the priest stop it long ago. I even hear that the Government pass a law against it.'

He was right. The piai-men, or witch-doctors, are now forbidden to practise their spirit contact rituals, known to anthropologists as shamanism. At one time they were the leading figures in Indian society. Their

1. Tobacco.   2. Maraccas.

69

main task is to heal the sick, by means of seances held in a darkened house. Any illness or accident is attributed to mischievous spirits. When he is summoned by a patient, the piai-man works himself into a trance, by fasting, smoking and drinking tobacco juice. Then he summons the relevant spirits to attend. When they arrive, he talks to them, asking them why they have caused trouble and threatening to punish them. A seance like this can last for hours, and any number of spirits may be called. Most of the Indians probably know the secret which lies behind the performance. It is all done by ventriloquism. Yet the piai-men still seem to believe in their own supernatural powers. Amongst the Akawaio, the next tribe I hoped to see, piai has blended with Christianity, forming a strange Indian religion, known as the Hallelujah cult. But elsewhere their rituals and beliefs, suppressed by the Church and Government, are rapidly dying out.

'Sometimes this piai-man had better medicine than the white man giving us,' Uncle Charlie added. 'But now it all finish and gone from here.' He paused for a moment and changed the subject. 'When you come back again we must talk about all the people you seen.'

I wondered what his comments would be when I had more news to tell him. By now the party was well under way. A gramophone was playing in one corner and shadows were mingling on the floor. The young people had started to dance to the tune of a coastal calypso.

'What happened to the village band?' I asked Eric, the curly-haired musician. Two years ago they had joined every party, with their banjoes, drums and shak-shaks, playing the old Indian tunes.

'We finish playing since you gone,' he said. 'Now they got the gramophone, they scarcely singing the old time songs or dancing the mari-mari.'

Another trace of the past had vanished. The dimly lit house, with its swaying figures, was a meeting-point of two worlds—one dying, almost unmourned, and the other emerging, still uncertain, groping for some identity. The mari-mari, a traditional dance, had still been popular when I left; now it seemed to be forgotten. I scarcely heard it mentioned that evening. Calypso had clearly come to stay. There was something unreal in this ambiguity—in the contrast between one of the old women, swathed in a karasuna, and Ellen and Clifton, neatly dressed and dancing together in European style. Few of the old people joined in; the younger ones took little notice of them. The new culture seemed to be mocking them, blinding them beyond recall to the dying strength of their own.

I danced with Albert's wife, Juliana, while Nelly and Henry watched in glee, holding hands and skipping round us. Her quiet face, with its deep brown eyes and high cheekbones, hardly came up to my shoulder. Gradually my spirits lifted. Despite its strangely confused appearance, the atmosphere was still Indian. I could feel it in everything around us— bare feet shuffling on the floorboards and half smiles caught in the flickering light, snatches of laughter and two old ladies jogging round together; a handful of children playing in the corner and one of the boys, who was slightly tipsy, dancing quite happily on his own.

There was also Carlita, the belle of the village. With shy, slightly pouting lips, deep-set eyes and a distant expression, she had one of the loveliest faces I had ever seen. Three years ago she had been a teacher, with high heeled shoes and her hair in a bun. Then, like many Indian girls, she had given birth to a child without being married. At the time the school was still run by the Church. Judged by an alien moral code, she had lost her job and returned to the old life, an Indian girl once more. Since then she had seemed completely withdrawn. I had seen her child occasionally, a pathetically neglected mite; she had learnt to be ashamed of it. Now I suddenly saw her smiling, her profile caught against the light. Her spirit seemed to be unbroken. There was something defiant in her figure, barefoot, in a pale green dress. I got up and danced with her. I could feel the weight of her jet-black hair, tumbling carelessly over her shoulders and reaching down almost to her waist. Once or twice she looked up shyly. Somehow, like all the others around us, she was still wild and free.

The hours slipped by. The dancing would last as long as the paiwari. When I left, a faint slip of light was spreading over the river. The village was on the edge of waking. Somewhere a child whimpered softly. The dogs stirred uneasily in their sleep, beside the last glow of the fires. It was hard to be leaving, even so briefly. By the time I was back I would have followed the whole changing pattern of their lives. Already it seemed to culminate in the carefree flicker of defiance I had shared with them that night. As I fell asleep, I could still hear the music, mingled with the chatter of parrots, winging their way across the pale dawn.

4

Hallelujah Indians

Two days after leaving Orealla I was on my way to the Kamarang, near the Venezuelan border. The makeshift Dakota juddered and shook as we sped over the dimpled green carpet of the forest, a few hundred feet below. The inside of the plane already suggested the roughneck world of the interior which lay ahead of us. A row of metal seats on either side, a cargo of machinery roped down to the floor and half a dozen passengers—a rather glum-looking European, three or four African porknockers,[1] all fast asleep, and a buxom East Indian girl, who probably also belonged to the diamond world.

'Are you stationed in the Kamarang?' I asked the European, who was sitting opposite me.

'Yes,' he said, looking up for the first time. 'I'm a missionary at one of the Indian settlements there.'

I hesitated for a moment, expecting some further comment. It occurred to me to ask him about the hybrid Hallelujah cult of the Akawaio. I had heard that it was dying out and wanted to know if it still went on. Then I realized that it might be tactless. Most of the local missionaries were strongly opposed to it.

'Perhaps we'll meet up there,' I said. 'I'm hoping to get around a bit.'

'What are you doing here?' he asked. His expression hardly changed as he spoke.

'Just travelling about,' I replied. 'I'm interested in the Indians.'

He nodded non-committally. One of the porknockers snored loudly. The missionary seemed taciturn. I couldn't help feeling that he found the company oppressive. Silence slid awkwardly back again. Perhaps the buxom East Indian girl had sensed the situation. She delved into her

---

1. Diamond-prospectors. They probably acquired this name from their traditional diet of salted pig-tails.

ample bosom, pulled out a packet of cigarettes and offered one to the missionary. He declined with a slightly injured look. She turned to me with a golden-toothed grin. The missionary looked away quietly as I accepted one from her. Most of the minor sects evangelizing in Guiana disapprove strongly of smoking.

I had heard a good deal about the Kamarang, mainly from Dr. Audrey Butt, the only anthropologist to have studied the Akawaio intensively. It was she who had told me about Hallelujah. The cult began among the Macusi tribe, as an attempt to combine Christianity with their own beliefs. At one time it was widespread, but now the Akawaio were thought to be its only remaining followers. It was this, above all, that I wanted to see, in the hope of finding out exactly what lay behind it.

The Kamarang is also inhabited by the Arecuna tribe, who came across from Venezuela under the influence of Seventh Day Adventist missionaries. The Akawaio, on the other hand, were once scattered throughout Guiana; but during the past few generations most of them have slowly withdrawn to the Pakaraima Mountains, which straddle the Guianese border for over two hundred miles. Until some fifteen years ago both tribes were almost undisturbed. But the prospect of change has slowly approached them. Some of the earliest diamond rushes took place in the lower Mazaruni, not far from Akawaio country. The porknockers brought with them a sinister echo of coastal life. Tuberculosis and venereal disease were two of its first ambassadors in the Akawaio villages. Meanwhile the Arecuna received no real help from the Adventist missionaries. They were taught to wear clothes and sing hymns, but little was done for their economy. Most of their culture was suppressed, along with much of their diet, which the Adventists considered unclean.

Under these pressures their old way of life was clearly unable to last. Realizing that they needed some positive aid in their development, the Interior Department established an Indian reservation and a Government post. For over ten years it was run by Bill Seggar, a District Commissioner who was deeply aware of the Indians' problems. Under his guidance they made steady progress towards the point where they could deal with the changes ahead of them. But diamonds suddenly intervened, when a strike was made at Imbaimadai, on the edge of the reservation. Another followed at Ikereku, a little farther north. Then in 1959 a third of the reservation was opened, in answer to the porknockers' demands. Many of the Indians were soon caught up in the whirl of diamond fever. Meanwhile the missionaries were trying to suppress Hallelujah. A few years ago it was still being practised in the outlying villages. But, like the rest of their traditions, it seemed unlikely to survive the influx of missionaries and diamonds.

In less than an hour we would be there. Outside the sunlight danced on the silver-studded wings. Below us, a world of massive green stillness. veined by the darkly meandering rivers, which rose in the Pakaraima foot-hills. Little tufts and spirals of cloud wandered aimlessly over the forest. The sullen span of the Essequibo had already disappeared. Soon we were over the Mazaruni, with a jigsaw puzzle pattern of islands jostling in each of its vast bends. Its waters were flecked with foam-white rapids. Like almost everything in the forest, they are explained by an Indian legend. In the old days the small fishes lived up river and the bigger ones down below. One day the small fishes held a paiwari spree. Their big brothers came to join them and on the way they performed the tugoit, the dance of the green humming bird. When they reached the small fishes' home, the unfortunate hassa, a large black fish, got stuck in the entrance by his whiskers. Eventually he turned to stone— hence the Mazaruni rapids.

I laughed as I remembered the story and shared it with the East Indian girl. By now we could see the low tableland of the Pakaraimas. Philip Jardim, the Portuguese pilot whom I had met at the airfield, beckoned to me from the cockpit. The local airways were no exception to Guianese hospitality. He sprayed the windows carefully so that I could take photographs.

He cupped his hands and raised his voice above the drone of the engines. 'We'll be crossing the Mazaruni again in about five minutes,' he shouted. 'Then over the Pakaraimas.' He pointed to the map. 'We fly through the gorge here—watch out for the waterfall on our left.'

Already the foot-hills were below us, rising slowly through the mist, until the mountains leapt up behind them, forming a rugged, defiant frontier. For a moment we flew straight towards it. A cloud swept by and as we emerged the sandstone gorge climbed up on either side of us. I glimpsed the waterfall Philip had mentioned, a silver thread spilling out of the forest, with its feet wrapped in spray. A few seconds later we passed another, slender, blown apart by the wind before it reached the ground.

'There's Roraima,' shouted Philip, as the gorge fell away. He pointed to a sugar-loaf mountain squatting on the horizon—the setting of Conan Doyle's 'Lost World' and the meeting-point of the boundaries of Guiana, Brazil and Venezuela. A few minutes later we saw the airstrip, a tiny scar of red sand, with buildings dotted along each side, dwarfed by the forest behind them. We dipped down towards the headland, which divided the Kamarang River from the Mazaruni. A little crowd of figures appeared, hurrying towards us. They were hidden for a moment by a cloud of dust, as we bounced along the airstrip.

The crowd of faces round the plane was typical of the mêlée of the past ten years. A group of porknockers rolled cigarettes and watched the scene with an air of boredom. Barefoot Akawaio women stood shyly in the background, wearing shapeless, tattered dresses. A huddle of schoolchildren, all neatly clothed, edged forward to look at us.

Suddenly I saw a familiar face. It was Mani, an Arawak from the Moruca, the first Indian district I had ever visited. He came forward and shook my hand. The dead-pan, rather suspicious air, which seemed a part of the porknocker's outfit, vanished from his face.

'I did think my eyes was fooling me, when I seen you,' he said. 'When you gone away to England, I didn't know you was coming back.'

'But what are you doing up here?' I asked.

'Going after the diamonds,' he said. 'Working with these two boys here.'

He introduced me to his friends—George, an Arawak from the north-west, and Albert, a strongly built young Wapisiana from the Rupununi savannas. Again I had the same impression; the hard, somewhat casual veneer, which they wore as a part of this knockabout world, gave way to a shy Indian smile.

The District Officer was away. His second in charge, who was genial, but pining for the comforts of Georgetown, pointed to a wooden rest house, where I could spend the night.

'I going carry this for you,' said Mani, shouldering my bag. We walked on down the runway, followed by a handful of children, whispering in curiosity. Most of them were Akawaios, with short figures and pinched faces, unlike the Arecunas, who were darker and lithely built.

It was not hard to imagine this spot as unbroken forest some twelve years before. The rows of little wooden buildings were a striking contrast to the leaf roofs of an Indian settlement on the far bank. Behind it, the mora trees towered upwards, a sheer grey wall trailing lianas from its topmost branches. A tiny wood-skin, the Akawaio brand of canoe, which is made from the bark of a tree, skimmed across the dark river. Against this peaceful Indian background, our surroundings had a distant echo of the old, lawless frontier point—dust-laden, roughneck and happy-go-lucky, with porknockers chatting in tight little groups and battered outboards and diving helmets at every other corner. An atmosphere of suspended fever, conjured up by the scent of diamonds, a day or two away.

75

The others left me to unpack, but in the evening they returned.

'The Indians here are shy,' said Mani, as we talked by the quivering light of a pressure-lamp.

'You know what makes them so,' said George. 'The missionaries tell them don't go near strangers. They say all outside people is bad—even we Indians from other tribes.'

The others laughed. But George was right. Partly for protective ends, but also for fear of losing their influence, the missionaries tend to seclude their Indian flocks. But here it was a dangerous policy. Sooner or later they were bound to mix. Their distrust of the other races would only add to their problems.

'Have you heard of a thing called Hallelujah up here?' I asked.

'Yes,' said Mani. 'Once we did dance it the whole night, in one of the houses over the river. They had special Hallelujah songs and plenty of paiwari—cassack, the Akawaio call it.'

'But the same thing happening with Hallelujah,' said George. 'The missionaries trying to stop it now.'

'Yes,' said Mani, 'is so I heard. If you want to see the proper thing you got to go far from here, to a village called Amokokopai. That's up the Kukui River, near the border with Brazil. We supposed to be leaving here tomorrow. We could take you to Jawalla, the village at Kukui Mouth. From there you could get a next boat.'

They seemed to have settled my plans for me. We chatted on until late that night. Their mood changed at every moment from light-hearted banter to diamond talk, as they counted the stones they were going to find. The three of them were close friends. I wished that I could have joined them for a while, to see how they had adapted themselves to the world of diamond fever; but by now I was thinking of Amokokopai and the Hallelujah Indians.

I was woken by the sound of bare feet in the kitchen. The school-children were cooking their breakfast. They had gathered from the neighbouring villages for an annual examination. Most of them came from Paruima, they told me, the Adventist mission up the Kamarang River. Once our brief introduction was over, they avoided my glance and kept to themselves. They had none of the coy curiosity of most Indian children. I remembered what Mani and his friends had told me. Only one of the girls seemed less withdrawn, smiling at me occasionally. She was taller than the others, with distinctive, finely chiselled features. I was sure she came from a different tribe—perhaps the distant Maiong-kong, who live in Venezuela.

The morning air was still cold outside, despite a watery sun. A thin blanket of mist lay over the Mazaruni, curling its way round Kako Mountain, a few miles up river. The faraway roar of the howler monkeys carried softly out of the forest, with the hills echoing in reply. A moment later Mani appeared. The engine was giving trouble, he said. It might be some time before we left.

At midday it still refused to start, but a boat had come down from Jawalla.

'They going back just now,' said Mani, when he brought the news to me. 'I think is better you leave with them. Perhaps we going meet you at Jawalla.'

We carried my bag down the steep little path which led to the water's edge. An Indian, who was bathing quietly, looked up as we arrived.

' 'Morning, yakko,[1]' Mani said to him.

He nodded in reply and came and sat down beside us on the bank. He was wearing a pair of blue bathing trunks which had an American look about them.

'Where you come from, yakko?' asked Mani.

'From topside, Paruima,' he said.

'Arecuna?'

'Yes,' he replied. 'And you, what tribe?'

'Arawak. This boy Wapisiana,' said Mani, pointing to Albert.

The Arecuna gazed at him in curiosity. 'First time I seen Wapisiana,' he said. 'Long time I been Venezuela. Only now I come this side.'

I offered him a cigarette, but he shook his head suspiciously. It was almost the first time I had known an Indian refuse one.

'Why no smoking?' Mani asked.

'Cigarette poison.'

'Who say so?'

'Priest tell we,' he said firmly.

Mani gave me a meaningful look. Just then the boat appeared—a little canoe with an outboard engine, driven by a slightly moon-faced young Akawaio, called Basil. Yes, he said with a grin, he would take me up to Jawalla. I said goodbye to Mani and Albert and in a moment we were off.

The sky was soon overcast. Suddenly a gust of rain spotted the dark, mirror-like water. Basil and I pulled off our shirts and thrust them under the seat. As we did so, the heavens opened. A clap of thunder echoed round us. The river and sky faded rapidly into a grey blur of water. There was nowhere to shelter, so we carried on. The throb of the engine

1. Little brother, friend.

was almost drowned by the drumming of the rain. A few minutes later a patch of blue sky broke slowly on to the horizon. The river grew still again, while the warm sun dried our shoulders.

As we turned the next bend, the low hump of Kako Mountain came into view, with the mist still lingering at its feet. The forest climbed up steeply on either side of us. The massive liana-tangled trees were smattered with bright yellow flowers, their blooms a delicate trumpet shape, spilling down towards the water. Cone-shaped ants' nests hung from the branches, some of them forty or fifty feet up—the equivalent of several miles climbing for the ambitious ants, I reckoned. The slow monotony of the big rivers encourages whimsical trains of thought.

The hum of the engines was almost lost in the heavy stillness around us. Occasionally there was a sign of life. A large flock of howler monkeys, with their young clinging on to their backs, peered through the leaves in curiosity and ambled along the branches. A flight of bats flipped over the water and vanished into the darkened forest. Then a lone wood-skin drifted by on the far side of the river. Basil slowed down and shouted to the boy who was paddling it. As his voice echoed from bank to bank, I caught an Akawaio word—'kapong', with which they refer to themselves. Its meaning is literally 'sky people'. Like the Warraus, they believe that their ancestors lived above the clouds.

Dusk was gathering by the time Jawalla came into view. Its two scattered groups of houses stood on each side of the Kukui River, at the point where it joined the Kamarang. I glimpsed a leaf roof here and there; but many of the houses seemed to be built in the style of the wooden shacks back at the Government station.

'We got fancy homes now,' said Basil. 'We build them on a housing scheme.'

I concealed my surprise in somewhat feigned admiration. This was rather different from anything I had expected to find in an Akawaio village. As we pulled into the landing, beside a cluster of wood-skins, a figure appeared in the half darkness above us. It was Joe Blake, the school-teacher, a lively, jovial character, of mixed African and Indian blood, whom I had met on the previous day.

We left my bag in the wooden school-room where I was spending the night. Joe asked me to join him for a drink. He ushered me into his makeshift little home. The door was opened by his wife, a quiet, wrinkled Akawaio, who rummaged mysteriously in a corner and produced a bottle of rum.

'We scarcely get visitors here,' said Joe. 'Just one or two people passing each year. But I like the work all right,' he added. 'The Akawaio is a friendly people, when you get to know them. Nice kids too—like a family to me.'

He patted the head of a tousled urchin standing by the door. His timid brown eyes were full of wonder, as he looked up at us.

'How long have you been here?' I asked.

'Six years now,' he said. 'These people change up a lot since then. When I first came here they had no school. They was scarcely wearing any clothes—the men just got a red loin-cloth, and the women their bead-aprons. But now you hardly see these things. The old people does still wear them, but underneath the new clothes that the missionaries give them.'

'What about their houses?' I asked. 'They seem to be changing too.'

'Yes,' he replied, nodding his head, 'all the old customs dying out. At first two or three of them got new houses and now they all want them. They get ashamed of the old way of living.'

'Yes,' I said, 'the same thing's happening up at Orealla. But do they still have Hallelujah—or has that died out too?'

'No, they still dance it here,' he said. 'But the best place for that is Amokokopai. Is there the blind old prophet lives, the man they call Aibilibing. I believe they getting a dance up there in a couple of days from now.'

A knock on the door. Basil sauntered in.

'You like to go to Amokokopai with this gentleman?' Joe asked him.

'Yes,' said Basil, 'I could go with him. They got a boat going up there soon. Not tomorrow, but the next day.'

'And they going to dance Hallelujah?' asked Joe.

'Yes,' said Basil, 'is so I heard.'

'They don't mind strangers coming?' I asked.

He laughed. 'No, they is friendly people. White man can dance Hallelujah too.'

At last I seemed to be within reach of one of the last remaining features of the Indian world.

The next day passed slowly at Jawalla. The little school was gay with children, wild mites with tangled hair, who sang their school songs proudly for me. The mission was run by the Anglican Church, which treats the Indians more tolerantly than the smaller, unorthodox sects. But in spite of this the older people seemed bewildered by the changes going on around them.

In the morning I walked round the village. The first house I saw was one of the few which still had a leaf roof and a rough wall of bark. A young Akawaio was sitting outside, chipping idly at a piece of wood. He beckoned and I followed him into the house. An old woman was crouching on the floor, scraping a heap of cassava roots, with their white flesh gleaming dully beside her. She glanced up suspiciously. Over her emaciated figure she wore a ragged blue dress, which looked as if it had never been washed. A motley necklace hung down in front of her, made of seeds, safety pins and the teeth of wild animals. A bracelet of blue and white beads encircled each of her wrists. Leg-bands of a similar pattern were wrapped tightly round her calves, above the ankle and below the knee. They are worn by the women from childhood, to strengthen their muscles for the long walk to the farm. Her face had a pale, sunken look; tuberculosis had been common since the diamond rushes. To complete her rather grim appearance, three blue-grey lines were tattooed across her upper lip, curling round on to her cheeks.

'Nice, no?' said the young man, following my gaze.

I nodded in agreement.

'That is scorpion charm,' he explained, indicating the twirls on her cheeks, which were similar to the upturned tail of a scorpion. 'They does help her to make good drink,' he added. 'The spirit like it and let she make good cassack.'

This was the first example I had seen of the symbolism which once played a leading part in Indian ritual. Most of the Akawaio still use these cassiri-binas, or charms, which are made by piercing the skin and rubbing in a mixture of burnt sugar-cane and wild honey. The sweet quality of these ingredients has a symbolic purpose. Among the more remote tribes, the drink is still made by chewing cassava bread and spitting the juice back into the cauldron. The saliva converts the starch into sugar, which causes fermentation. The sweetness of the cassiri-bina symbolizes and helps this process. The various patterns which they use are chosen for the same reason. One represents the honey bee and another the skin of the hassa fish, which is also noted for its sweetness. The symbol of the kansok, or scorpion's tail, a favourite among the Akawaio, has different associations; just as the scorpion has a sting in its tail, so the pattern which represents it adds to the sting, or strength, of the cassack.

As if to prove the power of the charm, the man went over to the corner and spoke to a girl who was stirring a large cauldron. Although she was young, perhaps eighteen or twenty, she still wore blue and white leg-bands. Her lip was tattooed with a single line curling up into a kansok pattern. To a Westernized eye it rather spoilt her docile, attractive features, but it would have appealed to a young Akawaio as a sign of her maturity and her skill in brewing cassack. She filled a calabash for the young man, and he brought it over to me. The drink had probably been made by the traditional chewing method, but there was no time to be squeamish. I raised the calabash and drank it down. It was thicker than paiwari, with a sweet, rather clinging taste, which reminded me faintly of peaches.

I smiled gratefully at the old lady. She said something to the young man, whose name turned out to be Philip.

'She ask if you got cigarette,' he said.

I handed her the remains of my packet. Her grim expression suddenly melted into a gleeful smile. She picked one out and I lit it for her.

'I could take her picture?' I asked Philip.

He passed the request on to her. The old lady muttered something.

'She frighten,' he said. 'She believe you going lock she spirit inside the machine.'

This was a new problem. Suddenly I had an idea. There were just two pictures left on the roll of film.

'If I open it after I take the picture, the spirit can't stay inside,' I said. 'And then you can all see how it works.'

Philip spoke to her again. She paused, then nodded doubtfully and we trooped out into the sunlight. When it was over, they pressed round to watch me removing the film. I held the camera up to the light and one by one they peeped inside to watch the flash of the shutter. The old lady sighed in wonder and showed her approval by bringing some more cassack.

'You like to see my home?' asked Philip.

He led me to one of the new houses, which was still in the process of being built. Inside, it was almost bare. A pair of hammocks strung across it and a heap of clothes lying in a corner, with a diving helmet and a cheap guitar beside them.

'I making money with this,' he said, pointing to the diving helmet. 'Finding plenty diamonds.' He smiled shyly, picked up the guitar and tried to strum a chord. 'I ain't learn as yet,' he explained. 'The man who buy diamonds give it to me. Fifty dollars I pay him for it. Is a good one, no?'

He looked at me anxiously. It might have been worth fifteen dollars, twenty at the most.

I tried to conceal my reactions. 'Yes, it's nice,' I said.

'You got wife?' he asked suddenly.

'No,' I said, 'not as yet. And you?'

He grinned broadly. 'I got plenty of wife,' he said, 'all about this place.'

I wandered back towards the school. That afternoon Basil took me across the river to see the other half of Jawalla. Here there was even more contrast between the old and new houses. Most of the former now stood at the far end of the village. The new ones had wooden walls, steps and curtained windows; but inside they were almost bare. Like Captain's house at Orealla, they looked completely out of keeping with the Indians' lives. There was nowhere for the women to cook, for the children to play, for hammocks to be slung—nowhere even for the men to drift in and out for their cassack. Most families had a camp nearby, made out of bark and leaves. It was here that their lives were going on, just as they always had done. The cassack was being handed round and hammocks were stretched from side to side. It looked as if their new homes were hardly ever used. Once more they were forced to choose between an unreal imitation and a retreat to the far end of the village.

This seemed to explain their suspicion in some of the homes we visited. I was a part of this new world which had so little perception. Some of them demanded money when I asked if I could take their pictures. Why not? I reflected. They had been taught that they were poor and the porknockers had exploited them. It was not a difficult lesson to learn. Now it was their turn.

But elsewhere they were still generous. As soon as we reached one camp, cassava bread and pepperpot were placed in front of us. One of the women walked round with a calabash in her hand. She moved gracefully, hardly aware of the child at her breast, asleep in a cotton sling. The men began to grow curious. Where had I come from and where was I going? Did God speak Akawaio and, if so, how had he learnt it? Their defensive suspicion had vanished; and yet this return to their natural friendliness seemed only to emphasize the way in which they were changing.

We left at dawn, with a long day's journey ahead of us. It was several hours to Philipai, a mission at the head of the river. From there a trail led to Amokokopai, just a few miles away. There were five of us crammed inside the canoe—apart from Basil and myself, a tall, reserved Akawaio called Johnny, and Ignatius, the Captain from Philipai, with his young wife, who looked hardly more than sixteen. For eight hours we droned up the Kukui, with the forest closing in on each side. The Akawaios were restrained at first, but soon their shyness disappeared, and they chattered and laughed gaily. By now we were heading directly south, towards the Brazilian border. The narrow river twisted and turned, with some of the bends almost blocked by a mass of fallen trees. Johnny turned the throttle full out each time we approached them, raising the engine at the last moment, as we scraped over the top. Once or twice we came to rest amongst a tangle of half submerged branches. But somehow we kept our balance, as Basil and Johnny jumped out and pushed the boat through.

By mid-afternoon we reached Philipai. It was run by a small American sect, similar to the Adventists, called the Pilgrim Holiness. The village was scattered over a wide clearing, backed by a steep little hill. In the centre stood the missionary's house, a gaily painted model for the changes going on around it, which were much the same as those at Jawalla. Ignatius led us to his house, which was different from most of the others—a low building, with a leaf roof, enclosed with long strips of bark.

It was just over an hour's walk to Amokokopai. Ignatius said he would come with us. He had heard that they were dancing Hallelujah. Although the missionary frowned on it, some of the people had already left for the cult centre. It was pleasantly cool inside the house and we paused for a cigarette. As soon as I produced a packet, hands appeared from all directions. Smoking was an abomination, in the eyes of the Pilgrim Holiness sect; but clearly the Akawaio still thought otherwise.

We trailed slowly up the hill which overlooked the village. Several other Indians had joined us to come and sing Hallelujah, including two stalwart little boys who insisted on carrying my belongings. We stopped at a house on the brow of the hill and Ignatius led us inside. An old man stood up to greet us—Ignatius's father. He was dressed in a picturesque combination of a red loin-cloth and a tattered old jacket—a vivid contrast to his son, with his striped T-shirt and plimsolls and a slightly American twang in his pidgin English.

We sat down on a rough bench, and cassava bread and pepperpot were brought forward. A little boy with a monkey on his shoulder peeped out from behind the old man, giggling and hiding his face whenever I caught his eye. Two girls lay in their hammocks, one of them spinning a fishing line and the other weaving a bead-apron on a wooden frame. Suddenly a child appeared, with the finished article slung round her waist, a little square ornament, attractively patterned with blue and white beads. She skipped shyly behind her mother, lithe and agile, utterly different from the subdued mission children whom I had seen before.

A round of cassack, sweet and refreshing, and the meal was over. As we set out, the sun glinted fiercely on the blue-grey line of the hills. Ignatius paused and pointed west. 'Look Mount Roraima,' he said. I caught sight of the mist-hung plateau, dominating the jagged horizon, the centre of an untamed world of broken crags and valleys. On one side the Brazilian hills; on the other Venezuela.

We trudged on past a deserted round-house. The ribs of its rafters stood out gauntly against the low horizon. Until the missionaries arrived, most of the Akawaio lived in these large circular houses. Each one contained several families, belonging to the married daughters who, by a system of matrilocality, stayed in their parents' home. The missionaries thought this undignified and immoral. It has now been discouraged in favour of single family houses. A moment later we were into the forest. The narrow trail was speckled and shafted with the sunlight that forced its way through the dense leaves overhead. A pigeon murmured up in the branches. Now and then we came to a creek, spanned by a single narrow log. Although I was used to these Indian bridges, I felt clumsy and hesitant beside the sure-footed Akawaios.

After an hour's rapid walking, the forest came to an end. We crossed a last, clear-watered creek at the foot of a sudden hill. It was here that they all bathed together—something I was unlikely to see—after the Hallelujah dances. The village of Amokokopai, which means literally 'old man's grotto', takes its name from the creek. Legend relates that an old Akawaio was bathing there after a cassack spree. When he reached the deepest spot, where Lato the water spirit lived, she lured him away to his death.

We hurried on up the path. Suddenly I paused. A low chant was coming from the hilltop. They were dancing Hallelujah. Basil looked at me in excitement. He had never seen the cult centre before. Two little boys in red loin-cloths scampered timidly away, as we entered the village. Its half dozen houses were all built in the traditional style. On our left stood a large round-house, with its pointed roof almost reaching the ground. It belonged to Aibilibing, the reigning Hallelujah prophet. In front of it was an open space, and beyond this a low wooden building, where the Indians were singing their slow, rather solemn chant.

Our surroundings had an awe-striking beauty. It was not hard to understand why the wandering cult had ended up in this remote little village. It had an air of magic about it, which must have occurred to the Indian mind, where mountains and the supernatural are closely associated. The level vista of the forest rolled away on every side, hemmed in by the blue Pakaraimas, with a single sharp crag in the foreground.

Basil looked up and pointed to it. 'Is there Piait'ma living,' he said— a mountain spirit whom the piai-men visit, when they need a cure for a patient.

Ignatius had already vanished. We followed him into the wooden building. As we peered in through the narrow doorway, the dance was coming to an end. A circle of some thirty Indians, with children amongst them, was just breaking up. Some of them looked round suspiciously. I saw Ignatius explaining my presence. The children all had bead-aprons and loin-cloths, but most of the adults wore ragged clothes. Once I glimpsed a splash of red, where a loin-cloth peeped over a pair of trousers, donned for the occasion. Most of the women had rough necklaces, made out of anything they could find—beads, pins, old coins, seeds and the teeth of wild animals. The building itself was completely bare, except for a single post in the centre. The light filtered in weakly through two small windows on each side.

They paused and then began dancing again, with Ignatius at their head. Linking arms, they formed a circle round the inside of the building. Their expressions were suddenly intent. Ignatius hummed softly for a moment, as if searching for a note. Then his head began to sway as he broke into a low chant. It was muttered and slightly indistinct, with a touch of fervour in it, repeated and slowly growing stronger. For a few seconds he sang alone, and then the others joined in, bodies swaying into rhythm and bare feet brushing the sandy floor. A step forward, back again, and then they began moving slowly round.

So Ignatius was a Hallelujah leader. In a moment he had changed completely, slipping back into something quite different from his Westernized exterior. I remembered how reticent he had been when I first mentioned Hallelujah—as if it were a topic to be avoided in the atmosphere of Philipai. The missionaries' disapproval must have put him on his guard; but clearly their influence was skin deep. The cult seemed to be dying hard, when the ablest young Indian in the mission was one of the prophet's leading disciples.

The others confirmed this first impression. The dance was not the shambling, uncertain performance which I had often seen at Indian ceremonies. They were all familiar with the words, and the same expression of quiet intensity had come over every face. Their voices rose in unison as they circled on, backwards and forwards, dipping their bodies in perfect time and stamping their feet together. After a while they broke into pairs, turning at right angles to the centre, with Ignatius and his young wife facing the other dancers. The chant had a low, monotonous rhythm, consisting, like their traditional songs, of two lines of a few words each, repeated over and over again. At first their blurred, nasal tone made it hard to distinguish the words. Then I began to pick them out—the fervid refrain of 'Hallelujah', after which the cult was christened, 'Papa', the Indian term for God, and 'Abel', the name of the first Akawaio prophet. The song described his vision of God and the message which he received for his people.

After some ten minutes the ritual came to an end. The dancers fell back into line, with their steps slowing down. Ignatius sang a final solo, his voice dying away to a whisper, and then, after a moment's silence, they stood back and raised their heads. This time the atmosphere was unbroken as they linked arms again. Ignatius looked up and beckoned to me, and I joined in the line. He clearly knew how to dispel the suspicion with which they seemed to regard me. A little old woman, with an elegant pattern tattooed on her face, grasped me firmly by the arm, scarcely looking up as she did so. The circle swayed and gathered speed. Slowly I fell in with their steps. The low hum welled up around us, with a somnolent yet powerful effect, like the pulse of a living thing which bound them together as they danced. For a moment I was held by their fervour, a slow, irresistible current, with its depths far down in their Indian blood. Then suddenly Ignatius led us outside, still chanting rhythmically, into the open space, now encircled with dusk. For a few minutes we danced round it, until we gradually came to a halt. The last Hallelujah echoed down into the darkened valley.

Ignatius spoke quietly. The others knelt down, with their heads bowed close to the ground. He started praying, slowly at first, until his voice gathered speed and grew louder. The others repeated the phrases after him, faster, carried away by his words, until exhortation and response were almost overlapping. I caught the word 'akwa', meaning light—they were asking for God's light and strength to be given to the tribe. The circle of figures, with the dusk around them, was a strangely moving sight. I felt sure that the missionaries' views would have crumbled, had they been there to watch the Indians, praying in a way that was still defiantly their own.

A few minutes later they rose to their feet. The day's ceremony was over. Benches were brought out and we sat down in front of Aibilibing's house for a communal meal. One by one the Indians came forward to break off a piece of cassava bread and dip it into the pepperpot. One of the women moved slowly round, handing cassack to each person, including even the youngest children. The hunters had been successful that morning; a wild hog had been caught and roasted. Two of the men stood in the background, cutting it apart. Pieces were passed from hand to hand and soon I could hardly keep up with their offerings. The firelight from inside the house flickered amongst the circle of faces. Once or twice a whispered comment, followed by a quiet laugh; but otherwise they talked very little. They were watchful, conscious of each other, yet intent on the meal they were eating.

I was sitting next to the old lady with whom I had danced Hallelujah. She was less shy than most of the others, patting me gently on the shoulder and pointing towards the pepperpot with a look of encouragement. She turned to Basil and asked him something. 'Mister Colin,' he replied with a grin, and I gathered that she had asked my name. Her brow wrinkled in bewilderment as she tried to pronounce it. The nearest she got was 'Mistakong', and so Mistakong I became.

She asked Basil another question.

'She want to know how many years you got,' he said.

'Twenty-one,' I replied.

He passed on the information. The old lady sighed and looked at me closely, obviously pondering something. She turned to Basil and muttered again.

'She say she going care for you while you here,' he said.

I laughed. She gave me a motherly smile and passed me a piece of wild hog.

The meal continued, in true Indian fashion, until the last scrap of meat had gone. Night had long since fallen around us. One by one, with hardly a sound, the Indians slipped away to their hammocks. Ignatius suggested that Basil and I should sleep in the 'chochi'[1]—the term which they used for the Hallelujah building. There was no particular reverence attached to it, now that the ritual was over. Two little boys clambered up into the rafters to sling our hammocks, while a handful of chickens and dogs followed us in as curious spectators. Five minutes later I was scribbling my diary, while Basil chatted quietly with one of the Akawaio boys.

Over an hour must have passed, when the stillness outside was suddenly broken by a tremulous voice. It was coming from Aibilibing's house.

'Who's that singing?' I asked Basil.

'Aibilibing,' he replied sleepily. 'The old man blind, he can't dance no more. But sometimes he does sing whole night. Tomorrow they say you could see him.'

I went outside for a moment. The old prophet's voice rose and fell against the hum of the crickets. I could sense that the others were listening to him, in the houses all around, where the firelight still flickered weakly against the enveloping darkness. After a while his voice died away. The chant was immediately taken up by a woman in the

1. An Indianized version of 'church'.

87

neighbouring house. I went slowly back to my hammock. As I lay there, half asleep, her lonely voice still ululated down the highways of the night. At brief moments, silence returned, but each time another song followed.

So Hallelujah had survived. By now it was a part of Indian history. Legend has it that the first prophet was a Macusi named Bichiwung. Adopted by a white priest, he left his people and went to England. Here he was taught Christianity. Suspecting that he was being deceived, he decided to visit God himself. One afternoon, while the priest was away, he went outside and walked up the path to Heaven—this being quite simple for him, because he had once been a piai-man. When he arrived he knocked on the door. God immediately opened it to him, and listened to all his troubles. His answer confirmed Bichiwung's suspicions— the priest was deceiving him; in any case the white man's religion was old and out of date. The Indians must learn Hallelujah, a new religion, designed especially for them. God taught Bichiwung some songs and gave him a special bottle of medicine and a piece of paper, to serve as the Indian Bible. Heaven looked an attractive place—the cassava grew of its own accord and was nearly as high as a house. Bichiwung naturally wanted to stay, but God said that this was impossible; he must go back and teach Hallelujah. If the Indians did as He told them, He would give them light[1] and strength and protect them from their enemies. They would even acquire the white man's wealth, without being dominated by him.

Bichiwung kept his religion a secret until he returned to the Macusi. At first they were sceptical about it. Even his wife refused to believe him. Returning from the farm one day, she found Bichiwung locked up with their daughter, praying for Hallelujah; suspecting rather less spiritual motives, she made quite a nasty scene. But eventually the whole tribe became followers of the cult. Bichiwung's power caused jealousy and in the end he was killed by kanaima.[2] Twice the medicine which God had given him brought him back to life. The third time the murderer cut up his body and scattered the pieces through the forest, His wife was unable to find them all and so he finally died.

The Macusi went on with Hallelujah. But one day they had a wild paiwari spree, and when they woke up, God took their religion away, to punish them for drinking too much. Meanwhile the Akawaio had learnt it. The next person to see God was a piai-man called Uraiak. God

1. Light (akwa) being a symbol of tribal regeneration.
2. An Indian who transforms himself into an evil spirit in order to take his revenge on an enemy. Their methods are said to be extremely bloodthirsty. Deaths amongst the Akawaio are still often attributed to them.

told him to call himself Abel and preach Hallelujah to the Akawaio. He started by building a wooden 'chochi' at Amokokopai. For a time he had a rival called Christ, an Indian who lived in a neighbouring village, but eventually Abel became sole leader and first of the Akawaio prophets. He was soon acknowledged by the whole tribe, with an ebulu, or disciple-leader, in most of the villages. One of them took his place when he died, and a line of prophets came into being. The name of each one is still remembered, and Aibilibing is the fifth.

Meanwhile Hallelujah had spread from the Akawaio to their neighbours, the Arecuna and Patamona tribes. Some fifty years ago there may have been several thousand followers; but now the cult is on the decline. The situation in the early nineteenth century could easily have witnessed the events which the Bichiwung legend describes. Rumours of Christianity were arousing intense curiosity among the remoter tribes. Anglican priests came and preached to them, while parties of Indians went down to the missions and then returned to their homes. These brief contacts with Christianity probably led to the hybrid religion, which attempted to reconcile them with traditional Indian beliefs. Bichiwung, if that was really his name, may have gone no farther than Georgetown; but certain aspects of his story suggest that he actually reached England. One of the Akawaio songs is about 'Hallelujah coming from England'; another, describing God as 'mist-maker', is attributed to Bichiwung's impression of the fog on the English coast.[1] But, wherever it was that he went, the outcome is clear. Suspecting the priest in charge of him, he visited God through spirit contact, just as he visited Indian spirits in his days as a piai-man. He then returned to Macusi country and started preaching Hallelujah. Historically, little more can be said; but certain details in the story seem to explain his revelation and the cult it produced. Some of these had already occurred to me. On the next day they grew clearer.

I was woken by a cold mountain dawn. The silence outside felt strangely deliberate, after the singing which I had heard at broken intervals throughout the night. I lay in my hammock for a moment, trying to recapture a little warmth. After a while the stillness was broken by the sharp, enquiring bark of a dog, and then the sound of children's voices, patched on the morning air.

I left my hammock and went outside. Basil, who had woken before me, was just returning from the creek, with his wet hair gleaming in the sunlight. One by one the women were appearing, bringing their

1. A selection of Hallelujah songs is given in Appendix C.

cooking pots from each home and setting them down in preparation for the morning meal. A few of the men were out hunting, but the rest of the Indians gathered round. Once more they ate quietly, as if to preserve the peace that hung over the village.

As soon as the meal had ended, Ignatius came over to me.

'Aibilibing going talk to you now,' he said.

He led me towards the old prophet's house. I stooped in through the narrow entrance. As I grew used to the half darkness, details began to emerge. A third of the village must have lived there, consisting mainly of the old man's daughters, together with their families. Their hammocks were slung from post to post in a curved pattern that mingled with the shadows. Overhead, on the rafters, lay a collection of bows and arrows, blowpipes, and a single shotgun. A dark cluster of baskets and gourds, some of them grotesquely shaped, hung beside the entrance. The pointed leaf roof was black with the smoke that curled slowly upwards. At least three fires were burning, with the women crouching beside them, scraping cassava roots. The children were playing on their own, tumbling each other out of their hammocks and laughing quietly. A plump, middle-aged woman, with a heavy tangle of bead-necklaces, sat in a corner spinning cotton. A younger man was squatting beside her, with his arm round her shoulder. Partnerships of different ages are fairly common among the Indians, until Christianity arrives. I was struck by their open affection. In the advanced villages, this would never be seen. I had always assumed that their modesty was something intrinsically Indian; but perhaps, like so many of their inhibitions, it was due to the influence of the missions.

Ignatius went over to the darkest corner and muttered a quiet greeting. An old man, wearing a tattered shirt and a loin-cloth, sat up slowly in his hammock, with his frail legs on either side. His hair was slightly flecked at the temples, over a strong, heavy brow. The lines in his face had drawn their expression from the void in his blind, centreless eyes, blind eyes turning towards us, laden with distance and gazing over our shoulders. Seventy, perhaps, it was hard to tell. His presence seemed to fill the house. He stretched out a wrinkled hand, and I held it in mine for a moment.

'Aibilibing,' he announced solemnly.

'Colin,' I replied, 'Engiland tawina'—from England.

The old prophet's features broke into a smile. He beckoned and two of the women came forward. One of them brought a wooden bench, while the other filled a calabash and placed it in his hand. He took a slow, ponderous sip and passed it over to me.

'I could hear about Hallelujah?' I asked.

Ignatius told him my request. A long exchange followed in rapid undertones.

'He like to tell you,' said Ignatius. 'But he say that some white people get angry with this Hallelujah. One time a priest come here to stop we. He did want to steal Hallelujah and he vexed that we got it. This thing is for Indian people. But if you come in a right way, if you like this Hallelujah, Aibilibing would sing for you.'

I reassured him. It was interesting, this defensive barrier which surrounded the cult. Even Ignatius seemed to share it. He hardly looked me in the face, speaking in a low, hurried tone, with his eyes fixed on the ground. But slowly the prophet's story emerged, told mainly in terms of the songs handed down by his predecessors.

'Aibilibing say the first man to get Hallelujah was Bichiwung,' said Ignatius. 'He was Macusi man, working with white priest, and he gone to England, far, far. He see God and get Hallelujah. That make white people want to thief Hallelujah, because it come from England. But Macusi people drink and sport and then they loss Hallelujah. God give it to Akawaio man called Abel. Aibilibing going sing you the song about how Abel get Hallelujah.'

The old man raised his head and began the chant which I had heard on the previous day. Sitting bolt upright in his hammock, he droned on for several minutes, repeating the half dozen words over and over again. The meaning was compressed and simple. 'Abel was praying, he got Hallelujah, Hallelujah from God, sisters.'

'Why sisters?[1]' I asked, when Ignatius told me the meaning.

'Well,' he said, with a straight face, 'the men did like this thing from the start, but the women not so much. They was sporting all the time. So Abel tell them about Hallelujah. Then he got a son called Moses. God tell Moses to dance Hallelujah. Before this they was only singing, but now they learn to dance. When Abel dead, they got a next prophet— he name John William.'

The old man sang once more. By now the others had gathered round, gazing at him intently. His face had an almost frozen expression, his lips barely moving. All morning he sang and talked, unfolding the Hallelujah saga. The third prophet was called William. After him there was Kwiabong, who had died a few years ago, and then came Aibilibing himself. The themes of the songs were brief and clear, asking for strength and help and messages from God. Finally he sang his own song—'Aibilibinge Hallelujah', 'Aibilibing has received Hallelujah'.

1. Bajeeko (Akawaio).

'Why does he have that name?' I asked.

'First time he singing and praying,' said Ignatius, 'he couldn't get Hallelujah. Then one day he got the thing, and the people hear him sing this song, with the word Aibilibing.[1] Is so he catch the name.'

'But what will God give to the Indians if they keep up with Hallelujah?'

Ignatius seemed vague. He was either uncertain or else reluctant to tell me.

'God give good thing,' he said. 'Light and strength and nice place for the Indians.'

'A place in Heaven?'

'Heaven, yes. Old people was saying God going give all this place to the Indians. Outsiders going away.'

'And who got Hallelujah now? The Patamona and Arecuna still got it?'

'We ain't know. Perhaps, yes. But I hear Arecuna people lost it. The priest stop Hallelujah, same like they wanting to stop it here. We can't say about Patamona. I believe they still got it. But now Hallelujah getting small, because outside people want to thief it. But this is we Hallelujah, nobody can't take it.'

Once more this sense of resistance, which seemed to be at the root of the cult. Aibilibing lay back in his hammock, obviously tired by his exertions. I asked Ignatius to thank him for me.

'He say you should stay more long,' he said, 'and then you could get good Hallelujah. He does like the way you talking.'

The old man spoke to one of the women. She took down a bunch of bananas and passed it over to me. Then he turned to Ignatius again.

'He ask if you want sūki-sūki,' said Ignatius. 'Look a nice one there.' He pointed to a slender blowpipe, some eight or nine feet long.

A little boy climbed up to fetch it. It was simply a straight, hollow stem, from which the pith had been removed by soaking it in water. Two labba's teeth were fastened to it, some eighteen inches from the mouthpiece. Eventually it would warp, said Ignatius, and you had to aim away from the target. The teeth enabled you to hold it in the same position each time.

'You like arrows?' he asked.

The little boy held out some bamboo slivers. Each one was about ten inches long, with a small wad of cotton at the end, to give it the required compression. The points were coated with a dull, blackish stain—curare, the notorious Indian poison, made from a strychnic vine, which gives the arrows their lethal effect. The boy took one and scampered outside to give me a demonstration. He raised the blowpipe to his mouth

1. Probably an Indianized version of 'I believe in'.

with an almost casual air. I heard a quick, sharp puff. A moment later the arrow was quivering in a mango which lay on the ground, some forty feet away. It was better than a gun, said Ignatius. If you saw a flock of monkeys, you could shoot them one by one, without alarming the others.

Aibilibing had something to ask me. Could I please send him some trousers? He would hardly be the same without his tattered shirt and loin-cloth; but it seemed a humble request and I promised to find him a pair.

We stumbled out into the sunlight. Over in the 'chochi' they were dancing again, with the low hum of their voices ebbing through the languid heat. I went and sat in the shade of a tree, overlooking the path to the creek. What was it in the Indian mind that had given birth to this strange cult? I felt that the morning's conversation had brought me closer to the answer.

Many of its details, from Bichiwung onwards, are far too striking to be the product of mere imagination. Its blend of Christian and Indian ideas is anything but haphazard. Some of the prophets were ex-piai-men; their visions of God were a legacy of the way in which they had once made contact with the Indian spirits. Perhaps the dimness of the chochi is derived from the total darkness in which they held their seances. The songs, which they often refer to as hymns, follow a traditional form and rhythm. But here a meeting-point occurs; the ideals and concepts which they express are predominantly Christian. There is no Indian precedent for the concept of a Supreme Being, or Heaven and an after-life which can be obtained by good conduct. The names of most of the early leaders—Abel, Moses, Noah and Christ—are clearly derived from Christian teaching, like their fashion of praying. The pattern seems to be quite simple. The cult is a form of Christianity, vague indeed, but none the less Christian, expressed in a wholly original Indian way.

But why did Bichiwung have his vision? And why did the cult obtain such a hold on the complex mind of the Indians? The explanation lies partly in their first impression of Christianity. Their curiosity was provoked by rumours of the white man's religion. This was largely because they saw it as the source of his power and wealth. They wanted to share these benefits, and the gifts and clothes which the missionaries gave them suggested that they could do so. But conversion had its drawbacks; it seemed to entail a loss of freedom, and in spite of becoming nominal Christians, the Indians were almost as poor as ever. How could they retain their freedom and still gain the white man's weath? How could they convince themselves that they had a real place of their own in this new religion which was absorbing them? A peculiar need arose from this crisis. They must have their own Christianity, designed for them by the same God, on new, essentially Indian lines.

Once this positive need occurred, it was almost bound to be satisfied. This naturally happened through the piai-men, who, with their supernatural powers, were best equipped to deal with it. Bichiwung's vision began the process. First his suspicions were confirmed—the white man was withholding a secret. Then he was given a new religion, similar to Christianity, but free of its subordination to European priests and their culture. The conflict which Bichiwung experienced was shared by all the remoter tribes in the early nineteenth century. His vision was inspired by a state of mind which Hallelujah answered. Even the modern Akawaio still have the same feelings—hence Aibilibing's suspicion of the white man wanting to 'thief Hallelujah', and their emphasis of the fact that it belongs to the Indians.

But exactly why did this feeling develop? Like most of their problems, it seems to have sprung from the gulf between the Indians and the outside world. They were faced with a new, confusing religion, opposed to most of their own way of life, which apparently had no real place for them. The missionaries failed to bridge this gulf by accepting Indian life as they found it; instead, they imposed their own standards. The Indians resisted them by means of their imagination, with its strong sense of the supernatural. They retained their identity by clinging to their old beliefs; but, at the same time, they tempered them with independent Christianity. Hallelujah came into being. It is, in fact, the spiritual expression of the Indians' entire dilemma—of a feeling of being misunderstood, which compels them to seek a place of their own in the new world closing round them.

The dancing continued all afternoon. The heat of the sun was dying away by the time the Indians emerged from the 'chochi' and knelt for their final prayer. Ignatius was going back to Philipai. We decided to leave together. I looked in at Aibilibing's house. The prophet was sleeping, but the others promised to say goodbye to him for me. Someone hurried after us, as we set off down the path. 'Mistakong, Mistakong'— it was the little old lady who had promised to 'care' me. She pushed a large loaf of cassava bread shyly into my hand. Long after we waved goodbye, I could still see her on the hillside, watching us disappear.

Dusk had fallen by the time we reached Philipai. A little crowd gathered in Ignatius' house. As we cooked and ate together, Amokokopai was discussed in eager undertones.

'Aibilibing is a fine old man,' said Basil quietly.

'But you know,' said another young Akawaio, 'the priest here ain't like him at all. He ain't been to Amokokopai. But he say the Bible ain't got Hallelujah and that make it heathen. He like it to finish right away. And the first priest been over there and try to stop them from dancing.'

'And he managed to stop them?' I asked.

'No,' he said. 'We can't leave it.'

Two hours later the only sound was the heavy breathing of the Indians, as I sat and made notes in my diary. What would become of the cult? I wondered. In the end, it seemed bound to decline, like the rest of their beliefs. But the struggle promised to be a long one. Some of its features were unique. Its history survived in striking detail in all their songs and legends. They sprang from emotions which really belonged to the Indian situation. The encroachment of new, alien ideas was consciously, almost fiercely resisted. The ritual expressed a set of beliefs which were part of the daily pattern of their lives. Its quiet fervour was very different from the passive acceptance of Christianity in the newly missionized areas. The young people believed in it as strongly as the old. I had never met anyone like Ignatius, who, though highly conscious of the change, supported something essentially Indian with such determined pride.

And yet there were few followers left. The cult centre was so isolated that it seemed to be a final stronghold. The Arecuna had been won over by the Adventists. The problem of the Patamona remained. Did they still have Hallelujah? Anthropologists were uncertain and even the Akawaio seemed vague. If they did, would it show the same symptoms of an Indian struggle for recognition, now at its last defiant stand? I would soon be in Patamona country with Andrew, the young Macusi who was coming down to Georgetown to meet me. Perhaps I would have a chance to find out if they still followed the cult.

5

A Patamona Secret

Looking back on the time we spent together, it seems almost inevitable that Andrew should have begun as something of a mystery. Georgetown snoozed in the afternoon sun, as I walked round to the Interior Department to see if he had arrived. I had sent a message, asking him to come, as soon as I was back from the Kamarang. The rest of my time there had been disappointing, compared to Amokokopai. I had gone on to one of the Adventist missions up the Kamarang River. The porknockers and missionaries had transformed its Indian inhabitants, leaving them diffident and suspicious.[1] I had found the atmosphere depressing and been glad to leave.

Jimmy Bamford had retired and no one at the Interior Department seemed to know that he had arranged for Andrew to travel with me. I had asked for him to be flown down by the afternoon plane from Lethem, a cattle-ranching township in Macusi country. One of the clerks rang the office there, to make enquiries for me. The plane had left some time ago. Had Andrew Macdonald been on board? Perhaps—they couldn't say.

If anyone knew where he was, it would be Alfred, the keeper of the Indian depôt, known to the Indians as Mr. Mac. He was a virtual intelligence service about the movements of all the Indians who came to Georgetown. But even he was unable to help. 'Yes, I know him well,' he said. 'He's a nice boy, if you're careful with him—but I haven't seen

1. The Seventh Day Adventists have even forbidden the Indians to eat most of their normal diet, which is considered unclean. Wild hog, labba and scaleless fish are all taboo; so too is cassiri, despite the fact that qualified doctors have warned that it plays an essential part in their diet. On one occasion emergency food supplies had to be flown to Indians who had destroyed their crops on being told by the Adventists that the world was due to end.

him around here. I believe he has friends in town, so he's probably stopping with them.'

By now I was feeling anxious. We were due to leave for Orinduik, a frontier point on the Brazilian border, early on the following day. How was I going to find him in time, even if he had arrived? Back at the Interior Department, we got in touch with the airfield. His name was on the passenger list, but apparently he had left for Georgetown. Suddenly Mr. Cassou, who had taken over from Jimmy Bamford as Commissioner of the Interior, had an idea. He knew one of the taxi-drivers who often met the plane. He picked up the phone. 'Andrew Macdonald?' said a voice at the other end. 'Yes, we just brought him down. He's staying in Ford Street, opposite the lighthouse.'

Ten minutes later I was there. I turned down a little alleyway, where the wooden houses leant close together, with the paint peeling off their brows.

'Up there, soldier,' said a little boy, pointing to a girl at a window, who gave me an alluring smile. The presence of the British troops, who had been in Georgetown since the riots, had obviously con-tributed to life in the back streets. The little boy grabbed me by the arm.

'Andrew Macdonald is here?' I asked him.

He looked disappointed. 'Is he you come for?'

I nodded and gave him ten cents to replace his lost commission. He scampered round to the next house.

'Andrew, white man come to see you,' he shouted.

The door opened and Andrew appeared. He paused for a moment, looked at me, and then came down the steps. He was short and stocky, with an open, rather hard face and a trace of his Scots blood in his light complexion.

He smiled and shook my hand. 'I just arrived from Lethem,' he said, 'but I didn't know where to find you.'

'The man with taxi said you were here,' I replied. 'We're leaving for Orinduik tomorrow. You have everything you need?'

I could feel him trying to size me up. 'I just going to buy some rations,' he said. 'Is only one thing I want to ask you—about my salary.'

Apparently the officer at Lethem had not discussed it with him. It was soon settled, but I couldn't help wondering how much his enquiry meant. At least he was uninhibited; but coming from the Rupununi, with its rough and confused atmosphere, he might be less easy company than the Indians at Orealla. There was something else that worried me. Any two people who travel together, especially through rough country, are thrown right into each other's lives. The fact that I was paying him had a slightly uncomfortable 'boss and boy' ring about it.

'But about this salary,' I said. 'Even if I'm paying you I don't want any boss story in it. We're just travelling together. If anyone's in charge it's you, because you know the place. So don't worry to call me "Sir", or treat me like a boss.'

'That's the best way for me,' he said.

I think he felt as relieved as I did. Now that we both knew where we stood, the matter would solve itself. He seemed reserved, but far from shy. We would probably get on well together. We still had to discuss our plans, so he promised to come round and see me that evening.

An hour or two later we were poring over a map of the interior. 'I living here,' said Andrew, pointing to a village called Moka-Moka, a few miles from the Brazilian border, below the Kanuku Mountains. 'We could stay there when we go down to the Rupununi. My wife going make parakari for you. That's the Macusi kind of paiwari—the best Indian drink.'

'You're married?' I asked in surprise.

'Yes,' he said, 'for a couple of years now. My father sent me to school in Georgetown. When I came back to the Rupununi I was living like a wild fellow, so I decide to settle down. Is that made me ask about the salary, because I got a family to keep. I reach twenty-four now and my wife is seventeen. We got two small children already.'

'And you've been to Patamona country?'

'Yes,' he said, 'I know it well.' He pointed to Orinduik, nearly two hundred miles to the north of his home village. 'I was working there about five years back, in the police force. But after a time I left the place and gone back to the Rupununi. They had too many regulations, so I didn't fancy the work.'

'You like the Patamona?' I asked.

'Yes,' he said, 'they're friendly people. Some of them is still living in the old time way. They just wearing bead-apron and loin-cloth. The missionaries scarcely reach them all yet. If we go up the Ireng River we going find them so.'

'We could spend a bit of time up there and then go down to the Rupununi.'

'Yes,' he said, 'that could work. From Orinduik, going south, is all Patamona people. Just before you meet the savannas you find Macusi villages. It's rough walking, but I know the trails.'

The country which we had to cross was almost blank, except for the mountains and an occasional Indian village. Unless the rains had ceased by then, all the rivers would be flooded. It promised to be a rugged journey. But Andrew seemed enthusiastic. I hoped it was a good omen.

We set out for Atkinson Field early the next morning. 'You see that man over there?' said Andrew, as we waited for the plane. He pointed to a tall, spare figure, in a panama hat. 'That's Irving Cheong. A couple of years back he was just a porknocker, like all the others. Then he found a big diamond, forty-eight carats, in a creek near Orinduik. He sell it to some American for seventy-two thousand dollars.'

Five minutes later the crowd of porknockers scrambled on to the plane. They joked and laughed as they helped each other with their rough baggage—shovels, shotguns, sifting pans and cartons of tinned food which would have to be eked out in the lonely diamond fields. Andrew introduced me to Irving Cheong, who was sitting just behind us. He looked about thirty-five, with a candid, rather handsome face, part African and part Chinese.

'So you're coming to Orinduik?' he said. 'I've got a little shop there now. You must drop in and see me. But the place isn't how it used to be. Once we were finding plenty of diamonds, but now they seem to be hiding.'

'Yes,' said Andrew, 'it used to be a fine spot. When I was there it was nothing but diamonds. As soon as the news got over the border, the Brazilian girls were coming in, a new plane-load every week—the diamond buyers used to bring them. And Orinduik was full with rum. Everything was a high price, three or four times more than Georgetown. For a few months the place was wild. Then the diamonds start to get scarce and all the girls gone back to Brazil. Is only Irving still getting luck.'

'Yes, it's quiet now,' said Irving. 'Hardly a diamond left.'

Andrew dozed off to sleep. Below us, the sluggish brown Essequibo glinted in the sun. Then it was hidden by a cloud savanna, level white, till it billowed up on to the pale horizon. After a while it drifted apart. We were over the endless forest again, rising towards the Pakaraimas and broken by the Potaro River, threading its way down from the mountains. A little settlement passed beneath us—Tumatumari, an old gold centre, which had been abandoned. Fifty miles ahead was Kaieteur, one of the world's highest waterfalls, with a sheer drop of over seven hundred and forty feet. Two years ago Vin and I had reached it on foot, with some boys from Orealla. Remembering our first glimpse of its furious, cascading splendour, I wondered how it would look from the air.

Broken waters lay beneath us, flecked with patches of foam. The forest

99

gave way to bare rock and suddenly the fall was ahead, a scar of white suspended in the distance. The sheer walls of the gorge leapt up towards a wild torment of water. The river seemed to pause in terror, before it thundered over the brink in towers of white-contorted anger. The spray was thrown up for hundreds of feet, spanning the gorge with a pale rainbow and drifting over the lame river that crawled on down the valley.

Long ago, the Indians say, there was a village in the nearby savanna. One of the inhabitants was an old man, so old that nobody knew his age. His relatives, finding him a burden, decided to help him on his way to the land of the Spirits, some two days journey beyond the sun. Gathering all his possessions into a straw basket known as a pegall, they placed him in a woodskin and sent him over the fall. Shortly afterwards his woodskin and pegall reappeared, in the form of two large rocks which can still be seen in the gorge. Awe-struck by this miracle, the Indians named the spot Kaieteur, meaning old man's rock.

Above the fall the water was strangely still. I caught sight of a tiny plateau where we had stood two years before. We had stayed there for several hours, fascinated by the fall, which had an irresistible lure, drawing us towards the brink until the spray whipped over our faces. Looking back, I could see the valley along which we had walked for three days, with Kaieteur's thunder growing closer. A moment later it disappeared, as we banked away from the river. The hills were still rising gently, broken by deeply shadowed gullies. Then the forest thinned out into a pale green savanna, divided by the Ireng River, which forms the Brazilian border. A rough airstrip came into view, and as we swooped down towards it, we flew over a series of rapids, with the broken white of their spray catching the sunlight.

I was almost bowled over by the heat, as we stepped down from the plane. The little crowd that gathered round seemed half curious and half indifferent to our sudden arrival. The usual motley variety of faces which every diamond spot attracts—a pair of policemen in blue uniforms, a relic, perhaps, of the wild days of a few years ago. A burly, heavily bearded Brazilian, with the remains of a straw hat pushed on to the back of his head, sitting on a gasoline drum and surveying us through half closed eyes. One or two African porknockers, a lean, watchful Chinese face, and in the background a few Indians—Patamonas, roughly dressed, with short, squat figures, and flat features; expressionless—only their eyes were alert, with a faint suggestion of withdrawal peculiar to the Indians.

Orinduik had an empty feeling. It was inert, as if exhausted by its spell of diamond fever. A few whitewashed adobe huts were strung out beyond the airstrip, blending in Mexican fashion with the blue-grey hills. The sun-swept savanna stretched all round us, rising into a stark peak on the Brazilian side of the river; below it, on the bank, stood a little settlement, with a handful of cattle grazing nearby, dotted in brown and white against a green background.

Andrew was soon caught up in a round of greetings. We chatted to the African policemen and one of the diamond-buyers. I learnt that there were two Patamona villages farther up the Ireng—Waipa, a day's walk by the trail, and beyond it Kaibarupai. Did they practise Hallelujah? I asked. They shrugged—yes, they had heard of it, but a long time ago. Waipa was under Catholic influence, which made the cult's survival unlikely; but someone had heard that it still went on at Kaibarupai.

We decided to spend the night at Orinduik and leave early the next morning. Andrew disappeared and came back with a little Patamona called William, who was scarcely more than four feet high. He was just setting out for Waipa in his corial. He offered to take our equipment for us—we could meet him there on the following day.

'A lady living here who would give us a place to stay,' said Andrew, as we walked towards the cluster of white buildings. 'Mrs. Correia—Auntie, we call her. She has a shop for the porknockers. She's always kind to strangers.'

The shop was a typical bush store, with a sleepy, improvised air. A weather-beaten notice hung outside. 'Orinduik Shop. Licensed to Trade in Gold and Diamonds.' The spasmodic smack of dominoes from its dark interior, where a pair of porknockers lounged over a table, with a bottle of rum between them. A jaguar skin hung on the wall, with a few faded pictures beneath it. Tinned food, bush knives and Indian baskets were ranged along the wooden shelves behind a makeshift counter. Mrs. Correia turned out to be a friendly, middle-aged Portuguese, with a keen business sense, which had been useful during the diamond days.

'So you're writing a book?' she said, when Andrew had introduced me.

'Yes,' I replied, 'about the Indians.'

She looked me briskly up and down, with a disbelieving air. What could she be thinking? Diamond-runner? Prospecting on the quiet? Or just on the run, like so many others?

'What shall I write about you?' I asked.

Perhaps this sounded more convincing. Her face melted into a smile. 'Don't worry about me,' she said. 'Just tell them I like it here. But one person you must write about is Joseph Tesarick. King of the Border, they used to call him. He was the first man who found diamonds here. Is he built this very shop. He died just five years ago. Come back this evening—I'll tell you about him.'

She pointed outside to a nearby building. 'You could sleep over there,' she said. 'Only one thing, take care with the toilet. It's getting proper rotten now and it nearly gone with me this morning.'

As we unpacked, the rain began. In a moment the hills were blotted from sight, but by the time we had eaten, it was over. Andrew and I wandered outside. After an hour or two with Irving, we crossed over to the settlement on the far side of the river. We were greeted by the local shopkeeper, another old friend of Andrew's. He insisted that my first taste of Brazil should be an alcoholic one. By the time we had staggered back to Mrs. Correia's, where a few porknockers had gathered for the evening, it was almost dark. She placed a meal in front of us with a motherly air, and then produced a battered folder, full of newspaper cuttings.

'There he is,' she said, as the others gathered round to share the story. 'Joe Tesarick, King of the Border.' She pointed to a faded photograph, which showed a good-looking Eastern European face with thin lips and pale blue eyes.

'I never heard much about his early days,' said Mrs. Correia. 'He was born in Czechoslovakia. They say he served in the Foreign Legion. Then he got away to Brazil on a Spanish boat. First he started looking for diamonds in the Matto Grosso. Then he travelled up from São Paulo to Rio and on to Manãos. He stopped there for a little time, working as a mechanic. In the end he reached Bôa Vista and crossed over to B.G. That must be about 1938. After that he came up here, right through the bush. In a couple of months he found a thirty-five carat stone, worth about fifty thousand dollars.' She gave a nostalgic sigh. 'Is then that Orinduik began. At the time there was just one Indian camp here, but Tesarick bought a little Auster. Then in 1947 they opened up the airstrip. The first place he built was this shop and soon the porknockers started to come. Then they really found some diamonds. They had about twenty houses here. The Indians began to change too, buying clothes with the money they earned as droughers.'[1]

She glanced at the Patamona boy who worked behind the counter. He had a silent, distrustful air, hardened, no doubt, by his experience of the diamond world. She turned to another page of photographs—Tesarick standing beside his Auster, surrounded by a crowd of porknockers; the first adobe houses going up in the bare savanna, and Orinduik shop, with its wooden notice hanging tipsily outside.

1. Bearers.

'Things were really bright then,' she said. 'Diamonds, Brazilian girls—we even had a lighting plant. Right here we used to sit, gaffing till late at night, with Tesarick telling us about his life.'

'You wouldn't meet another man like him,' said Vincent, a dark, curly-haired diamond buyer. 'Without Tesarick, the stones would still be in the creeks, every one of them. He scarcely drank and he never smoked, but every woman from São Paulo to Georgetown knew his name. Everyone here used to like him, Indians, porknockers and all—but they were all afraid of him too. You never knew what the man was thinking. Only when he was getting angry, the tips of his ears would start getting red. Otherwise you wouldn't know. In the end he married an Indian girl from the Pomeroon River. They got a son in Georgetown now. But since he died, this place just faded away.'

Mrs. Correia brought out another newspaper, dated November 16th, 1957, with the now familiar face splashed across the front. Above it, in broad headlines: 'Joe Tesarick, King of the Border, makes his last journey. Three die and one lives, in blazing plane.'

'Nobody knows how it happened,' she said. 'The plane caught fire in the air. They were crossing the border, just south of here, near a place called King's Mine. They buried him over in Brazil. His son still wants to be a pilot. Three days after his daddy died, when he was just fifteen, he landed a big Dakota right here at Orinduik.'

The gas lamp spluttered in admiration. There was a moment's silence. A few minutes later we said good-night, but not without a final toast to Tesarick, King of the Border.

Dawn had already slipped out of our grasp by the time we woke on the following morning. A pale sun was slanting over the hills, as we set out past Irving's shop and along the bank of the Ireng. Andrew seemed disgruntled at having to carry his belongings. Perhaps it was just the effect of the previous evening, but it worried me slightly. He was reluctant to use a wareshi, an Indian carrier made from vines, like the one which I had adopted. He preferred his awkward Georgetown suitcase, which seemed to be a status symbol that he never expected to carry. He wasn't used to a load, he said; in the old days, when he worked as a policeman, he had a drougher to carry his things for him—only the Indians used wareshis. I thought that he would soon forget it, as we were sharing the load. But I wondered about his use of the word 'Indians'. Did he regard his Georgetown education and Scottish blood as something which set him apart from them? He could easily have acquired this complex from the strongly divided, half Indian, half coastal society of the Rupununi.

But it might be awkward if it persisted, as the watchful Patamona would sense it immediately.

For over an hour we walked in silence, fighting off the clouds of kaboura, little black savanna flies, which covered our faces and hands, leaving dots and smears of blood behind them. The stern silhouette of Mount Sipu grew closer, on the far side of the river.

After a while we lowered our burdens and sat down for a cigarette. A herd of cattle were grazing on the far bank, dwarfed by the distance around them. The foot-hills were peppered with sandpaper trees, scrawny, contorted little shrubs, named after their coarse leaves. Behind them, the low table-land of the mountains vaunted its bare ribs to the sky, red sandstone parched by the sun. A cool breeze ruffled the grass. The valley was still and silent.

Andrew slapped at the kaboura. 'These things biting hard,' he said. He laughed. His spirits seemed to have lifted. His long silence came to an end as he told me about his time in Georgetown. His father had been appointed a Ranger, or Field Officer, in the Northern Rupununi. When the small American sect, called the Unevangelized Fields Mission, moved in among the Wai-Wai, the Government sent him to keep an eye on the work they were doing. But the missionaries had their own way. A few months later he returned as a convert, and sent Andrew to their school in Georgetown.

'What was it like there?' I asked.

His strong features hardened a little. 'I wouldn't forget it in a hurry,' he said. 'It was like a prison. You could hardly go outside—Bible class every day and regulations all the time. They used to make us go in the street and preach about how we had God's word. One time, when I was fifteen, they caught me smoking and give me sixty-four lashes. Those people got me confused.'

His descriptions sounded exaggerated, but there must have been a good reason for them and obviously they weren't unfounded. The missionaries seemed to have thought that this was the easiest way to conversion. But Andrew, unlike most of the Indians, had been too much for them.

'Is that got me wuthless and wild,' he said. 'As soon as I met back to the Rupununi, I started on the drink and the girls. Then I had to leave the police force. One time I met this same missionary down in the Rupununi, at Lethem. He was sitting in the hotel, so I called some boys and walked up beside him and ordered some cigarettes and a bottle of rum.'

'What did he do then?' I asked.

'He didn't say anything—just walked away. After that I felt all right. We Indians don't forget it when a man treats us bad.'

One moment 'the Indians', and now 'we Indians'. I could see what must have happened. With his Indian sense of independence, he had reacted strongly against the missionaries' assumptions. But despite this, their education, together with his mixed background, had set him apart from Indian life. Perhaps this explained his behaviour over the wareshi.

All day we walked on, without seeing a single person. Occasionally we had to wade through shallow swamps and past groves of ité palms, with the mud pulling us down at every step. The landscape grew harsher as we approached the hills. The quiet green gave way to arid red sandstone, weathered and wind-carved into grotesque clumps and ridges. As we crossed a narrow creek, cobbled with purple and brown stones, we could hear the sound of rapids below us. Once we passed a waterfall, tumbling down from the hills towards the river.

Around midday we reached an abandoned camp. 'We could eat lunch here,' said Andrew. We crept into its welcome shade. 'An Indian was sleeping here last night,' he added, glancing at the remains of a fire. The leaves rattled drily overhead, as a lizard skittered across the roof, searching for insects. Over in the corner lay the bleached skull of a steer, watching us with a hollow-eyed grin.

'This thing dangerous,' said Andrew, pointing to a large cow-fly which buzzed monotonously round him, as he opened a tin of corned beef. 'If you take a hair from a man's head and tie it on one of these flies, his head going to ache with the noise, until he die. Indian people know all these things. A next thing the Macusi can do is to take some grains from a man's footprint in the sand. They throw it inside a rattlesnake and sew up the mouth. The snake gets thin and then it dies—and just how the snake coming thin, is so the man gets, until he dies at the very same time. Is so a Macusi girl did to my father. Some Brazilians were vexed with him. They pay her to kill him so.'

'You believe it happened that way?'

'Yes,' he said, 'is so it happened.'

I wondered if he was playing up to me. Educated Indians usually lose faith in their old superstitions. Perhaps he had his tongue in his cheek, or maybe he was just reacting against his imposed education. He was full of Indian stories, many of them unprintable and others clearly made up on the spur of the moment; but, to the end, I never discovered how far he himself believed in them.

Soon we were on our way again. By now we had reached the hills. We climbed steadily upwards, until the river suddenly reappeared on our left, sweeping through a mist-hung gorge. Beside it the forest began once more. We followed the narrow trail into its semi-darkness. The creepers and branches, cut off at Patamona height, snatched at our shoulders as we stumbled on. Once we heard a flock of monkeys chattering overhead; otherwise, hardly a sign of life. It was late afternoon by the time we reached the first Indian field, slashed out of the heavy forest at the foot of the mountains.

'Waipa,' said Andrew, as we emerged into a little clearing. An old lady peeped out timidly from the first house. Beyond it were about half a dozen others, most of them with leaf roofs, but smaller than the old round-houses. Their traditional kinship system, with several families in one home, was clearly on the decline. A moment later William appeared, with the things which he had brought up for us on the previous day. He led us over to a wooden building at the far end of the village. A little crowd of women and children gathered outside, led by the wrinkled old lady whom we had seen before. Like the Akawaio, many of them had cassiri-binas tattooed on their faces and coloured bead ornaments round their ankles and wrists.

The old lady waved at us shyly, while the others giggled in the background. Andrew produced a large bag of sweets which he had brought for the occasion. He beckoned to the nearest children. They paused for a moment, torn between shyness and curiosity, and then came forward one by one. Glancing up coyly from beneath their distinctive Patamona fringes, they held out their hands and retreated hurriedly to inspect the booty. Even the old lady joined in. She looked at the sweets suspiciously. I picked one up and placed it in my mouth to reassure her. She followed my example cautiously and suddenly grinned with delight. She muttered something to the children. They scampered off and reappeared with a large bunch of bananas which she handed to me.

'We should go and see the tushau,' said Andrew.

'The tushau?' I asked.

'Yes,' he said. 'Is so the Patamona and Macusi call the village headman.'

We walked outside, followed by the children.

'First time I came here was five years back,' said Andrew. 'The tushau was living in a round-house then, with about twenty people inside. But I see some of them changing now, with each family living separate. Look his new house over there.'

He pointed to a large, square building, with walls made out of bark. The news of our arrival had already reached the tushau, who came forward to greet us, surrounded by his relatives. He was dressed in an old pair of trousers, with a string of wild hogs' teeth round his neck, and a pair of elegant wooden ornaments in the lobes of his ears. Once more I was struck by their low cut fringes and unusual build, light skinned and sturdy, with short, squat necks above their powerful shoulders. None of the old people were more than five feet high, though some of the younger men were taller. Clearly the sparse medical attention and changing diet of the past decade was affecting their physique.

Few of them spoke any English, but Andrew explained our arrival, as they gathered round. A large bowl of cassiri appeared. They watched me closely, as I drank. This gesture of hospitality is often refused by visitors, for fear of contracting tuberculosis; but this offends the Indians deeply, making them apprehensive about the reactions of any stranger. The cassiri was pleasantly sweet—a familiar end of a sun-parched journey, on reaching an Indian village.

'You know how they make this thing?' said Andrew, as he drank his share. 'They still chew the cassava bread. I know from the taste. They wouldn't tell you, if you ask, because they get shy about it. But it tasting really nice this way.'

This reassured me slightly. He was not entirely sceptical about the customs which the more civilized Indians had abandoned. The tushau led us into his house. Although its style had changed, it was much larger than any of the others in the village. Here they still lived in the communal way, with the tushau's daughters and their families acknowledging him as the head of the household. Some twelve or fifteen hammocks were slung on one side, while the other seemed to be used for cooking and preparing drink. A fire was burning in one corner, with a large clay bowl over it—a relic of an art which had now died out amongst the other tribes. In the centre lay two wooden objects like miniature corials, both full of cassiri.

'Those things really big,' said Andrew, glancing at them. 'When every house has cassiri like that, these people can drink for two or three weeks without stopping.'

I gazed at them for a moment. The tushau saw me and turned to his wife, who refilled the calabash for us.

'Tell them her cassiri-bina is working well,' I said to Andrew.

He passed on the message. They laughed in approval, and the tushau said something in reply.

'They asking us to come back later,' said Andrew. 'They going to sing some old time songs for you.'

'Tell them we've got a surprise,' I said. 'They going to see it when we come.' I wondered how they would react to the miniature tape-recorder which I had brought with me.

It was dark by the time we returned. A fire had been lit outside the tushau's house. Some thirty or forty Indians were squatting round it, with the children huddling close together to escape the cold. The silence was broken by a whispered enquiry, as I produced the tape-recorder. I switched it on and they sighed and laughed at the little green test light. I let it run for a few seconds. Then I stopped it, reversed the tape and played back their reactions. For a moment they were completely silent, with incredulous, half bewildered faces. Suddenly the spell was broken. They edged closer, laughing in delight and pointing at every detail.

An old man came forward and muttered something to Andrew.

'He wants to know how the talking machine learnt Patamona,' he said.

How was I going to explain this one? 'Tell him it just listens to them—like a parrot,' I answered.

The old man was still curious. 'He's asking if it would take away his voice,' said Andrew. 'But I told him it wouldn't trouble him.'

The old man stroked the tape-recorder with a look of awe. He moved back, paused for a moment and then broke into a slow, lilting chant. Someone began to shake a maraccas. Its steady rhythm lifted his voice, which filled the heavy darkness around us, rising through almost motionless lips, its tempo quickening until it softened and died away in a whisper.

'That was a song for the tugoit dance,' Andrew explained. 'He was saying welcome to the people who arrive, and telling them to paint their skins for the dance.'

I played it back on the tape-recorder. The old man smiled with quiet pride. Then he began singing again, this time in a different key. Somehow the tune was familiar. And then I suddenly realized—it was a Hallelujah chant, muffled, but ending with the usual chorus, repeated over and over again. Slowly I picked out the words—'Awaishaloo, Chrisinbe, Hallelujah'. Some of the others were humming in the background. The intonation was almost the same as that of the Akawaio hymns. As his voice faded away, it might have been Aibilibing or Ignatius singing.

Andrew asked him what it meant. They didn't know any more, they said. It was just a song which the old people taught them, a long time ago.

I repeated the words to them slowly. 'What does "awaishaloo" mean?' I asked.

The old men discussed it in whispers. 'They say it means something like kindness or mercy,' said Andrew. 'When a man dead and his spirit leaving his body, he goes up to Heaven singing this song.'

'So Chrisinbe is Christ?' I asked.

They nodded.

'It's a Hallelujah song, then?'

Perhaps, they said, they weren't sure. They muttered quietly and looked away. Had they really forgotten its meaning, or were they afraid to talk about it? They were still whispering to each other. Suddenly I caught the word 'Aibilibing'.

'Tell them I've been to Amokokopai,' I said. 'Aibilibing is a friend of mine.'

Their expressions changed as Andrew told them. Yes, said the old man, he knew Aibilibing. It was he who had taught him the song. Did they still dance Hallelujah? I asked. Not at Waipa, they replied, the priest didn't like it. But up at Kaibarupai there was plenty.

Opposition had made them reticent, like the Akawaio. But even these suppressed hints suggested more than I had expected. Hallelujah still persisted, in spite of the missionaries. The Patamona obviously knew of the cult centre at Amokokopai. The two outposts were isolated, but they seemed to be in touch with each other. If the old man's case was typical, the Patamona had learnt their doctrine from the Akawaio. Why had it not reached them first, since they were closer to the Macusi, from whom it had come after Bichiwung's death? Had we been staying longer, their restraint might have lifted. But it looked as if there was more to be learnt at Kaibarupai, and we decided to move on early the next day.

A slow moon was lifting over the mountains by the time we said good night. They still seemed apprehensive about my curiosity. As we reached the building where we had slung our hammocks, a figure appeared behind us. It was the tushau. He said something to me in Patamona.

'He's asking if you could give him the talking machine,' Andrew explained.

I smiled. The Indians are quite uninhibited about demanding anything which takes their fancy, from a camera to a comb, or even a pair of shoes which may be several sizes too big for them. They had given me their songs and cassiri—so why shouldn't I give them my talking machine? But I had to keep it, I explained, so that the people in England could hear their songs. Instead, I gave him a large packet of Brazilian cigarettes. He smiled, apparently quite content, and vanished into the darkness.

Andrew and I sat on the steps, talking quietly. We could still hear the murmur of voices by the tushau's house. What were they discussing? I wondered. Perhaps they were sizing up my motives for asking about Hallelujah.

'These people change a lot since I was here,' said Andrew. 'The first time we came they scarcely had clothes. When they seen how we was policemen they all scatter and hide. But now they get clothes they ain't so shy. And the young girls scarcely using the cassiri-bina on their faces. The houses too—these small ones are new. Before, they were all living ten or fifteen people in one house.'

'You think Kaibarupai will be the same?' I asked.

'I don't know,' he said. 'The tushau say it ain't change so much. And they don't like to tell you, but I believe they got plenty of this Hallelujah up there. Tomorrow we going see.'

6

A Fading Millennium

EARLY the next day William appeared with a troop of little boys, who carried our equipment down to the landing and packed it into his long, powerfully built corial. As we pushed out, they threw off their shorts and loin-cloths, and leapt into the water. They kept up with us for a while, swimming strongly, then waving goodbye as we disappeared round the first bend. William had brought a paddle for each of us—his son Regis, Andrew, myself and Launcelot, a short, thick-set Patamona, who sat in the bow to guide us between the rocks.

We soon slipped into a steady rhythm, paddles knocking on the stern, as we pulled against the current which swept down from the rapids. Below them the water was still and dotted with wandering patches of foam. But already the smooth surface was shadowed by the rocks beneath it. Then, as we reached the rapids, a torrent of water leapt up around us. The paddles were exchanged for long sticks. The corial nosed its way through the channels, scraping uneasily over the rocks, swept aside for a brief moment, then regaining its balance. Once or twice we dragged to a halt, and Launcelot jumped out, struggling for a foothold and heaving at the bow, with the brown muscles of his back flexing in the sunlight. Otherwise he scanned the dark water, silent, apart from a few terse comments to warn William that rocks lay ahead. A lonely pride in his squat figure, now relaxed, now fiercely tensed in conflict with the river.

'You see this thing?' said Andrew. He pointed to a plant growing on the rocks, which was carried out into pale green streamers by the current. 'That is the ireng that gives the river its name. The Patamona really like it. The old men dry it and mix it with salt and tobacco. Then they chew it just so—you going see them at Kaibarupai.'

All day we paddled on. The silence was broken by an occasional mutter from Launcelot, or a comment from Regis, as something caught his eye —an evil looking, copper-brown snake, curled up on a branch, and once a gaudy splash of colour, as a macaw spread its wings, red, blue and yellow against the dull green of the forest. The first sign of the village was a cluster of corials at a small landing. They were larger than those of the other tribes, some of them almost thirty feet long, designed to face the blows of the rapids. By now we were all wet and hungry. The corials were a welcome sight. We struggled through the last of the rapids, until we saw a leaf roof, perched on the bank beneath a grove of bamboos.

There were twelve or fifteen houses in the village, huddled close together, with the forest climbing up steeply behind them. They were all built in the old style, and walled up for protection against the cold riverside dawn. As we appeared, a crowd of children scrambled out of the water and ran up the bank, concealing themselves behind the bamboos. They watched us timidly from their hideout, scattering in all directions as we followed them into the village.

Shy faces at every entrance, as the news of our arrival spread from house to house. Suddenly, three men appeared, dressed with almost grotesque variety. One of them came forward to greet us with a solemn expression. He was wearing trousers and a tattered jacket, with an old leather belt strapped round his waist. His features were sharper and more wary than those of the Patamona. I was not surprised when he told us that he was an Akawaio. His name was Henry, he said, and he was the only man in the village who spoke any English. I wondered what had brought him to Patamona country.

He turned and beckoned to the other two men. The first was the tushau, a sturdy, round faced Patamona, with a pair of shorts and a rough necklace, made from jaguars' teeth and scraps of tin. The third of the trio, David by name, wore only a red loin-cloth. He was more heavily built than the others, with an open, seemingly ingenuous face, crowned by a wispy moustache and a rough mop of hair. Unlike Henry and the tushau, who seemed more reserved, he grinned broadly, holding on to my hand to stare at my watch in admiration.

Slowly the Indians emerged from their houses, standing a little way off at first, then gradually coming closer. Nearly all the children, with their neat fringes, wore bead-aprons or loin-cloths. The smallest of them simply had pieces of string around their waists. Like most of the old people, several of the young and middle-aged men were still unclothed. Their natural grace compared vividly with the miserably tattered dresses which most of the women and girls had acquired.

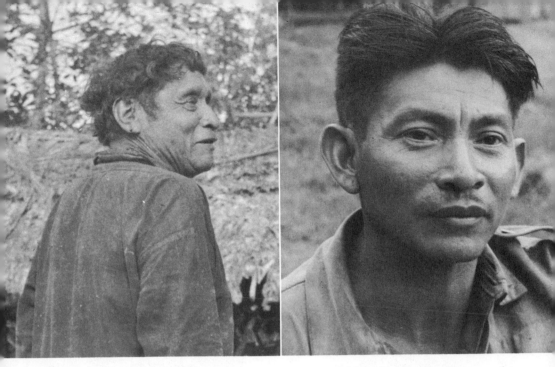

Aibilibing, the reigning Hallelujah prophet, pictured at Amokokopai, the Akawaio cult centre

Aibilibing's disciple Henry, the Hallelujah leader at the Patamona village of Kaibarupai

The Patamona praying at the close of a Hallelujah meeting. The 'chochi', in which the meeting is held, is in complete darkness. (Flash)

A Patamona mother at Kaibarupai, wearing a necklace of coins obtained from a neighbouring mission . . .

. . . and her child, with a traditional bead apron, woven in blue and white patterns

A Patamona on a fishing expedition. He is beating the roots of the narcotic haiari vine, which stupefies the fish and enables his companions to shoot them with their bows and arrows

The tushau muttered to one of them. She disappeared into a nearby house and returned with a ceremonial bowl of cassiri. Andrew produced our diplomatic store of sweets, to return the compliment. After a moment's hesitation they all lined up to receive them. The boys watched us in excitement. One of them stroked my leg boldly, provoking a rustle of whispered comments. The little girls clutched their sweets and hurried back with downcast eyes. The old women came forward nervously, set expressions on their faces, most of them with necklaces of the usual motley style. The old men were much less shy. At first they stood quietly in the background, observing us carefully. Some were chewing dark wads of ireng, turning them slowly between weathered lips that were blackened with the juice. Then, one by one, they approached us. They asked for cigarettes rather than sweets, and touched my clothes and camera in wonder, showing their appreciation with wide, gap-toothed grins.

Henry took us over to a half built house in the centre of the village, where we could sling our hammocks. Already there was a hint of dusk in the air. Andrew and I went off to bathe. The water was cold and refreshing, washing the sweat of two long days off our backs. With the rapids above and below us, there was no danger of pirana, the savage little cannibal fish, which often made it impossible to bathe in the Corentyne.

Henry and William were waiting for us by the time we returned.

'I tell them about the talking machine,' said William proudly.

I brought it out and showed it to Henry.

'We could let it work in my house,' he said. 'I living over so in the chochi.' He pointed to a large, oval-shaped building by the bank of the river.

'The chochi?' I asked.

'Yes,' he said. 'Is there we dance Hallelujah. I is leader for it, and so I living there. The people waiting on you now. They hear about the talking machine.'

'But you lived here all your life?'

'No,' he said, 'I come from so.' He pointed north, up the river, towards Akawaio country. 'From Amokokopai.'

So he came from the cult centre. The link between the two outposts of Hallelujah was even stronger than I had suspected.

'I been to Amokokopai a couple of weeks ago,' I said. 'I was dancing Hallelujah and talking to Aibilibing.'

Henry's face lit up at this news. 'Is good time since I seen him,' he said. 'Is he who teach me Hallelujah and send me over here. I come like a kind of preacher-man, to lead the Patamona.'

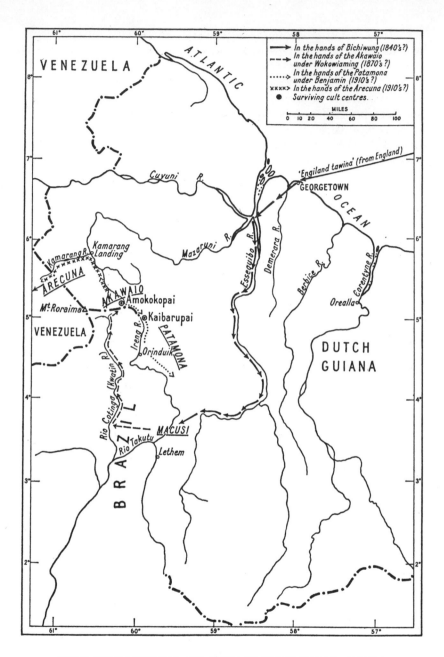

THE EXPANSION OF THE HALLELUJAH CULT
(AS RELATED BY INDIAN TRADITION)

At last I was discovering the network which lay behind the cult. It still had a stronger, more organized hold than anthropologists had suspected. The prophet-leader, Aibilibing, was acknowledged by both tribes. He was still sending his disciples to the Patamona. The two cult centres were closely linked, overriding tribal distinctions for the sake of a final, remote alliance, in the name of Hallelujah.

Henry led us across to the chochi. As at Amokokopai, it was the largest building in the village. Some sixty people were waiting inside. Like the Akawaio, they seemed less inhibited than the missionized Indians, with the men and women sitting together, some of them with their arms round each other. As we appeared, an old woman brought forward a lump of sheeba, a dried gum from the bark of a tree, which she placed on the ground. She lit it with a piece of wood. The flames leapt up, with their shadows dancing on the watchful faces around us. Henry seated us in a corner and looked around, surveying the crowd sternly. He started talking in Patamona.

'He telling them about the tape-recorder,' said Andrew. 'He say you going to play something for them.'

They watched me expectantly, as I turned on the tape from Waipa. They listened in the same awed silence. When it was over, they whispered excitedly, while the children laughed in glee. A little boy scrambled towards it, only to be pulled back, out of the reach of its strange power, by an indignant mother.

'You could catch we voice on it?' said Henry.

'What are you going to sing?' I asked.

'I tell them to sing Hallelujah song.'

He turned back towards the others and broke into a slow chant, quiet at first, almost enquiring, then rising in volume like those of the Akawaio. As he was carried away by the rhythm, the others joined in, with their voices blending into a powerful hum. The words were obviously well known, part of a familiar ritual, even for the children.

When it was over, all eyes were turned on the tape-recorder. Their curiosity was mounting, as I reversed the tape. I switched it on. Henry grinned, as his voice carried through the half darkness, followed by those of the Patamona. The experiment was such a success that they paused for a round of cassiri, taken from two large gourds, which stood in the centre of the chochi.

'We does sing every morning and night,' said Henry. 'And sometimes, when we got plenty drink, we does dance all day.'

He stood up again and broke into song. They continued for over half an hour, with a brief pause between each chant. Then, at a sign from

Henry, they all knelt down to pray. He led them just as Ignatius had done, with his exhortations repeated by the others. His voice rose to fever pitch, almost to a shout of triumph, never once pausing for words, until, after a few minutes, he slowed down again.

'We asking God to give us he place,' he explained, when the prayer was over. 'Special country for the Indians. This life nasty—we Indians poor, so God give a new place for us.'

He turned to the others and said something more. His voice had a sharp, emphatic tone, quite different from the usual subdued mutter of the Indians. The meeting was a slightly one man affair. Henry was clearly a powerful figure, with something of Aibilibing's prophetic stature, perhaps reinforced among the Patamona by his more independent, domineering Akawaio character. On the spiritual level of Hallelujah, his authority seemed to be unquestioned, even by the tushau. The others listened without a word, until one of the old men asked a question. He sounded anxious about something. A rapid dialogue developed in short, staccato exchanges.

'They talking about us,' said Andrew. 'The old man asking why we come. This Henry telling them you know about Hallelujah. He says they must trust you, not to get frightened, because you been to Amoko-kopai, and you like this Aibilibing.'

Suddenly Henry asked a question, in which I heard my name mentioned. The men answered in unison. The same question was repeated, and this time the women replied.

'You know what he say?' Andrew whispered. 'He ask the men, you like Mr. Colin? And they all tell him, yes. Then the women, you like Mr. Colin? And they say the same thing. Then he ask them to treat us nice.'

After another round of cassiri, the Indians drifted away. Andrew and I said good-night to Henry and walked back to the camp. His strange personality had made an immediate impression on me. His isolated, mystic figure obviously had a strong hold on the quiet Patamona. They seemed to regard him with a half cowed and half reverent air.

Andrew started cooking a meal. The light flickered in the breeze, as I wrote my diary. Our pressure lamp had already collapsed. Andrew had replaced it with an effective, but slightly explosive-looking 'bushman's lantern'. It was made from an old Nescafé tin, full of kerosene, with an improvised wick passed through a hole in the lid. I was finding it hard to write, as Andrew was in a cheerful mood, chatting incessantly, ranging from his wild Rupununi days to comments on the local Patamona girls.

We could still hear the sound of voices from the nearby houses. Now and then an Indian figure stirred in front of the firelight. Suddenly someone appeared beside us. It was David, with his wife and two children, who hid behind him, clutching their mother's hand. He pointed shyly at our equipment and showed me a hideous sore on his leg.

He was obviously asking for medicine. I looked at the sore. It seemed to be a bad form of bush-yaws, a tropical skin disease contracted from a combination of mud and scratches, along with a poor diet. As I had once caught it myself, in a much milder form, I had some ointment for it. Ten minutes later it was washed and bandaged. David grinned and patted me on the shoulder.

Their shyness seemed to be short-lived. When the operation was over the whole family sat and watched us, noting each detail of our belongings, and reaching out occasionally to touch some object of special interest. The parents and children were strangely alike. David and his wife had a childlike curiosity, while the children were quiet and grave, as if they already belonged to the adult world. After a while they left us, melting away into the darkness. Their presence seemed to linger behind them. They had a spontaneity which the missionized Indians had lost.

Dawn at Kaibarupai, the dawn of a day spent in watching the last of the old way of life. The village is woken by the thrumming of rain on the dark roof of the forest. It dies away, as the last hint of night slinks off the silent river. The first Hallelujah song begins; Henry is calling the village to prayer. The Patamona move like shadows towards the silhouette of the chochi. They kneel, carried away by the rhythm that summons the cold light of day.

Inside, the shadows are lifting. A circle of passive faces—the whole of the village is there. Independent though they are, there seem to be no exceptions to their way of sharing life. The prayer for help and strength is over, a moment of age-old ritual that links the vanishing night to the new-born day. The women have brought their gourds of cassiri. The cassava bread is broken up and passed from hand to hand. Old Daniell comes forward, peaked cap and loin-cloth, a stolid figure, with a wad of ireng turning slowly in his mouth. He was Hallelujah leader once. Now he is old, too old to sing, but when the morning prayer is over he still comes forward to fill the first calabash. The drink is carried round by the women, sweet and cold, thick with cassava. The children watch them. Their eyes gleam as night hunger dies away. From the women, hardly a word. One or two of the men talk quietly. The babies, in their cotton slings, are still half asleep at their mothers' breasts. As the meal comes to an end, the first family slips out of the chochi—the tushau, who is going to hunt, followed by his two wives and their children, unquestioning eyes beneath their dark fringes. Bare feet follow obediently, a part of their parents' shadows.

A few minutes later the building is empty, apart from Henry and his family. His wife is crouching by the fire, with a long, dark cassiri-bina across her upper lip. The sun has risen over the trees, lacing the river with shadows. The mist still lingers in the branches, while the faint, warm scent of decaying leaves drifts out of the heart of the forest. The startled laughter of the parrots, high up over the river. A splash of water below the bamboos, where the children are bathing. The sunlight plays across their shoulders and gleams on the back of the river. Uncrowned king of the children's world, Marcello is standing out on the rocks, with his bow and arrow, body tensed as he waits for the glint of a fish.

The women are leaving the village now, along the path that leads to the farms, a little way down river; moving quickly and yet unhurried, empty wareshis on their backs, with the children close behind them. A little girl hums as she passes—the Hallelujah song of this morning, still turning over in her mind. Some of the men have gone to fish, scouring their traps at the scattered creek mouths over on the far side of the river. Others have vanished up the hill, to hunt for wild hog and labba in the unbroken silence of the forest.

Somehow they belong to its stillness, which cloisters the tiny village. Its strength is an ally, secluding them from an outside world which is still afraid of its mysteries. For the Indians, this isolation is freedom, while the forest and river draw their meaning from the people who live between them, hunting their trails, fishing their waters, and weaving legends around their spirits. It is here that their relationship lies—men and animals, trees and the river, all have their place in the spirit world. The lack of any real distinction binds them into a single life. It seems to be the same with their pets, the parrots and monkeys, a solemn toucan, and a mischievous, striped kibihee.[1] They come and go, from village to forest, sharing the Indians' lives of their own free will.

The village is dozing, half empty beneath the languid sun. A world for old men and children now. Two little boys are wrestling intently, young warriors, eyes alert, watching each other's every movement. A whistle from the far end of the village puts an end to their battle. Someone has glimpsed a parakeet, high up in the bamboos. Snatching their

1. A small type of racoon, which is easily tamed, and a favourite pet among Indian children.

blowpipes, they creep forward, crouching, searching overhead. A sharp puff and a cry of triumph. They have no sense of cruelty in a world where life is lost and gained with unquestioned simplicity.

The old men drowse in the shadows, hunting in their dreams. Once or twice a figure moves slowly down to the waterside. Moses, bent and lined with age, his thin legs feeling their way beneath a tattered loin-cloth. Daniell is back in the old days again, when he learnt Hallelujah. The first time he led the dance, in the chochi his father built, when they lived farther up river. His voice grows strong again as he dreams, carried up by the stamping of feet, refreshed by another round of cassiri, until the day-long dance is over. The ireng begins turning between his lips, as he hears the sound of children's voices, drifting from far away, in the somewhere between sleep and waking.

The sun is stooping over the river, as the time of day mounts up and turns. The women are returning now, heads bowed beneath wareshis which are laden with cassava roots, bananas and firewood. There seems to be no sense of hardship when a woman is born for toil. The children need food, and the men cassiri. The roots are scraped, grated and squeezed, and the slow scent of cassava bread begins drifting through the village.

Soon the men are back from the hunt. The fish gleam silver in improvised carriers, woven out of reeds. The tushau has the pride of the day, a wild hog, carried over his shoulder; the best of Kaibarupai's hunters, his skill has given him two wives, sisters, perhaps even twins, their faces are so alike. A single haunch of meat is smoked and hung up in the corner of their home. The rest will be cooked and carried to the chochi, for the others to share.

For the men, there is time to relax. They are sitting by the tushau's house, with the calabash passing from hand to hand, talking of the day's events—the wild hog, the fish, the cassiri, and perhaps the two strangers who have come to the village. Outside his home by the river bank, David is weaving a wareshi. The straw passes through strong fingers, falling into a careful pattern.

Children's laughter drifting up from the waterside. A little girl passes, a shy smile—yesterday all downcast eyes. Lithe and agile, poised in her movements, blue and white bead-apron, hair running wild over bare shoulders. A moment later she returns, gourd in hand, with the dying sunlight trapped in the water on her pale brown skin. A trail of footprints in the sand. The other children will recognize them. Strange, how conscious they are of each other. They seem to speak by their very silence, gathering round, half shy and half curious.

Dusk is sliding over the river, deepening in a moment. The night sounds stir into life. The spasmodic, enquiring call of the frogs, so deep that it seems to come from somewhere beneath the river. A distant, falling cry from a night bird. The drowsy monotony of cicadas, humming their one note chorus.

The Indians are moving back to the chochi. At first a few tremulous voices, then the song rises, pulsing between them, the voice of the village, led by Henry, eyes half closed and head swaying slightly. A song which comes from deep down among them, a message woven into their lives, from Bichiwung to Aibilibing, apprehension finding a refuge in their imagination. Their faces have a wisdom about them, remote, intangible, somehow withdrawn beyond the force of change.

Henry's voice rises in prayer, an emotion which seems to be speaking through him, echoed by the others. '*Papa, wakobe goolibage, maimuge yelemuge, Hallelujah melundage.*' (God, give us words and strength, give us Hallelujah to sing). '*Aibilibinge ulibage sililidule, wakundage wehoromai, selaiou uliou, ulibage Hallelujah.*' (Father, give it to us now, send it to us, we are suffering in this harsh world, give us Hallelujah).

Fever pitch slowing down to a whisper, as the prayer dies away. Food and drink are handed round by the wavering light of the sheeba. After they have returned to their homes the murmur of voices can still be heard, at broken intervals through the night. The tribal legends are retold, while the old women talk in whispers which still rule the family. Figures move quietly through the shadows, renewing the fires beneath their hammocks against the cold night air. Just before dawn a brief silence falls over the village. Another day of ritual is over, a link in the unbroken rhythm of life. The old men dream of the trail and the river, the things of which their fathers dreamed. For the young men, perhaps, it is different. They have seen a new world down river. Their dreams have changed, and soon the rhythm will vanish into the past.

One day was much the same as another at Kaibarupai. William had returned to Waipa with Launcelot and Regis. Every morning and evening, unless we happened to be in the chochi, a large bowl of cassiri was brought to us, no doubt at Henry's instigation. I noticed that it was thicker and sweeter than the Indian drinks I had tasted before. The grated cassava was left in it, increasing its nutritious value, while its alcoholic content was low. Although both children and adults drank it in large quantities, it hardly ever made them tipsy. Here, unlike the advanced areas, where substitutes had reduced it to little more than the means of a spree, it remained an essential part of their diet. Perhaps this explained the elaborate symbolism behind their cassiri-binas, which only they and the Akawaio still used.

Their restraint began to lift, as they grew used to us. At first they seemed self-conscious about their own way of dressing, but even this was short-lived. Some of the younger men, who had worn clothes ever since our arrival, reverted to their loin-cloths. The women no longer thrust their children into ragged shorts and dresses, provoking a wail of indignation, whenever we passed their homes. The old men were much less inhibited; they and the children were the first to gather round our camp. One by one they brought us presents—a piece of meat, a bunch of bananas, fish and, on one occasion, two little pouches made of jaguar skin. They clearly expected something in return. Like the tushau at Waipa, they made some difficult requests, centering on the tape-recorder and my only pair of trousers. But here, too, they seemed quite content with the cigarettes which were all we could give them.

Often they simply stopped to demand one, as the Akawaio had done. Already, in the Kamarang, this habit had been a strain on our limited supplies. At first I imagined that they had learnt it from the porknockers. But I soon had second thoughts about it. The Patamonas' requests were never made in a begging tone. Whenever I produced a packet of cigarettes, the men nearby would ask for one as if it were an assumed right. It was clear what lay behind this. None of the Indian dialects have any terms for 'please' or 'thank you'; they would have no use for them. In a subsistence level society the individual requires only enough to satisfy his own and his family's immediate needs. If anyone has more than this it is shared as a matter of common sense, rather than generosity. Being instinctive, this outlook dies hard; even at Orealla, where money had been in circulation for two or three generations, few of the Indians ever tried to save it.

This lack of the concept of property, with its time demanding, long-term values, gave them a freedom which is lost to Western society—the freedom of living from day to day, of basing their lives on a sense of each other and their environment. Perhaps this was the main reason for their curiosity. Many of the older people were quite content to sit and watch us for an hour or two on end, observing every movement we made. Our hammocks were of special interest. They had never seen them like that, they explained—Andrew's being woven in Macusi and mine in Arawak style. The children also clustered round us, led by Henry's son, Marcello, who seemed to have inherited his father's strength of character. They were equally curious. If one of them were allowed to touch my several days' beard, or dip his fingers in a tin of butter, the others would be there in a moment to share the novelty.

It was David whom we got to know best. Often, as I woke up, I was conscious of somebody watching me. Usually he was squatting on his haunches in a corner of the camp, like some faithful retainer. I never knew how long he had been there. He would greet us with a benign smile, nodding his head wisely, as if advising us to relax—the world was the same as ever. Sometimes he wanted his bandage changed; at others he was just paying a visit. It was strange, seeing a grown man with this childlike personality. We seemed to have won his trust completely. Like the others, he would sit and gaze at us, following our expressions closely. Whenever we laughed, he joined in, though clearly unable to understand a word of what had been said. Sometimes, when I was writing my diary, he would come and peer over my shoulder, watching the pen with a knowing expression. Then he would return to his corner, nodding every now and then, as if the whole performance had become a matter of special confidence between us.

One day Andrew and I went to see him in his home. We found him still weaving his wareshi. His wife, who was just back from the farm, was preparing cassava bread. She brought us a bowl of fresh cassiri and David laid down his work to share it with us. As he had no married daughters, his house was fairly small. Baskets and gourds were piled high in each corner. The usual pattern of hammocks stretched from side to side. Apart from the firelight and the sun, which crept in through the narrow entrance, it was completely dark.

I asked if I could take his photograph, but he suddenly seemed bashful. Andrew passed on his apprehension—he was afraid that people would laugh at his picture if they saw him wearing a loin-cloth. But after a while he relented, on condition that we found him a piece of clothing. It seemed sad that this was his first ambition, but Andrew produced an old yellow singlet. Although it was much too small for him, David beamed with delight as he struggled into it. As soon as he had tried it on, he folded it up affectionately and tucked it away in a corner. Later that afternoon we saw him strutting round proudly, displaying his sudden change of status, with the bright yellow singlet combining garishly with his red loin-cloth.

Henry and Marcello were passing by. They offered to take us round the village. The first house we came to was larger than David's with three or four families living in it.

'This man called Thomas,' said Henry, indicating the head of the family. 'And this is his wife,' he added, pointing to an old woman who was grating cassava. 'He got a next wife too—this same lady's daughter by a first man.'

This is a fairly common practice. By the time she settles down with a man, the average Indian girl already has at least one child. Her husband is often younger than herself; when she is past child-bearing age he takes a second wife. This is accepted by the first, who remains in charge of the female side of family life. If she happens to have a daughter by a previous man, the young girl, now of marriageable age, is often the one who takes her mother's place. Thomas's son, who also lived there, was equally uxorious; but his two wives were sisters, another frequent Indian custom. The house, not unnaturally, was crowded with children of every age. At this rate there could be little danger of a decline in their numbers; but polygamy had been stamped out in the nearby mission-ized areas.

I had noticed something which rather surprised me. 'All the people here have English names?' I asked.

'Yes,' said Henry, 'all of them. Long time back, a priest come, and he give them just one name. Then the son take the father's name and a next one with it. They got Indian names too, but they don't like to tell you.'

I had heard about this before. Indian names are much more attractive than the English ones which replace them. They are usually taken from animals or plants, such as Yuri-tokoro, tobacco-flower. But no Indian will disclose his name to a stranger. As it is generally based on some aspect of his character, the knowledge of it immediately reveals something about him. This can be turned to his disadvantage, or even used by an enemy who wishes to put a spell on him. Even when speaking to each other they usually avoid names. Instead, they use terms of relation-ship like 'yakko', 'little brother' or 'friend'. This meant that the first itinerant priests were obliged to give them English names, after which their own died out. They are always eager for new ones. Amongst the three and four year old girls in many Indian villages there are even several 'Princess Margarets', dating from the latter's visit to Guiana in 1958.

As we passed from house to house, I noticed that some of the young men had long, parallel scratches on their arms and legs.

'That is to make them hunt well,' Andrew explained. 'They take special plants and rub juice in the cuts. The Macusi got a different way. They did this thing to me once, in the Rupununi. They take some big black ants and tie them between some straws. Then they set them on my shoulders. When they start biting I nearly fainted. They said it would make me shoot well.'

123

'Did it work all right?' I asked.

'Must be so,' he said with a grin, 'because I shoot proper straight.'

This custom of the ant ordeal is practised by many tribes in both North and South America. It is often connected with puberty rites, which coincide with the stage when a boy is old enough to hunt alone. Early anthropologists thought that the concept behind it was the derivation of alertness and endurance from the pain involved. This idea may play a part, but amongst the Guianese tribes its purpose is mainly symbolic, like that of the women's cassiri-binas. The ants are noted for their industry, and their bites are thought to transfer a part of their spirit, which gives the victim a similar energy.

There is also a symbolic aim in their custom of rubbing juice into the cuts in their arms. Uncle Charlie at Orealla had once told me an Arawak legend about how the Indians learnt to hunt. One day a man killed a camoudi and chopped up the body. On the following morning, several different plants had grown on the spot where he buried the snake. Each one enabled him to shoot a different animal—one for deer, one for wild hog, one for monkeys and so on. This suggests that specific plants are thought to have the power to attract particular animals. This is clearly the idea behind their hunting charms. Most of the plants which they use have special features resembling those of animals. The Akawaio, for example, cultivate a plant called caladium to attract the tapir, or bush cow, because of the creamy spots on its leaves, which resemble those on the skin of young tapir. This symbolism is a natural outcome of their animistic beliefs, where spirits with peculiar powers are attributed to men, animals and plants alike. It was not long before I discovered that even Andrew was still influenced by this way of thought.

I had wondered how he would react to the Patamona. His remarks on the wareshi had suggested that he might be sceptical about their primitive way of life. For a day or two he made no comment, but when he did begin talking about them, I was pleasantly surprised. He had noticed how much healthier and more contented the children were, when their ragged clothes were removed. He seemed almost affectionate towards them, without being patronizing. I often noticed him feeding them from the rations we shared. Perhaps he was unconsciously moved, seeing in them a trace of the past which had vanished among the Macusi.

'You like the people here?' I asked, as he was cooking our supper one evening.

'Yes,' he said, 'I like them all right. They got a nice way of living.'

'How do you mean?'

'The way they share everything. Even if you got no food you wouldn't ever starve up here. These people got no worries about what they going to eat the next day. When you got food, you share it out. When you got none, a next man gives you. Is that makes me like them.'

'What about Hallelujah? Do you think they really believe in it?'

'Yes, they must believe in it. I don't know why the outside people always want to stop it.' He was silent for a moment. 'They say they going dance tomorrow.'

'You want to dance with them?'

'No,' he said, 'I wouldn't do that.' He suddenly seemed diffident. 'These people giving me worries. I believe they going to blow on me if I start dancing with them. You ever heard about this blowing?'

'Yes, I heard something about it when I was with the Akawaio. But they didn't tell me much.'

'The Macusi know how to do it,' he said. 'When they want to hurt a man they take a cup of parakari and blow on it, using special words. When you drink the thing you fall down sick. The only way you can get well again is if you know the right words. You take a next cup of parakari, and blow on it, using the words. Then you drink it and feel all right.'

'But did this ever happen to you?'

'Yes, a man tried it on me, a cousin to the girl I marry. He wanted to make her get power over me. So one day he come to shake my hand, because he was going away. You can blow on people that way too. He was saying the words so I couldn't hear them, but I knew he had blown on the hand. So I give him one helluva cuff, and tell him to take this thing out of me. Then he get frightened and blow again and take it out, like I tell him. Since that time I ain't seen him no more.'

'But this man was a Macusi?' I asked.

'No, he was a Patamona. They don't like the Macusi people. In the old days they were fighting us, and we used to put arrow behind them and send them running back to the mountains. But they still trying kanaima on us, and this same blowing.'

'But how do you know?'

'They was trying it on me today. A family call me to their house and ask me to drink some cassiri. I said I couldn't drink it—I knew they was blowing on it. They see how I got clothes and money, so they want to put a spell on me, to make me live with their daughter. And if I dance this Hallelujah they going do the same thing. If they know I'm Macusi, all these people going blow me. I tell them that I'm Arecuna—so you got to say the same thing.'

I promised to try and keep his secret. His anxiety seemed quite genuine.

125

Life among the Patamona was clearly more complex than I had realized. I had heard occasional talk of blowing in Akawaio country. Though once practised by all the Indians, it is now confined to the more remote tribes. A man's breath is identified as the physical part of his spirit. When one Indian wishes either to cure or harm another he mutters a special charm and blows in his direction. As he does so, a part of his breath-spirit leaves his body, and enters that of his patient or victim, acting according to the charm. The target need not be another human being. Given the right charms, blowing can fulfil almost any purpose, such as the prevention of rain, or the exorcizing of imawali, the mischievous bush spirit. Distance is of no account. The victim can be anything from a few inches to several miles away from the blower. Sometimes he is approached through the medium of drink or a hand-shake, as in Andrew's case; at others, simply by blowing in his direction. If the charm is a bad one, it can bring him under the blower's influence, or even cause his death. Clearly, if Andrew's suspicions were true and he really believed in blowing, he had every reason to be alarmed.

He was right about the dancing. On the following morning Henry himself brought us a bowl of cassiri, along with the news that they would be performing Hallelujah all day. Their dawn ritual was already over. An hour or so later, as Andrew and I went over to the chochi, the Indians were drifting back again. The gourds had already been refilled, while Henry's wife was still boiling cassiri over a fire in the corner. The old men had been there since dawn, half asleep inside the dark building. We sat down and chatted to Henry, while the others arrived.

'How did the village get the name of Kaibarupai?' I asked.

'I never hear about it,' said Henry. 'But I going ask these old people.'

He turned to Moses and Daniell, and spoke to them in Patamona. A hesitant, terse debate followed, with hardly the flicker of an expression crossing their wrinkled faces.

'They say they ain't know,' said Henry.

The old men never liked to be hurried. This was their usual response to a question of this kind. I bided my time. A long pause set in.

'They studying this name,' said Henry, glancing at the two old men— an optimistic conclusion, I thought, as Moses was staring into space, while Daniell's only sign of life was the steady movement of the ireng between his dry lips. Suddenly Moses muttered something. The conversation was renewed, with a slow, conclusive nodding of heads.

'They catch it now,' said Henry. ' "Kai" is old man, because an old man was first living here. "Baru" is creek, and "pai" meaning village. So Kaibarupai is old-man-creek village.'

Daniell offered another comment, slow and strung out, like a series of afterthoughts.

'This Daniell was a young boy when they come to live here,' said Henry. 'Before that they was living up river, at a place called Kanabia in Sequabi Creek. Is then they first get Hallelujah from Akawaio people.'

'They learnt it from Akawaio?' I asked. I was still wondering how the latter had acquired it before the Patamona, who lived closer to the Macusi founders of the cult.

'Yes,' said Henry, 'from Akawaio. You heard about this Bichiwung?'

'Yes, but he was a Macusi.'

'Yes, a Macusi man, the first who get Hallelujah. When he dead a next man take over. Some of the Akawaio people was living near the Macusi, Kwatin River side, in Brazil. They was travelling all about, and so they see this Hallelujah, how Bichiwung get God story. One of them called Wokowiaming. He gone to Macusi people. Then he come back to Amokokopai, trying to teach Hallelujah. They get a big cassiri spree, sport and dance Hallelujah. But they drink too much, get sweet, tumble up, fall down and sleep. When Wokowiaming wake up, he lost Halle-lujah, can't remember it. God take it back from him because he drink too much cassiri.'

'But what happened after that?'

'Is only one man catch it,' said Henry. 'Abel they call he, a young man, living Amokokopai. He ain't drink so much cassiri. He really want this Hallelujah. He study how Wokowiaming get it. He gone back to Amoko-kopai, praying, praying all the time, until he see God and get Hallelujah.'

So this was how Hallelujah had reached the Akawaio. 'How long ago was that?' I asked.

'Long, long, long,' said Henry. Reconstructing a piece of history is not always easy with the Indians.

'But when did Abel die?'

'A little time before I born.' He himself looked about forty. So Abel must have died between 1910 and 1920.

'But the Patamona live near the Macusi. Why didn't they learn it first, before the Akawaio?'

'Me ain't know,' said Henry. 'Sometime is only the Akawaio want to learn Hallelujah. These Patamona live in the mountains, Macusi ain't go near them. When Macusi people travel, they gone Brazil-side, to Kwatin River, meet Akawaio.'

So this was why the Akawaio, rather than the Patamona, had been the first to adopt the cult from the Macusi who lay to the south. The Patamona were secluded, as they are to this day, by the Pakaraimas. The southernmost Akawaio group stretched farther than I had realized, down to the Kwatin, or Cotinga River, over in Brazil. As a tributary of the Takutu, which is linked with the Ireng, this forms a natural highway between Akawaio and Macusi country, skirting the Pakaraimas and their Patamona inhabitants. Before the arrival of European goods it was a popular Indian trade route, conveying the Arecunas' blowpipes to the southern tribes. Later it was used by explorers, who travelled northwards to Mount Roraima, into Akawaio country, often with Macusi droughers. With these frequent contacts provoking their curiosity, the Akawaio were naturally the first to learn Hallelujah from the Macusi.

Only one major problem remained. 'When did the Patamona learn it?' I asked.

'Long before I come here,' said Henry. He consulted old Daniell again.

'He say he father Benjamin learn it from Abel's son Moses. This Moses was travelling about, and he come and teach the Patamona. Then Benjamin gone to Amokokopai. After this he build a chochi at Kanabia village, up river, where they living that time. Then all the Patamona get it. A next man called Chen Charlie was leader at Paramakatoi, but the priest stop Hallelujah there. This Benjamin seen God and get Patamona songs. When he dead, he son Daniell take over, and then I come here. That must be about seven years back.'

At last a complete pattern had emerged. Hallelujah began among the Macusi, probably in the 1840's, as a result of Christian doctrines diffused from the earliest missions in Indian territory. In the hands of Bichiwung it had evolved its own philosophy, providing the Indians with an escape from their initial contact with Europeans. After his death, in about the 1870's, it was carried northwards to the Akawaio, via the Kwatin River, by Wokowiaming. A roving, curious tribe, superstitious and fairly secluded, they made much more of it than the Macusi founders. The first Akawaio prophet, Abel, probably learnt it around 1880, and died some thirty years later. His successors all lived at Amokokopai, which became the cult centre. Soon after Bichiwung's death it must have faded out among the Macusi; but meanwhile the Akawaio were spreading his word to neighbouring tribes. About fifty years ago the Patamona learnt it through Benjamin, the first of their leaders. It must have been about the same time that it reached the Arecuna, over in Brazil. When Benjamin died, his son Daniell took over as leader of the Patamona, but he still acknowledged the supremacy of the Amokokopai prophet.

Now that Daniell was growing old, Henry had come to take his place, at Aibilibing's instructions.[1]

In its life-span of over a century the wandering, hybrid cult has passed through four of the nine Indian tribes—the Macusi, the Akawaio, the Patamona and Arecuna. At one time or another nearly half the Indian population, stretched over an area of two hundred miles along the borders of Guiana, Venezuela and Brazil, have believed in Hallelujah. Had it survived among the Macusi, it might have become a uniting, almost revolutionary force, strong enough to resist the approach of the orthodox Christian sects and the European rule they brought with them. But now it is clearly on the wane. It is forgotten by the Macusi, almost suppressed in Arecuna country and driven into isolation among the Akawaio and Patamona. Its remaining followers, perhaps two or three hundred in number, are confined to a single mountain stronghold, based on two remote villages. Although its history is still remembered, only three of its leading figures are alive—Aibilibing, Daniell and Henry. None of their younger disciples seem to have any prophetic status, and the cult is ringed round by orthodox sects, with the higher material attraction of their European culture. Within a generation or two it may easily be forgotten.

By the time we finished talking the whole village was there. The cassiri was being handed round, no doubt to give them strength for the dancing, as Henry had once told me. Before the ceremony began, he stood up and spoke to the others. I found myself almost resenting the slightly domineering way in which he treated the quiet Patamona. But clearly he was no mean orator. The circle of eyes hardly left his face. Indian harangues are usually brief, but Henry continued with hardly a pause for almost half an hour. It was only towards the end that he broke into a dialogue with Daniell, the former leader, while some of the other old men added their comments. I later discovered that their curiosity had been aroused by our conversation, reminding them of the Bichiwung story, which they were now discussing.

When this was over they started dancing to a chant led by Henry. Their movements were like those at Amokokopai; three paces forward and one back, with the circle swaying round, lowering their bodies in time to the rhythm, heads rising again. Most of the older children were

1. Henry's description of the early expansion of Hallelujah adds very little to Dr. Butt's information on the subject (see Bibliography). My own summary is also indebted to her research. The only new piece of information is the story of Patamona Hallelujah. Apart from the Arecuna details—which are probably beyond discovery, due to the influence of the missions—this completes the history of the cult, at least in the vague outline which is all that the Indian memory allows.

familiar with the words and steps, while even the smallest of them, tagged on to the end of the line, were following the others carefully. Despite its similarity to Akawaio Hallelujah, the atmosphere was more intense—the chanting was clearer, the rhythm stronger and their expressions completely absorbed. With sixty or seventy people dancing, there was a sense of power about it, something expressing a bond between them which seemed indestructible.

Soon their shoulders were gleaming with sweat. The half darkness thinned out slowly, as the sunlight crept through the chinks in the walls. They had all dressed up for the occasion. Some of the men had a pair of trousers over their red loin-cloths. Many of them wore necklaces, made of wild hogs' teeth, a sign of a man's hunting prestige, varied with jaguar fangs, which act as a charm against illness. One of the younger men stood out, with a pair of small tortoise-shells, painted in yellow and black, tied to his arm with coloured cotton. The women's blue and white bead-necklaces matched their bracelets and anklets, while long strings of deers' tails hung down the backs of the little girls.

After a while old Daniell got up and joined in, with his peaked cap still perched on his head. At the end of each dance he went through his usual ceremony of handing out the cassiri for the women to pass round. Andrew was watching every movement, leaning against the entrance in a slightly nonchalant pose, perhaps to conceal his fear of being blown on. Otherwise everyone was dancing, apart from the old men; even they took what part they could, with their tremulous voices joining in, as they squatted quietly in a corner, chewing their pensive wads of ireng.

I danced with them for a while. Andrew betrayed no reaction. I wondered if he would rebuke me for exposing myself to their blowing. After one of the longer pauses Henry suddenly withdrew. It was Daniell who took over the lead, apparently rejuvenated, as his husky voice intoned the songs which he and his father had learnt from God.

Henry and I went and sat outside. The village was almost deserted; the sound of the Hallelujah song ebbed out into the drowsy sunlight.

'He father Benjamin get that song,' said Henry.

It had a strong, lilting rhythm, which remained in my head long afterwards. 'Pada wela terope, uwi yapong tabichi-co' (Take me up to Heaven, Father, let me touch my bench there).

'Benjamin sleep and gone to Heaven,' Henry explained. 'When he meet there, God show him the place, nice, nice, with plenty cassava. He see the old people who dead. They was all sitting on benches. He say he going give Hallelujah people some benches in this same Heaven. So they asking God to send the benches and take them up to His place.'

'Do you think these young people are going carry on with Hallelujah?' I asked.

He paused. 'Me ain't know,' he said. 'Other Patamona people lost it. It finish at Paramakatoi, the village below Orinduik. This white priest come from America. He say the people going burn in the big fire if they keep up with Hallelujah. That make them frightened so they leave off and take the white man's Bible.'

'But this priest ever spoke to the people here?'

'No, he never come this side. But they got a next one coming to Waipa who say this Hallelujah is bad. He tell me I thiefing people, making them dance Hallelujah. He say the same thing, how I going burn in the big fire, when I dead and left this place. But I ain't get so frightened. This place is for the Indians. God give we Hallelujah—the white man ain't supposed to trouble we.'

He was silent. Perhaps, underneath it all, he knew that the strength of the cult at Kaibarupai might be its final defiant stand, with himself as the last of its powerful leaders.

'Have you ever seen God?' I asked.

'I trying,' he said quietly. 'Daniell and Benjamin seen Him, same like Aibilibing. Four or five times I was sleeping, and coming near to see God, but people bring cassiri and stop me in the way. But up to now I still trying. When I see Him, He going tell me what to do this side.'

He paused again. The chant had ended. A moment later, another began. Daniell's day was not yet over.

'When I gaff with the old men this morning,' said Henry, 'we talk about this Bichiwung. You like to hear about how he see God?'

I nodded, and Henry began. He must have talked for almost an hour, while I tape-recorded the story. It agreed fairly closely with the version which I already knew. Bichiwung had gone to England with the white priest for whom he worked. Here he visited God and received the message of Hallelujah which he brought back to his people. But Henry's account gave a new emphasis to its psychological aspects. Bichiwung had distrusted the white man; something was being hidden from him. God told him specifically to keep his new religion a secret until he returned to the Macusi. The white man's beliefs were outdated. Hallelujah was a new creed, designed especially for the Indians, who were now God's chosen people. He would give them a place of their own, with freedom, wealth and security. Although Henry omitted to say so, early versions of the story even suggested that the Indians would acquire white skins and regain control of Guiana.

This anti-European streak was not mere racialism. It had a much more positive meaning. The Indians seemed to be reacting against the white man's misunderstanding, his refusal to share his knowledge, and his desire to dominate them. The main factors behind the cult were a new sense of poverty, resulting from contact with Europeans, and anxiety for their vanishing freedom. God solved these problems for them. He gave them a Bible and a moral code similar to those of the white man. Bichiwung and the subsequent prophets built churches and started to preach, in the fashion of European priests, though with a different doctrine. It was not a retrogressive movement. The Indians were making a constructive attempt to solve their new dilemma. By combining methods of their own with those they had seen the white man using, they hoped to create their own place within the new scheme of things which the white man had imposed.

Hallelujah is not unique. During the last two centuries, similar circumstances have produced hybrid millennial cults of this kind all over the world.[1] They express the reactions of primitive peoples to the new standards—religious, cultural and economic—which European colonialism has suddenly revealed to them. This haphazard, unexpected experience disturbs them on every level. Before it occurs their behaviour follows a traditional, unquestioned pattern; but once they are deprived of their freedom and made aware of their poverty, they lose faith in this old way of life. Eventually they are either absorbed or destroyed by the new, stronger society, but first there is a transitional phase, when their old concepts are dying out, without the new ones being grasped. Faced with this vacuum, they withdraw and search for some form of adjustment. The type of solution which they often find has given this phase the name of charisma, meaning divine inspiration. It is based on a revelation experienced by one of the people, usually an ex-shaman, or witch-doctor, who becomes a prophet-leader. The message given to him by some divine power is passed on to his followers, who act on his instructions.

Charismatic cults have been frequent amongst South American tribes. Hallelujah has at least two predecessors in Guiana. Although they were both short-lived, they apparently had the same inspiration—a prophecy commanding the Indians to imitate the white man, by way of gaining their independence. The first was in 1797, when a strange disturbance was reported from the Essequibo River. Two Indians called Maypoerie-Poerie and Caycoeco were assembling the tribes from all around with news of a revelation. God was hiding in the sea, as a prelude to the day when the Indians would all be given white skins. Neighbouring tribes

1. They are discussed in Appendix D.

would come from Venezuela and Brazil to join the movement. Together they would drive out the Europeans and regain possession of their land.

This cult seems to have petered out, but fifty years later there was another, which led its followers to disaster. An Arecuna called Awacaipu, who lived at the foot of Mount Roraima, began to preach a new creed which attracted the Indians from hundreds of miles around. The Great Spirit, Makunaima, had appeared to him in a vision and told of his pity for his Indian children, who were poor and naked, and oppressed by the strangers; he had promised a day of resurrection, which would bring them all new wealth and enable them to regain their freedom. All those who killed each other, in obedience to his command, would return on the night of the next full moon. They would come down from Mount Roraima, with white skins instead of brown, to defeat their European masters and rule over the rest of the Indians. His followers took him at his word, and after a few cassiri sprees, the terrible slaughter began. In the course of the next three nights, some four hundred Indians killed each other. Following Awacaipu's instructions, the survivors sat down to await the full moon. Dawn came. There was no resurrection. Awacaipu received a new message, saying that the dead would return in five days' time. When this prophecy also failed the survivors clubbed him to death and returned to their villages, disillusioned.

European accounts of these movements often describe them as impostures. But clearly the leaders' beliefs are as genuine as the stress which provokes them. They follow a consistent pattern, which is expressed in their songs and mythology—moving from the initial despair towards a search for a solution, until they end in resignation, when the prophecy fails. These symptoms are still apparent in the Hallelujah songs. The oldest of them describe the sense of poverty and collapse which first inspired Bichiwung:

> 'Disaster is coming towards us,
> But we are praying for Hallelujah,
> Sorrow is coming, evil is near,
> But we are praying for Hallelujah.'[1]

From this despair there emerged the hope of an Indian millennium, which would solve their problems:

> 'God the Maker-of-Mist is coming,
> God who made the earth is coming,
> God the Maker-of-Mist is coming.'

1. The original versions of all these songs can be found in Appendix C.

The millennium would bring wealth and freedom. At first it was thought to be near at hand. Its followers' hopes still survive in the Hallelujah prayers:

'Father raise up my voice, put Hallelujah in my heart, give me strength and wealth, give me, this very day, good things to eat and see and hear, give me happiness.'

But the promised day has failed to arrive, and the Indians' original hopes have waned. Their ideals have shifted towards the concept of an after-life in an Indian Heaven. Most of the Hallelujah songs now express this conclusion. The one we had just heard them sing, which was given to Daniell's father by God, was typical of this final stage:

> 'Take me up to Heaven, Father,
> Let me touch my bench there,
> Take me up to Heaven, Father.'

The increasing vagueness of their hopes shows that the cult is dying out. Their prophecies have failed to produce any concrete results; at the same time there are new pressures, mainly from the missionaries, who see Hallelujah as a barrier to their own doctrines. But although the cult is declining, outside attitudes towards it are still important for the Indians. Veiled terrorism of the kind which Henry described—threats of the 'big fire', for example, and the condemnation of the cult leaders as mere impostors—is giving them a sense of defeat from which they may never recover. If only the cult were understood, they might receive more sympathy from those who oppose them; Hallelujah could then be absorbed, rather than suppressed. In its hey-day it probably created a degree of unity which had never previously existed within the loosely knit structure of Indian society. Given some genuine understanding, this might have been adapted into the form of an independent sect, or even a secular co-operative movement. But the time when this could have been achieved is almost certainly over. For the Europeans who deal with them, Aibilibing, Daniell and Henry are just a handful of false prophets whose beliefs must be suppressed. But, for their few remaining followers, they are still the leaders who tried to find a solution to the collapse imposed on them by the civilized world.

Andrew's anxiety was increasing. Although he watched the Patamona all day, until they emerged from the chochi to pray in the shadow of the bamboos, he carefully avoided joining in the dancing. He seemed to respect their beliefs, but was still afraid of being blown on. As we talked that night, I sensed that he was getting restless, with his thoughts turning south to the Rupununi. Our time was already running out, so I promised that we would leave fairly soon.

The next day we were woken by a series of wild whoops and shouts, piercing the cold dawn air. Andrew looked out of his hammock.

'They beating haiari,' he said. 'That's the vine to poison the creek. I hear them say they going fishing today.'

'But why are they shouting like that?'

'They calling out the names of the fish. They telling the haiari to poison them, so they can get plenty to eat.'

They were still singing inside the chochi. A few of the men were sitting outside, drinking cassiri and beating the haiari. Most of them had been up half the night, drinking and sleeping alternately, but none of them looked the worse for wear. Several large bundles of haiari lay on the ground beside them. They were squatting in front of a log and beating the roots to a pulp, so that the poisonous sap would flow as soon as they were dipped in the creek. As they worked, they laughed and shouted, calling out the names of the fish. 'Loka-loka, kanyu, kanoit, come to us. Big ones, small ones, poison them all, haiari.'

'Where are they going to fish?' I asked Andrew.

'Over on the Brazilian side,' he said. 'They aren't allowed to use haiari here, because it spoils the creek water.'

Kaibarupai was too remote to feel the pressure of a distant law code. But once more the outside world seemed bound to clash with the Indians' customs. The juice of the haiari has a narcotic quality, which stupefies the fish in the creek. As they float down, semi-conscious, the Indians wait at the bends to shoot them with their bows and arrows. The power of the vine is accounted for by an Indian legend. There was once an old man who noticed that the fish were always suffocated when his son bathed nearby. For some time he used this as a means of obtaining his food, until one day the fish got together and decided to kill the boy. The next time he came to bathe, they attacked him. The wound from the sting-ray proved fatal, and as his father carried him home, the blood dripped on to the ground. At each point where it fell, a poisonous haiari vine sprang up.

As soon as they finished the beating, an inexplicable pause set in. The morning's Hallelujah was over, and some of the others had joined us— Daniell, Henry, the tushau and David. All of them were stripped to their loin-cloths, ready for the fishing. For a while they sat round in a circle, sipping their cassiri; a laugh every now and then, but otherwise they were silent. I wondered if they had changed their plans. In view of the amount of cassiri which still remained to be drunk, it looked quite possible. But suddenly the tushau stood up. He turned and spoke to Andrew.

'He ask if you coming,' said Andrew. 'He say you must take picture of him.'

The tushau laughed merrily. Their camera-shyness seemed to be over. Gathering up the haiari, they set off down to the landing. Half the village was following, including both women and children. The troop was led by Daniell and David, with knives tucked into their loin-cloths and bows and arrows in their hands—a picture relieved by the comic touch of Daniell's ubiquitous peaked cap, worn on every occasion.

As we reached the landing, Henry's son, Marcello, turned round modestly and pulled off his loin-cloth, wrapping it round his bows and arrows. He held them up and plunged into the river with a shout of glee. I watched him as he swam underwater, with his progress marked by the little red beacon above him. Once or twice he bobbed up in the rapids, splashing and waving cheerfully, quite undisturbed by the foaming current, which was sweeping him down river. A moment later he reached the far bank, some fifty yards below us, at the mouth of the creek they were going to poison.

The others piled into the corials. Inspired partly by the cassiri, they had a festive air. Now that they were used to us, their inhibition had vanished. They were less passive than before, chatting and laughing among themselves, and still whooping with excitement. There must have been some eighteen people in the corial which Andrew and I had joined. Their paddles cut into the dark water, as we steered towards the rapids. Suddenly we hit a rock. The corial lurched from side to side, turning at right angles to the current. The Patamona shouted with mirth, as the first rush of water came into the boat. I made a despairing lunge at my cameras. A moment later the river closed over my head. I must have been under for three or four seconds, groping for them, before I emerged. We were hardly out of our depth, and the Indians were still laughing gaily, but by the time I reached the far bank I had rather lost my sense of humour. A flood of water poured out of the camera case, adding to their amusement. I tried to restrain my annoyance. It is part of the Indians' philosophy to laugh at any mild misfortune, but at the time it was hard to share. All my pictures of the previous day's dancing were bound to be damaged, if not destroyed.

The others hurried on unconcerned, while Andrew and I returned to the village to try to salve the two films. We were met by a crowd of old ladies, who stood round and giggled quietly at our bedraggled appearance. The damage was less than I expected. The mechanism of one of the cameras had escaped the water. Both the films were fairly wet, but I placed them in some desiccator, in the hope of saving a part of them. I began to calculate hurriedly. A plane due at Orinduik, around noon on the following day. With the heavy rains of the past few weeks, the river was running down fast—the return journey would take us less than half the time we had spent in reaching Kaibarupai. If we left at dawn, we might catch the plane. I could send the films down to George-town, which meant that they might be saved.

The old ladies were still amused. One of them came forward and squeezed the water from my trouser legs; another round of giggles. By now my temper was getting frayed, but their laughter must have been infectious, as Andrew and I suddenly found ourselves joining in. A moment before I had been in despair. Their fatalistic, good-natured philosophy seemed to be a solution. They clearly approved of our sharing it. One of the tushau's wives hurried off and came back with a bowl of cassiri.

After reloading the drier camera, Andrew and I set off again. Within half an hour we heard their voices, farther up the shadowed creek. The women and children were in the water, catching the stupefied fish which floated down towards them. Occasionally one of their victims leapt up, contorted, white belly turned to the sunlight. A shout as each one appeared, tensing the Indians into action. The boys always had the first chance—this was part of their training as hunters. They crept up with their bows and arrows, crouching close over the water, pausing, and then pouncing forward, as an arrow flashed out, vanished for a moment, and then lay still on the water. Once, as a lone fish jumped, Marcello transfixed it in mid-air, with a loud shout of triumph. The few that escaped were netted by the women, a little way down stream. Already the piles of fish were mounting, silver and brown in the baskets which lay on the banks.

Farther up, we met the men, standing by a fallen tree, beating the haiari again and dipping it into the water. The milk-white sap flowed out, yellowing the creek's complexion. Even here a few fish had been shot, as they struggled to escape the first wave of poison. Every few minutes the men moved down, dipping the haiari and driving the fish into the arms of the women and children, who waited around the next bend.

An hour later it was over. The catch was a good one—four or five baskets filled with a strange variety of fish, some bewhiskered and some armour-plated, loka-loka, yarrow and hassa. We returned to the village in high spirits, though Andrew and I took the precaution of travelling in Henry's corial. As we arrived, the old ladies met us, with bowls of cassiri for the men. The women disappeared to their homes, to clean the fish and start cooking, while their husbands sat down in the tushau's house, to drink and wait for the meal that would follow.

Andrew and I made plans for our journey to the Rupununi. With nearly two hundred pounds to carry, in the form of rations and equipment, we would need someone to help us. We talked to Henry about it. He soon brought two young men, called Pablo and Michael, who were willing to join us. But when they heard how far we were going, their enthusiasm began to wane. It might be hard for them, they said. Pablo had a new wife, and was worried about leaving her; Michael had a field to cut, so he might not have the time. As they muttered to the tushau, I heard them use the word 'kanaima'. Neither of them, as it turned out, had been outside the Ireng Valley before. They were apprehensive about the Macusi, who might blow on them, or use kanaima, the avenging spirit.

Eventually the problem was solved, when Henry found a young Patamona, called John, who agreed to come with us. He had once worked with Government surveyors on the Brazilian road scheme, so the outside world had no terrors for him. The tushau agreed to take us down in his corial—he knew the rapids well, he assured us. His enthusiasm seemed to be roused by the prospect of trying to catch the plane—the 'kurung-ganawa', or 'carrion-crow-boat', as the Patamona called it. We decided to leave at dawn.

Dusk was shifting over the treetops. By now I had learned the words of some of the Hallelujah songs. I joined the Indians in the chochi, where the darkness was filled with the familiar rhythm. Afterwards there was food for all, fish from the morning's expedition and gourds still full of cassiri. As we ate, I chatted to Henry.

'You leaving in the morning?' he said.

'Yes, as soon as it starts to get light.'

'Is one thing I want to ask you—about these outside people. First they want to stop Hallelujah, and now we hear a next story. Some people come and give us a thing, a vote they call it. They say the Government changing up, and people going take away we land. Is so it going to happen?'

The others were watching intently. I wondered if any of them knew what Henry was asking about. Even here, at Kaibarupai, the future was making itself felt. But at least it still seemed remote. I tried to reassure Henry. He had probably been misled, I replied—there was no immediate cause for anxiety.'

'Is there anything I can send for you from outside?' I asked.

'Please for some pictures,' he said. 'The ones of Hallelujah.'

He was quiet, reserved again. Perhaps our departure reminded him that I came from a world which was hostile to his beliefs. A strangely enigmatic figure, who stood for so much in the Indians' lives. Lonely, powerful and defiant, in his silent Indian way.

He began to speak to the Patamona. He was telling them that we were leaving early next morning. Their passive faces betrayed no reaction, apart from David and the old men, who came to pat me on the shoulder, by way of saying goodbye.

As we lay in our hammocks that night, Andrew told me, with great relish, what I should do if we sank in the rapids; I must let the water carry me down, without fighting against it. It was always useful to know, he added, especially when the river was high and running down hard, as at present.

The murmur of voices still carried round us, from beside the fires in the Indians' homes. Andrew was suddenly silent; it could only mean that he was asleep. I lay awake for some time. Later, when the village was still, I heard Henry singing on his own in the chochi, as Aibilibing had done. Perhaps he was reminding me of all that we had talked about. It was probably the last that I would hear of Hallelujah.

7

The Southern Trail

BACK at Orinduik the next day, we seemed to have returned to another world. Only then did I realize just how remote and enclosed Kaibarupai had been. Our journey down the Ireng was fairly uneventful; leaving the village at dawn, we skimmed safely through the rapids, only to see the weekly plane vanishing over the hills. We had missed it by a matter of minutes. When we reached Orinduik, the tushau and one of his wives came over to the shop with us, and then disappeared hurriedly back to Kaibarupai. By the time we had said goodbye to them, it was late afternoon. We decided to spend the night there and set out early in the morning.

Mrs. Correia welcomed us back with her usual benevolence. As we ate our supper that night, in the half darkness of her shop, Andrew chattered gaily. He seemed relieved at our return to semi-civilization. John, the Patamona boy, sat beside us without a word, eating unobtrusively and observing all that went on around him. I pulled the map out of my pocket. We still had to plan our route down to Macusi country.

Andrew was already excited at the prospect of reaching home. 'You see this part?' he said. 'That's all good diamond country, up in the Pakaraimas.' He ran his finger down the long stretch of mountains through which the trail wound its way to the south. 'All hard walking,' he added. 'When we meet the Rupununi, I going to want plenty of parakari.'

'These mountains high,' said John. 'Sometimes you can't go more than ten or fifteen miles one day.'

'True,' said Andrew, nodding his head. 'Look Karasabai here.' He pointed to a settlement at the foot of the Pakaraimas. 'That's the first big Macusi village. After that, one more day's walking—then you meet the open savannas.'

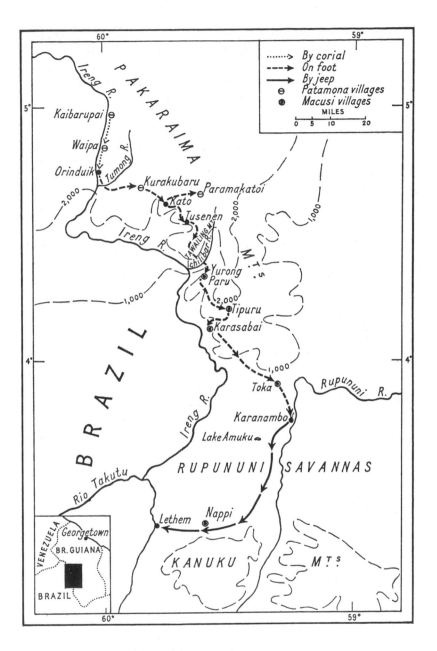

THE SOUTHERN TRAIL

I glanced back at the map. The trail followed the rough direction of the Ireng River, which formed the Brazilian border for a further hundred miles. Round it lay the Pakaraimas, rising to over three thousand feet, until they finally petered out into the northern savannas. Apart from a few Indian villages and a network of rivers and creeks, there was hardly a mark on the map.

'How long do you think it will take us?' I asked.

'I can't really say,' replied Andrew. 'By now we getting so much rain, all these rivers going to flood and that might hold us up. If we stop at some villages on the way it might take about two weeks. We could sleep at Kurakubaru tomorrow.'

He pointed to the nearest village, set on the edge of a plateau, some fifteen miles away. It looked as if the next few days might be heavy going. We drained the last of a bottle of rum and said good night to Mrs. Correia, who wished us a happy journey. Andrew and John were soon asleep, but for some time I lay awake, listening to the chitter of bats in the darkness above us.

The whitewashed adobe huts were gleaming in the early light as we left Orinduik. We paused at the crest of the first hill. In front of us lay the Tumong River, a tributary of the Ireng. The dark green of the valley was almost like an Italian landscape. Then the broad sweep of the hills, crowned with stray patches of forest and splashed by the shadows of the clouds; horizontal ribs of sandstone, dun-brown and distance-purple, with an air of rugged cruelty beneath the mounting sun.

As soon as we reached the Tumong, we heard the familiar sound of rapids. A rusty notice caught my eye. 'Irving Cheong, Claim Fair.' It was somewhere round here that Irving had found his forty-eight carat stone. Walking through diamond country, one often comes across old claims, with their names echoing the hardships and hopes of the por-knockers who staked them—Joyce, Love, God's Mercy and Lucifer were typical of those I had seen.

We stared at the dark, swollen river, rushing pell-mell over the rocks.

'We got worries already,' said Andrew. 'We can't swim with all these things. I didn't know it was so deep. Plenty of rain must have fallen last night.'

'How are we going to cross?' I asked.

'We got to use ropes,' he replied.

We stripped and stepped into the water. The current immediately swept us away. We struggled back and tried again, well above the rapids. Although we were just within our depth, the current still made it impossible to cross without using ropes. We unpacked our wareshis and tied our hammock ropes together; when we reached a lone tree on the far bank, there were just two feet to spare. If we lost the cameras this time we were unlikely to retrieve them.

As we carried our baggage across, each of us slipped several times; but somehow the ropes held. When everything was safely over we stopped for a cigarette. By now the kaboura were descending in a gleeful cloud. I watched their tiny, transparent bodies darkening and swelling up, as they sucked at our blood. I noticed that Andrew and John had a ceaseless jiggling and swatting technique which seemed to discourage them. I did my best to imitate it, without much success. Already my hands and face were freckled with red bites.

Tiring of their company, we trudged on up the next hill. The bark straps of the wareshi began cutting into my shoulders. It was only the sight of John, with his far heavier load, which still kept me moving. He and Andrew carried on, while I stopped at the brow of the hill to take a picture of the valley, stretching away beneath us.

A few minutes later I caught them up. They had paused for a rest, but when I arrived they both looked away from me glumly. Something was obviously wrong. I sat down beside them and started chatting. The two of them glanced at each other, and Andrew suddenly broke in.

'I never drough such a load before,' he said. 'Never in me whole life.'

'And I getting weary too,' said John. 'I forget how bad these mountains are. I studying to go back home right now.'

I knew that the reticent John would hardly have complained on his own. Andrew must have put him up to it, still remembering the days when his things were carried for him. John was probably quite sincere, as his load was heavy; but Andrew's was no bigger than mine, which was fairly light. I had the impression I was being sounded. I decided to call his bluff.

'Your load's too big,' I said to John. 'When we reach Kurakubaru, Andrew and I can take a part of it.'

Andrew's strong face darkened. As soon as the words were out of my mouth, I knew I had made a mistake. Although generally good-natured, he was not easily appeased when upset.

'Let's go,' I said, trying to sound casual. I turned on down the path, hoping that they would follow. By now it must have been almost noon, with the sun standing high overhead. The roofs of Kurakubaru were in sight, perched on a distant plateau, still several miles away. Below us lay another valley, carpeted with deep forest. There was no sign of the others behind me. I sat down to wait for them. After a while they appeared, walking with obvious reluctance. I decided on a mild demonstration. As they passed, I stopped John and exchanged wareshis with him. I hurried on without a word and they followed me down into the valley. I had soon begun to flag. Though John was sturdier than myself, I realized that I had given him far too much to carry. But I still felt put out by Andrew's part in the incident.

In half an hour we had reached the forest. We stopped for lunch by a narrow creek. The other two avoided my glance and we ate in complete silence. When we had finished, Andrew came over and offered me a cigarette. He had an apologetic air, which made me laugh as I took one from him. They looked at me and joined in, a little nervously at first, then louder, until we were suddenly shouting with amusement. A flock of sakawinki monkeys peered down with startled expressions. We relieved John of a part of his load and decided to find an extra drougher at Kurakubaru. Five minutes later we were off again, all of us feeling slightly foolish at our petulance.

As we approached the village, we caught sight of a family in front of us, bowed beneath their wareshis. They looked back and hurried on shyly, to spread the news of our arrival. We were greeted by a chorus of dogs, which were called off by the women as they peeped out to giggle at us. I saw the children pointing at me and realized what was amusing them. It had only just occurred to me that a European with a wareshi was an unusual sight.

The village had a strange appearance. A single round-house survived, but the others were much smaller. All of them had adobe walls, for protection against the cutting wind which swept across the plateau. Huddled together on the curve of the hill, with the pointed round-house in the centre, they looked like a film set for something out of Grimm's Fairy Tales. A few years ago the Catholics had chosen it as their headquarters in Patamona country. A neat little church and the missionary's house stood on the neighbouring hill, a few hundred yards away.

The Indians led us to an old building, once used as a school, which was now unoccupied. As we unpacked our wareshis, the clouds began lowering over the hills. The sky was soon overcast. A dark, sloping pattern of roofs crouching against a sullen grey background. The village was almost deserted. Quick, angry gusts of rain began lashing at the houses. Suddenly a jagged fork of lightning lit up the outline of the forest, followed by a crash of thunder. The wail of a baby rose in protest above the fury of the storm. The brick-like surface of the ground was rapidly turning into a lake, flecked by a hail of raindrops.

'You think this will hold us up?' I asked Andrew.

'It looks so,' he said. 'I believe we should stay here tomorrow. All the creeks are going to be full and running like the Tumong.'

It hardly mattered—we had plenty of time, and Kurakubaru looked interesting. We cooked a rough meal together—cassava bread, corned beef and farine, a Macusi type of cereal, made from dried cassava. By the time we were in our hammocks, the rain had died down to a gentle patter. Overhead, in the leaf roof, the bats were beginning to stir.

'You know about these bats?' said Andrew. 'The Macusi got plenty stories about them. Sometimes they can be proper useful. If you want to visit a girl-friend, you just kill one of these things and take out the brain. Then, when her parents sleeping, you put a piece on their hammock ropes and they can't wake up and trouble you. Only one thing—you got to remember to take it off before you leave the house. Else they can't wake up at all. Patamona people know about that?' he asked John.

'I never hear about it,' said John, perhaps out of modesty.

'You ever tried it?' I asked Andrew.

'Yes,' he said with a laugh, 'in the old days. You like me to give you some to carry back to England?'

'But they don't sleep in hammocks there,' I said.

Andrew was taken aback for a moment. But he wasn't easily discouraged. 'They got a next story,' he said, 'about how all these bats come here. Down in the Rupununi we got plenty of them. They got a place in Macusi country called Bat Mountain. Is from there the small bats come. In the old days they had none at all, just one big bat living there, in this same mountain. It used to come down every night and carry off Macusi people. They all wanted to kill it off, but they couldn't find the place where it lived. Then one day an old lady was standing in the middle of the village. When the bat come down to catch her, she light a big fire-stick and the people seen where it was flying. So they all gone with bow and arrow and find the place full with people's bones. They shoot the bat and kill it right there. When it died it gave one vomit and all the small bats came out. Since that time they got no big bats, only these small ones.'

We woke long before it was light, shivering in the cold dawn of the Kurakubaru plateau. I heard Andrew swing out of his hammock, muttering to himself. The snap of wood as he built a fire, and a moment later a cheerful glow broke through the lifting darkness. Soon we were warming ourselves with coffee.

That morning we met the local school-teacher, a slim, wiry Portuguese, who had lived in the village for several years. Like many Guianese working in the interior, he was generous and easy-going, yet sceptical about the Indians.

'They're still so primitive,' he said, as we chatted about them. 'They live just like animals.'

'But how are you judging them?' I asked. 'Our standards don't belong to their world. So how can we claim that our way of life is really better than theirs?'

'But it's not only that,' he said. 'These people aren't even honest. They just love to lie. They'll tell you anything.'

'But maybe that's simply because they always want to please you—or else because they're afraid of something?'

'No,' he said, 'they just love telling stories.'

'Or maybe they behave that way because outsiders think badly of them?'

He shook his head. 'I don't believe so. They're really difficult people.'

We seemed to be at a dead end and so I changed the subject. His views on the Indians were probably due to his years of solitude. He was generous as well as critical. Before we left, he took us round his kitchen garden and gave us an armful of vegetables, a luxury in the interior.

As we walked slowly back to the village, I noticed that several changes were already taking place. New building methods were being adopted. Forty or fifty years ago, in the days of the earliest travelling priests, most of the Patamona lived in round-houses. Like Aibilibing's home, at Amokokopai, each one contained some twenty people who always worked and hunted together. Following the laws of matrilocality, the daughters of the house remained there long after they were married. They and their families obeyed the old people and provided for them. Under this kinship system, the concept of marriage was vague. Young couples lived together for a while and if a partnership went well— especially for the girl's parents—it became permanent. The missionaries, feeling that this was licentious, encouraged the idea of single families living in separate houses. This change destroyed the customs attached to the former system. The sons-in-law were glad to move out and escape their obligations, leaving the older people without their traditional means of support.

This was still happening at Kurakubaru. Three or four years ago, Andrew told me, there had been several round-houses. Now there was only one left, where they still lived in the old fashion. Another, just below the hill, had been almost abandoned. Beside it were three separate houses, where the married daughters lived with their own families.

Clearly, within a generation, their own married children would be living completely apart from them.

Andrew and I went down there during the afternoon. We were ushered into the round-house by an old Patamona called Sebastian. Inside, it was almost bare. Only one corner was occupied, with three or four hammocks slung across it. A few years ago, Sebastian explained, there were ten or twelve people living there; but now both his sons were married, while his daughters lived in the neighbouring houses. Life was getting hard, he added. It was different from the old days. There was only himself and his wife and two small children left. Now that they lived on their own, his daughters and their families no longer helped them. I glanced round the half empty house. The standard of living looked no higher than that of Kaibarupai. Apart from their new religion, the Indians had little to compensate for the loss of their former customs.

That evening I went to see Father Banham, the local missionary. I was met by a patriarchal figure, wearing a pince-nez, with a face tanned by years in the tropics. He led me into a little room which had a homely air about it, despite its ascetic bareness. Dusk was already falling. He lit a pair of white candles and placed them on the table.

Perhaps it was this simplicity which gave the Catholic missionaries their understanding of the Indians. Father Banham was one of a long line of priests who had worked in the interior for nearly half a century. Starting in the Rupununi, they gradually moved northwards into Patamona country. The first of them, Father Cary-Elwes, walked the mountains and savannas for almost fourteen years. He was finally invalided home, poisoned by a Wapisiana woman who had been deprived of her husband when he adopted monogamy.

All his successors maintained a tradition of wandering solitude. Most of Father Banham's life had been spent in Guiana. Shortly after arriving in the country, in 1927, he was stationed in the Rupununi. From here he followed Father Cary-Elwes' footsteps into Patamona territory. As soon as he saw Kurakubaru, he thought it an ideal site for a mission; but malaria suddenly intervened and he had to return to the coast. In 1942 he came back and took up his wandering post again. When he retired, fourteen years later, the new mission had just been established. Now he was back for a few months, to act for the resident priest, who was away on leave.

At first he seemed a little uneasy, but soon he was talking volubly. He smiled. 'When I was here in the old days, a visitor was quite an event. It's very different now, of course. Quite a few people fly in from the coast just for the weekend. I hardly recognized the Indians when I came back here—all these clothes they've got and the children learning English.'

'I suppose that's really the work of the mission?'

'Yes, we've tried to help,' he said. 'We provide them with clothes and run the school. But I never feel quite certain about it. I think their clothes are a change for the worse—they were probably better off without them. But these things are bound to occur, so we just do what we can. We have a little store, for example, where they can buy their goods quite cheaply. But, of course, our work is mainly spiritual.'

'But what do you think will come of these changes?'

'Well,' he said, in his nervous way, 'I sometimes wonder how much we've achieved—we missionaries, I mean. The Indians are very independent. I often feel, even now, that the white man is here and the Indian there, right where he was before.' He paused and placed two thin fingers on far corners of the table. 'Perhaps our methods weren't quite right. But I sometimes think there may be a gulf which can never be properly bridged.'

I wonder if this were really true. Was the Indians' temperament simply too strong for adjustment? Perhaps this was only the case if one thought in purely spiritual terms. With a policy like that of the worker priests, both material and spiritual, change would have been more complete and the gulf less evident. The Catholics understood the Indians better than most of the other sects, yet they hardly tried to help them on a practical level. But the opportunity was still there and their aims were already broadening. The permanent priest was now encouraging agricultural progress. If this new policy continued, it could do a great deal for the Indians.

John had grown tired of waiting and returned to Orinduik. Meanwhile Andrew had found two more Indians, called Joseph and Pablo, to come with us to Paramakatoi, the next Patamona village. A day's walk from Kurakubaru, it served as the local headquarters of the Pilgrim Holiness sect. It was closely linked with Philipai, their mission in Akawaio country, where they were leading the opposition to Hallelujah.

By the time we left the village, the sun was already over the mountains. A few minutes later we were looking down from the edge of the plateau. Below us, a sea of clouds. As we edged our way down, they began to drift apart, revealing a long stretch of green. Here and there, dark patches of forest, scattered amongst the gullies and lining the banks of the creeks. Beyond, the low purple swoop of the mountains, enclosing the far end of the valley.

We were lucky—there had been little rain during the previous night. The water level had dropped in the creeks. The sand at the first crossing was dotted with the fresh tracks of animals which had come to drink before sunrise. The sharp print of a deer's hoof and a jumbled pattern left by a flock of acouri;[1] over on the far side, the paw-marks of an ocelot or a small jaguar. We followed the valley for over an hour, until the last creek brought us to the edge of the forest. Its dank scent was still heightened by the rain of the previous day. The slow, funereal echo of water, tapping the leaves around us.

The deep forest alternated with stretches of open savanna. The narrow trail twisted its way past broken rifts of dull red sandstone, gnarled sandpaper trees and the skeletons of dead bushes, strangled by the sun. The heavy, monotonous hum of the crickets rose through the almost tangible heat. Once or twice the sound of a lizard, scuttling through the dry leaves, emerald green, turning to watch us in beady-eyed curiosity.

We stopped at Kato, a small diamond centre, with an airstrip beside it. It was run by a Portuguese called Brazao, who gave us lunch in the cool of his shop and drove us on for the next four miles through the empty savanna. From here the path to Paramakatoi branched off to the east, away from the southern trail.

The hills began rising again, green slopes mottled with brown. In a month's time, Andrew told me, when the rains were over, the landscape would be transformed to a waste of dead grass and sandstone. Every now and then we passed through another strip of forest, ending in a sheer wall at the edge of the next savanna. We climbed the last slippery ascent, searching for footholds amongst the rocks. Then, as we emerged again, the roofs of Paramakatoi were immediately below us.

We sat down for a cigarette. 'Look how these people dress up,' said Andrew. He pointed at two colourful figures down in the village. 'That's the missionary story again, giving them fancy American clothes.' He turned round and looked at me glumly. 'When you meet this place, you can't smoke or dance—you can't even take a drink, or you got the missionaries chasing you tail.'

The other two laughed nervously. They seemed apprehensive at Andrew's comments on an authority which they had probably never questioned. As we entered the village, we passed a neatly built concrete house, belonging to the American missionary, with a large hangar and a private plane in front of it. The Indians' homes were farther on, scattered round a low hill. Many of them appeared to be in the process of reconstruction. The younger people were less shy than elsewhere.

1. A large rodent often hunted by the Indians.

Two girls, looking curiously ungainly in mission dresses and white plimsolls, took us to a rest house at the far end of the village. As soon as we arrived, several boys crowded round, asking where we had come from and how long we were staying. Most of them spoke good English, with a slightly American accent. My first impression was of a rather over-civilized but intelligent group of young people, a world away from Kaibarupai and even Kurakubaru.

We chatted to them for a while and then walked over to the missionary's house. We were joined by a young Indian called Derek, who turned out to be the tushau's son. He and Andrew paused at the door, obviously shy at the prospect of entering a white man's atmosphere. When they eventually followed me, they faded inconspicuously into the nearest corner.

Pastor Basset, the missionary, was a stolid, middle-aged figure, with an earnest brow. He welcomed us with a friendly handshake. Supper was just over, and he was sitting at the head of the table, with his quiet, grave-looking wife beside him. The dining room was well furnished. Several other people were there—his two sons, both wearing T-shirts, a pair of Guianese families who ran the local Bible school, and also the superintendent of the sect's South American missions.

We had scarcely introduced ourselves before the chairs were lined round the wall for a prayer meeting. Andrew and I exchanged a wink. We were each handed a volume entitled *Inspiring Hymns*; Sister Basset stood in the centre and launched into a rollicking tune on an accordion. As the others joined in, the hymn sounded like a cross between a rock and roll hit and something out of an early Western. When they had sung several more hymns, they prayed for the future of the mission, including a request that we should enjoy our visit. It made me feel slightly guilty about the wink which had passed between Andrew and myself. But how would this evangelical sect, with its intensely American character, have affected the Patamona?

The evening ended with a large bowl of popcorn. As we wandered back to the rest house, I realized that Andrew had felt an old strain. He relieved his feelings with a string of jokes, most of which victimized a missionary. The night was dark, almost starless, and faintly shadowed overhead. The houses were wrapped in a strange silence. As we said good night to Derek, he promised to show us round the village on the following day. There was one man up on the hill, he said, who used to sing Hallelujah before the missionaries came. He would take us to visit him and some of the other families.

Derek joined us again for breakfast. As we ate together, he told us about his home, which stood next to the rest house. It was a large, gaunt building, still only half complete.

'We started to build it a few years back,' he explained. 'My father was wanting a new house, a big one like the missionaries got, with two storeys and a wooden roof. But we didn't finish the top half. We hadn't the money for the wood or the nails, so we left it just so.'

I glanced at the house again. The gaps in the upper half were covered with rags and newspapers.

'Do you think you'll finish it?' I asked.

'I don't believe so,' he said. 'The old man decide to leave it now and build a smaller one.'

As we walked through the village, I realized that Derek's case was not exceptional. Twelve years ago Paramakatoi had been a small settlement, consisting mainly of round-houses and a Hallelujah church. Since then the neighbouring Patamona had been attracted by the missionaries; the population had now risen to almost five hundred. There was only one round-house left, inhabited by a single old man, whose family was living elsewhere. The new houses were set wide apart, and the lack of communication between them gave the village a dejected air. Some were built in the old style, with a leaf roof and adobe walls, but many of them were badly in need of repair. Others were similar to Derek's, but most of them were incomplete. In either case the inhabitants would have been far better off with a well built house of Indian style.

'Why are so many houses only half built?' I asked Derek. 'Is the same thing as happen with yours?'

'Yes,' he said, 'the very thing. You see most of them got an old house, with a new one close by? They all want a new style, with a shingle[1] roof and wooden walls. They want to live like the missionary. But they got no money for the nails, so none of them finish yet.'

'But if they haven't any money, why don't they keep to the old ones?'

'Well,' he said, 'they get ashamed because they're the Indian kind. So they don't bother to repair them. But most of them still living there, because they got nowhere else.'

Inside them, the standard of living seemed as poor as ever. Some of them were completely dark. The gaps in the roofs and walls had been roughly filled with bundles of leaves. The Indians themselves seemed diffident, rather than shy. Once we were offered a bowl of cassiri, but this was unusual, Derek told me—the missionaries disapproved of it. But they hardly ever visited the Indians' homes, he added, and so it was still quite easy to find. This remark seemed to explain a great deal of all

1. Wooden slats.

that we had seen. Apart from their work in the school and church, and their medical clinic, the missionaries kept very much to themselves. Perhaps they had never recognized the sense of inferiority which their higher material standards induced amongst the Indians.

'Is here the Hallelujah man living,' said Derek, leading us towards a large house on the crest of the hill. The room we entered was completely bare. A middle-aged woman was scraping cassava. Beside her sat a man of about forty. His clothes, including leather shoes and a white shirt that was far too small for him, gave him a garish, uncomfortable look. Andrew offered him a cigarette. He shook his head politely.

'No smoking,' he said firmly.

'Why not?' asked Andrew roguishly, knowing the answer perfectly well.

'Because God loves me,' said the man, with startling rapidity. 'God say smoking is bad.'

'But who give you brain to make cigarette? Is not the same God?' asked Andrew.

The Indian replied with a vacant grin. I nudged Andrew and changed the subject.

'You used to sing Hallelujah?' I asked.

As it turned out, this was equally tactless. He looked away, obviously abashed.

'Yes,' he said, 'I used to sing it, but I forget it all. Hallelujah no good. I going to the white man church now.'

Derek had supper with us that evening. We talked far into the night, by the quivering flame of Andrew's improvised lantern. The mosquitoes whined monotonously; but outside all was quiet, as Derek told us about Paramakatoi.

Life had changed completely, he said, during the past few years. As soon as the missionaries arrived, the size of the village began to increase. The economic effects were the most hard felt. The Patamonas' ambitions had changed. They were no longer satisfied with their old way of life. They wanted new types of food, clothes and supposedly better houses. But within the village there was no way of satisfying these demands. Things had got worse, rather than better, because of the growth in population. With their shifting agriculture, each family used a piece of land until its fertility was exhausted and then simply moved on to another. This meant that the district could support only a limited number of people, which had already been exceeded. Soil exhaustion was setting in, while the game had died out completely. When a crisis like this occurs, there are only two solutions—either new farming

152

methods or else some form of cash employment. Neither of these had been attempted. The missionaries considered the problem outside the scope of their work, and there wasn't a single government officer in the district to deal with it.

'Ten years ago, I was wearing a lap,[1]' said Derek—a remark which sounded strange in his slightly American accent. 'There was plenty of food then. If someone was short, a next man would help him—you scarcely see that happening now. One time things got really bad. Some of the people was nearly starving—the Government had to send relief rations.'

'But what do you do now?' I asked. 'Do you buy your food from the shop?'

He laughed dispiritedly. 'There's only one shop here—the one the missionaries got. How can we buy their goods? You seen the prices there?[2] We can't find any money because we got no work. The missionaries used to give people work and pay them with a shirt or a trousers—an old one from America. As soon as you wear it, the thing tears. When the Government heard about it, they made them pay money. Now they give a dollar[3] a day. But I know how much people pay outside—I would starve before I work for that.'

'But can't you get work elsewhere?' I asked.

'It's not so easy,' he said. 'A long time back, when we were free'—and he used this phrase quite unconsciously—'the men used to leave the village to work. They were going out to find diamonds and bleed balata[4] and so.'

'But don't they do it any more?'

'Not so much,' he said. 'The missionaries used to stop them. They say if the men leave the village they going to learn to drink and cuss, and they can't go to church on Sundays. Now we can go again. But the old people got accustomed to staying at home. They don't want to work no more.'

'Do the young people go out?'

'Yes,' he said, 'sometimes. But it's not so easy for us. We got to go a good way and outside people don't treat us well.'

'But when the missionaries stopped you, didn't anyone complain?'

1. Loin-cloth.
2. The articles in the two shops run by the Pilgrim Holiness missions averaged twice the price charged on the coast. The Catholic store at Kurakubaru was run on a non-profit basis. In cases like this, where the Church holds a lease, no Indian can open a shop without the sect's permission.
3. The minimum Government wage is over three dollars per day.
4. A form of wild rubber, drawn from the latex of the bullet-wood tree. It is bought from the Indians, for industrial use, by a subsidiary of Booker Bros.

'Well,' he said, 'I was young at the time. The old people didn't know what to do. They were afraid to say anything.'

This reminded me of some of the answers I had heard at Orealla. The Indian tends to suffer in silence rather than protest about his situation. The present one had clearly arisen during the past ten years. Change had set in on every level, but it seemed to have brought collapse instead of development. The Indians had learnt to be ashamed of every aspect of their way of life. Cassiri, Hallelujah and their housing methods were the most obvious examples. But what had they got to replace it? A semi-Americanized culture which had no meaning in their world. Their sense of community had also vanished and with it their kinship system and communal working methods. Even their economy had suffered. They were no longer satisfied with their former standards, while their means of subsistence were threatened by increasing numbers. No solution had been provided. When the men tried to find one, by going out to bleed balata, the missionaries opposed them on religious grounds. In their concern for the souls of the Indians, they scarcely seemed to have recognized the practical effects of their work. The critical human elements—the Indians' own way of life, and their reactions to novelty—had been completely ignored.

Early the day, Derek brought some of his friends to see us. They were anxious to leave the village, they said—they found it dull and oppressive. Where they could find work? they asked. There was none to be had nearby. There was little that I could do to advise them. Unless they went down to the coast, their only chance was at Lethem, the small town in the Rupununi; but even there, as I later discovered, their prospects would have been poor.

Pastor Basset was not responsible for this situation. He had been stationed at Paramakatoi for only a year or two. But when I met him again that evening, I wondered what he thought about it.

'Want a lift to Kato?' he asked, as we appeared in the doorway. 'I'm hopping over there tomorrow to meet the mail plane. Hope they've brought some gasoline for us. We really need some gasoline.'

I thanked him for his offer. We were already thinking of leaving, and it would save us half a day's journey.

'How long does it take?' I asked.

'To Kato? Just a few minutes,' he said. He paused. 'So how do you like the place?'

'I found it interesting,' I said. 'The mission seems to have quite a hold. But do you think there's been much change in the actual standard of living?'

'Well, I'm not sure,' he replied. 'But they've all got clothes now and their morals are much better. And our clinic's made them healthier.'

This last point was true. The missionaries had done some valuable medical work. But this had been partly counteracted by their attitude to cassiri and their effects on the Indians' economy. And did clothes and Christian morality compensate for their new situation?

'Do you feel there's any danger of the young people getting discontented with this atmosphere?' I asked. 'With your opposition to smoking and drinking, for example?'

'No,' he said, 'I don't think so. Of course we've got a few bad eggs who are always spreading trouble. But it never comes to anything.'

I found it hard to believe that this was really the meaning of all that I had seen and heard. But I was beginning to feel tactless. I refrained from pressing him any further.

It was just as well that we were leaving. Andrew was obviously depressed by Paramakatoi. When Derek and his friends were about, he incited them to rebellion. Otherwise he lay in his hammock with an air of boredom. He still talked of the Rupununi, but it would be at least a week before we reached his home village.

We left early with Pastor Basset. His single-engined Cessna lifted slowly over the forest and the sun-bleached savanna. Kato was soon below us. We coasted down and bounced to a standstill on the dusty runway.

Half an hour later we were followed by the weekly Dakota from Georgetown. Some new films had arrived for me. At last I was able to send out the two which had been submerged at Kaibarupai. A hurried exchange of news with the passengers on the plane—Independence in Jamaica, a bank robbery in Georgetown and rumours of more political trouble within the next few days. It all sounded strangely unreal in the heat-laden silence of the savanna.

The plane soon set off again, dwindling to a silver speck on the horizon. We were left in the shade of a lone hut with two porknockers from Orinduik—a young Chinese and an African, whose names turned out to be Mike and Trenton.

'Where are you heading for?' I asked.

Trenton looked at me casually. My question suddenly felt naïve— the sort of thing, he seemed to be saying, that only a greenhorn would ask in the bush. Enquiries like this were unnecessary. Time would answer them sooner or later. But his lean, rather quizzical face was unpredictable. He suddenly gave me a broad grin, that vanished as quickly as it had appeared.

'Tawailing,' he replied. 'One day walking, no Mike?'

'About that,' said his companion.

Tawailing Mountain lay on our route. Judging from the map, Trenton's reckoning was optimistic. But so, as I later discovered, was his whole outlook on life. Andrew suddenly reappeared. All but three of the men in the nearby village were away, he said. One of them was willing to join us, but the other two had been booked by Trenton. The porknocker's indecisive façade was obviously deceptive.

'You going Tawailing way?' he asked.

'Yes,' I replied. 'To the Rupununi.'

'Man, that's a long walk. You better join up with us. We could manage all these things together.'

'You leaving today?'

'Maybe,' he said, 'we can't tell. This sun terrible hot, man. Today almost gone already. Let we take a five, Mike.'

Soon they were both snoring contentedly in their hammocks. Only Trenton's feet were visible, twitching occasionally in response to a cloud of kaboura. Clearly he was not to be hurried. I glanced at his pile of equipment, stacked in a corner; picks and shovels, a sifting pan, an old shotgun and a battered panama hat. Resigning myself to the situation, which seemed to be commanded by Trenton, I decided to follow his example of sleeping time away.

I woke suddenly, an hour or two later. Someone had touched my hammock. I opened my eyes and came face to face with a wide-eyed little Indian girl, peeping at me in curiosity. She jumped back in surprise and watched me from behind a wareshi. Trenton and Mike were already awake, with a handful of Patamonas beside them, waiting to help us with our baggage.

When we reached the village, they showed us an empty camp where we could spend the night. As we unpacked our wareshis, they stood round, gazing at us. One of the women brought us a calabash full of fresh cassiri. When we had finished it, she led forward a little boy with a large sore on his neck. I washed it and put on some ointment. The women whispered to each other and pointed to the other children. They were all in the same plight and the sores were completely untended; with their fatalistic turn of mind the Indians often ignore illness, unless they can find a piai-man.

When we had seen to the rest of the children we made our plans for the next day.

'We got to leave soon morning,' said Trenton decisively.

'Do you think the creeks will hold us up?' I asked.

'No,' he said, 'I know these trails and all the right crossings. And I is a man does believe in luck. Is only that keeping me now as a wuthless ole porknocker.'

I glanced outside at the silhouette of the nearby houses. The whispering in the shadows had ceased. The Indians had vanished without a sound, back to the fires that flickered and danced through the surrounding darkness.

Andrew and I were awake shortly after dawn. Trenton was still slumbering with a blissful grin on his face. Mike was completely hidden in the folds of his hammock. Our droughers had already looked in, bringing us a bowl of cassiri. Finding the others asleep, they had slipped away again. At last Trenton began to stir. He sat up slowly in his hammock.

'What o'clock now?' he asked.

'Nearly seven,' I replied.

'I was awake all the time,' he said. 'Just waiting on those Indians. Wuthless fellows them, look how they hold us up.'

He poked Mike into life. In half an hour we were off. The droughers went on ahead, but by the time we reached the last house, they had completely vanished. Trenton diagnosed cassiri and turned back to collect them. We waited until he reappeared, with the reluctant Indians behind him. Their wives, who were coming with them, had taken the greater part of their loads. Knowing that any comment on this would simply have perplexed the men, we left them to their own devices. They hurried on in single file, taking short, rapid steps, with their toes splayed to give them a grip on the slippery path.

We picked our way down a hill, into a valley lined with ité palms. For a while we followed the bank of a creek, until we reached a fallen tree. The sure-footed Indians filed across it without a moment's hesitation, and led us over a brief savanna before the hills began rising again.

By midday we were into the forest. Suddenly the rain began, a hollow, drumming sound on the dense leaves overhead. We trudged on through the sodden green stillness, a trail of figures dwarfed by the massive trees. As the rain came to an end, the mocking whistle of the marsh birds echoed all round us. Once we glimpsed a lone cock of the rock, the most colourful of Guiana's birds, which is famous for its mating dance; a sudden, chattering cry, and a flash of orange across our path, as it disappeared into the branches.

By the time we emerged from the forest, the sun was stooping over the hills. We paused for a much needed cigarette. Trenton shook his head solemnly.

'Can't meet Tawailing tonight,' he said. 'We got to stop at Tusenen.'

He pointed to a lone round-house, set on the crest of the next hill, with two adobe huts beside it. We were met by a large family of mixed Indian and African blood. A bowl of cassiri appeared and one of the huts was swept out for us. Andrew and I slung our hammocks and went outside to bathe in a nearby creek.

Andrew pointed south, towards a massive sugar-loaf mountain, a few miles away. 'That's Tawailing,' he said, 'the biggest mountain we got to climb. After that the Ichilibar River. If we get more rain tonight it might be hard to cross. But if no rain we could reach Karasabai in three days.'

'Is there the Macusi start?' I asked.

'No,' he said, 'before that. These people living here is the last Patamona family. From here down to the Rupununi is all Macusi country.'

I had thought the first Macusis were situated farther south. But already we had seen the last of the mild Patamona, the most retiring and independent of the Indian tribes. As we continued south, the signs of civilization would increase, until we finally reached Lethem, the cattle-ranching town in the centre of the savannas.

After supper we chatted quietly, while Trenton's battered radio wheezed out a cheerful string of calypsoes.

'I believe we going find some good diamonds in this Tawailing Creek,' he said. 'They got some people working there does always get plenty of luck.'

Mike nodded doubtfully. 'I was working here before,' said Trenton. 'All the Indians know me well. They give me the name of Diamond Trenton. I never find the right diamond yet. But one day I going to find he, and then I really going to sport—sport till I fall down dead.'

The lamplight flickered weakly, throwing the criss-cross shadow of our hammocks on to the crumbling walls.

'What time we leaving here?' asked Mike.

'Soon morning,' replied Trenton. 'We got to meet Tawailing early.'

Andrew laughed under his breath. 'Proper talk-man,' he whispered. 'I don't believe he going leave this place tomorrow.'

'No rain last night,' announced Andrew, as he woke me the next morning. He passed me a cup of coffee. 'If it holds off today, we going to cross Tawailing Mountain and the Ichilibar River.'

I glanced at Trenton, still dead to the world.

'What about him?' I asked.

Andrew sucked his teeth. 'He wouldn't meet Tawailing today. This boy from Kato says he going to come with us. But if we go on ahead we going to need a next drougher. We could ask the people here.'

He disappeared and came back with one of the boys from the round-house. His name was Peter, he told us shyly. How far were we going? he asked. To Karasabai—had he ever been there? No, but people said it was far. Three or four days walking, beyond the end of the mountains. Down there was Macusi country. He glanced at Andrew and then at Simon, the boy from Kato, who was still coming with us. Andrew reassured them both. They could trust the Macusi, he said, and we needed someone to help us. Peter still looked anxious, but eventually he agreed to come.

Trenton was stirring by the time we were ready. He looked at us reproachfully. Perhaps he felt that our hurried departure was a rebuke to him.

'You leaving so soon?' he asked with a frown.

'Yes, man,' I replied, 'we hustling to cross the Ichilibar before we get more rain.'

'You does hustle too much,' he said. 'But don't worry to say goodbye. Mike and me going to catch you before night come.'

I pretended to take him at his word. But somehow I was fairly sure that we were unlikely to see him again. He seemed to have guessed my thoughts.

'In case we don't catch you,' he said, 'remember to ask about Diamond Trenton next time you coming this way. All the people here does know me—Indians, porknockers, all of them. If I ain't dead by that time, I surely going to be rich.'

Our journey would be quicker without him. But already, as we set out, it seemed to have lost its original flavour. Somehow he spoke for a whole way of life shared by Guiana's old time porknockers. Improvident, happy-go-lucky and idle for a few weeks in the year, while their slender profits lasted; then, for the rest of their time, roughneck, half starved and lonely, sustained by the gambler's dream of the diamond that comes to one in a thousand.

The round-house disappeared behind us. Led by the two boys, we passed through a short clump of forest, over a narrow creek, and into the next savanna. The creek, which was called the Malipa, snaked its way through the valley, crossing the trail several times before we left it behind. In front of us lay the Tawailing foot-hills, climbing slowly up towards the gaunt, level crest. By now the sun had risen, leaving hardly a shadow around us. The rugged, ungainly face of the mountain was strewn with mis-shapen outcrops of rock, like the work of some pre-historic sculptor, abandoned long before it was finished.

159

Within an hour we had reached the first ridge. Andrew and I sat down to wait for the others. We could still just see the peaked roof of the round-house at Tusenen. A thin column of smoke rose over it, veiled by the shimmering heat. To the north, the hills rolled on, parched and crevassed by the sun.

'Look, Mount Sipu,' said Andrew, pointing to the left of the round-house.

I recognized the square-cut mountain, now barely visible, which we had passed on the way to Waipa. Below it lay Orinduik, concealed by a faint ridge, and then the quilt-work of hills and savannas which we had crossed in the past few days. The Ireng River had disappeared, winding away to the east. Once we were over the crest of Tawailing it would be in sight again.

'Beautiful country,' I said.

Andrew looked at me sceptically. 'Beautiful for you,' he replied, 'but it got me cussing. You does measure it with your eyes, but I measuring with my feet. Wait till we meet the Rupununi. That is really beautiful country.'

I laughed at his local patriotism. 'Anyone living down there?' I asked, pointing to a lone shack on a ridge below us.

'I don't believe so,' said Andrew. 'A Yankee was living there once, a real gangster man. A porknocker came to him with some diamonds and this man shot him and take the lot. Then he heard the police was coming, so he hustled over to Brazil. Nobody heard of him since then. This place is really wild. You get plenty of men like that round here. When I was in the police, a fellow was murdered near the Ichilibar River. Two boys kill him and take all his diamonds. Me and a next man find the body. The boys got away to Brazil, same like this Yankee man. These diamonds give people a kind of madness. When they got a big shout up here, most of them carry guns.'

Suddenly Peter and Simon appeared, toiling slowly up the path. We carried on, turning east for a moment, along a narrow escarpment. The muffled thunder of a waterfall echoed up from somewhere below us. We glimpsed a foam-white torrent of water, cascading down a rocky slipway and drifting, almost in slow motion, into a hidden ravine. Beyond it lay the blue expanse of the Southern Pakaraimas. Somewhere in their midst was the trail which led to the Rupununi.

Soon we reached Tawailing village, the first Macusi settlement, set in a narrow vale below the final crest of the mountain. Two old women disappeared shyly as they saw us approaching. We came to a small house, surrounded by mango trees. A few chickens were scrabbling beneath

Children of Kaibarupai village. Young warriors . . . but still friends

Crossing a swollen creek in the Pakaraima Mountains, with the porknockers Trenton and Mike. Indian women (third from left) usually carry more than their husbands

Karasabai village in the Northern Rupununi. A sunset over the Pakaraima foothills

A Macusi girl weaving a hammock at Karasabai. The whole process usually takes several weeks

Most of the Wapisiana in the Southern Rupununi own one or two head of cattle. Bullocks are now their main means of transport to and from their farms

them in the dusty yard. Andrew tapped at the door; no answer. He said something in Macusi. Two wrinkled faces peeped out and lit up in recognition. They chattered excitedly and brought us some parakari, a thick, greyish type of cassiri, peculiar to the Macusi.

'Cousins to me,' Andrew explained. 'My mother was from this side. I ain't seen them for a couple of years.'

Soon Peter and Simon arrived. The two old cronies sat and watched us, as we ate our lunch.

'They looking old now,' said Andrew. 'But they only got about forty years.'

I glanced at them in surprise. Both of them looked at least sixty. But this was not unusual among Indian women. Back at Kaibarupai, I had noticed that early middle-age scarcely seemed to exist for them. Their continual work and child-bearing soon gave them an appearance well beyond their years.

As we walked on through the village, a few Indian faces peered out in curiosity. At the far end there were several new shacks, built mainly by porknockers who had come in response to rumours of diamonds in Tawailing Creek. It was here that Trenton hoped to work, but as yet there was little activity, due to the heavy rains, which kept the creek in full spate. We stopped to chat to a group of Africans, lounging against a doorway, and then a sun-tanned Portuguese, with a revolver slung at his hip.

As we reached the last shack, we caught sight of a strange figure, like something from a West Indian carnival. A middle-aged African woman, with a large cigarette in her mouth, was reclining in a Brazilian hammock. She was dressed in billowing slacks, for protection against the kaboura, with a time-worn, but colourful dress over the top. She gave Andrew a broad grin, revealing a set of golden fillings.

'So you come back again,' she said. 'Is a long time I ain't see you.'

'Yes,' said Andrew, 'we just passing through. This lady is an old friend to me,' he explained. 'The only lady porknocker in all of B.G. Auntie Stella we always call her, the queen of the diamond creeks. Whenever they got a new shout, she's always there on time. She can work a creek as fast as any porknocker.'

Stella chuckled in agreement. 'Could I have the favour of knowing this fine gen'leman name?' she asked.

Andrew introduced me to her. 'And where does the fine gen'leman come from?'

'From England,' I replied.

'Ah, England.' She nodded thoughtfully. 'I been studying to go that side for a few years now. But every time I ready to leave I hear a helluva shout some place and I got to go swinging my pan again, after these same diamonds.'

'You've had plenty of luck?' I asked.

'Yes, man, I've had my luck. I find some gold in the Cuyuni. Kurupung was my best shout, five or six years back. I find plenty of stones there, a hundred and fifty-seven carats. But I don't know what happen to it all. One day you rich, the next day you poor. Is the same with all we porknockers.'

Before we left, I took her photo, sitting proudly in front of the shack with her sifting pans beside her.

'Go easy up there,' she said, as we set off again. 'That is mighty Tawailing, the God of all the mountains.' She gave us another flashing grin and waved goodbye.

'She's a fine old lady,' said Andrew, as we climbed up the steep slope. 'First time I seen her was at Orinduik. She hadn't scarcely a cent left, so I give her some rice from my rations. Next time she was at Monkey Mountain, over to the west from here. If you see diamonds then—she really knows how to find them. Because she had a bit of luck, she was giving a sport for the boys there, with plenty of rum and dancing. She take me inside and show me the diamonds. Then she say because I help her, I got to take the biggest one. She really got a kind heart. When they had the Kurupung shout, she was down in Bôa Vista. She hadn't a cent to pay the fare, so she walk all the way from Brazil, she alone, without a gun. She scarcely stop till she meet Kurupung and find all those diamonds. But now she look like she poor again.'

Up on the crest of the mountain, a stiff breeze was blowing. The vegetation had changed suddenly. The scrawny sandpaper trees had vanished. Instead there were purple flowering shrubs and a handful of lilies sheltering beneath a rock. Farther on, a splash of scarlet, where a lone cactus had burst into flower. The slopes which had risen slowly behind us fell away almost sheer to the south, an unbroken bulwark of stone, gazing over the Ireng River, which looped its way through the valley. Beyond it, on the Brazilian bank, stood a small settlement.

'King's Mines,' said Andrew, pointing to it. It was here that the pioneer Tesarick had died a few years ago. 'And look Yurong Paru,' he added, indicating a cluster of houses, farther to the east. 'That's the next Macusi village. We could sleep there tonight.'

We scrambled down into the valley, slithering from rock to rock, with the jagged silhouette of Tawailing rearing up behind us. Slowly the ground levelled out towards the banks of the Ireng. An hour's walk through the waist-high grass brought us to the Ichilibar, the next tributary. Although it was wider than the Tumong, the lack of rain in the past few days had tamed its usually powerful current. We crossed without using ropes. Already dusk was settling down over the God of all the mountains. The others had quickened their pace. After crossing another creek, we saw the welcome flicker of firelight from a house above us. We had reached Yurong Paru, the Macusi village which we had seen from the crest of Tawailing.

We were met by a handful of women and children. All the men were away, they explained, bleeding balata in the forest. They offered us maize and parakari, and took us over to the little school-room, where we decided to spend the night. Peter and Simon watched silently, as Andrew cooked a meal. Soon after we finished eating, they both retired to their hammocks. I tried writing my diary for a while, but found that I could do no more than scribble a few terse notes. Outside, there was hardly a sound, apart from the heavy drone of cicadas. It was only just past nine o'clock. But Tawailing had left its mark on all of us. I was already half asleep.

By now our early departures were a familiar ritual. We left the village before sunrise. The trail we followed was an anticlimax after the awe-striking scenery of the previous day. The forest soon closed in around us; stillness, broken occasionally by the chatter of a flock of parrots or the rustle of sakawinki monkeys in the branches above us. A bright green parrot snake wriggled across our path and disappeared into the leaves. For a while we were followed by a pair of cow-birds, with their uncanny, whirring call breaking into the booming note after which they were named by the Indians. Otherwise, hardly a sign of life to break the mono-tony of the forest, starved of light by the green vaults which stretched high overhead.

The hills were already less rugged by the time we reached open country. Shortly after midday we suddenly heard the sound of voices. A large bullock came into sight, with two Indian children perched on its back and their mother and father behind them—the first travellers we had passed since leaving Orinduik. It was the school-teacher from Yurong Paru, returning to the village with his family. He came from the Moruca, he told us, up in the north-west of Guiana, a district inhabited by Arawaks with some Spanish blood in them. He had several relations farther south, teaching in the savannas, amongst the Macusi and Wapi-siana. If we made good time, he added, we would reach Tipuru, the next large village, well before nightfall.

We said goodbye and carried on. Later that afternoon we passed a few more Macusi houses. The children came running out to meet us, then paused in momentary shyness, until their mother appeared and offered us some parakari. An old lady with faint tattoo marks sat up in her hammock and talked to Andrew. Another relation of his, he explained —he had some in most Macusi villages. The children pressed round and touched our belongings in whispered curiosity. Their bright-eyed, expressive faces were very different from those of the children whose sores we had treated a few days ago. At first glance the Macusis' lives appeared to have taken a different course from those of the Patamona.

We reached Tipuru just before dusk. Most of the houses were built in the neat Macusi style, with leaf roofs and adobe walls. A few sheep and pigs routed round them, beneath the citrus trees. Andrew's spirits had already lifted at reaching Macusi country. As at Yurong Paru, the men were away, bleeding balata; but the women and children gathered round, as Andrew described our journey to them. Even Peter and Simon were getting over their reticence. During the last two days they had scarcely offered a word, but after supper they began chatting with us. They seemed impressed by the look of prosperity in the Macusi villages. Perhaps they would stay down here, they said, and try to find work somewhere. Had they never found any at home? I asked. No, there was none back there. Though neither of them looked more than sixteen, they seemed completely independent and ready to leave their families without a moment's warning. They would have to look far afield to find any outlet for their ambitions. I wondered if they would continue south with us after Karasabai.

The warm morning air already suggested that the mountains were almost behind us. Someone was ringing a bell in the little adobe church, summoning the women and children, who filed demurely past us. It was Sunday, I suddenly realized, the 2nd of September. There was hardly more than a month before I was due back in England. Outside the sky was shifting from grey to pale blue. The silhouette of a mango tree, thrown up in sharp relief against the first rays of the sun.

Although it was late, we lay in our hammocks, watching the sunrise and reassured by each other's reluctance to move. Trenton would have approved, I thought idly, had he still been with us. Suddenly Andrew came to life. Our brief reverie was over.

The trail swung towards the west, past the last house in the village. The flash of a green humming bird, and a purring of wings as it hovered in front of us, poised, until it darted sideways and vanished into the bushes. A pair of macaws rose into the air, with their scarlet wings bathed in sunlight. A harsh, broken screech of derision, thrown back in paradoxical contrast with their exotic colours.

All morning we walked through the cool of the forest, with the trail still falling steadily towards the level of the savannas. We stopped for a while by a clear-running creek. The two boys were still talking about the Rupununi. Was there a shop at Karasabai? they asked Andrew eagerly. Yes, he replied, a Government store where they could buy food and clothes. They seemed half nervous and half excited at the prospect ahead of them.

As the forest opened out, I realized how far we had descended. Already the mountains lay behind us, stretched in a wide semicircle. We scrambled down the last gully. Suddenly, the level savanna, like a distant glimpse of the sea, framed by the jagged foot-hills.

'We almost reach,' Andrew announced. 'Is here the Rupununi begins. Now you going see some beautiful country.'

After several weeks in the mountains the level horizon looked unreal. We rounded a steep, saddle-backed hill and heard the thoughtful tinkle of cattle-bells from a herd in front of us. They turned their heads slowly to watch us, lowing and jostling close together in the shadows of the sandpaper trees. As we approached, they stirred nervously. Suddenly they stampeded away, leaving a trail of dust behind them. With its six thousand square miles of sparse grazing land, the Rupununi is the last spot in the world with a partly open ranch system. The cattle are allowed to roam freely, until they are often semi-wild.

The savannas were still half flooded. As we came to a narrow swamp, the boys looked round apprehensively, watching for alligators and camoudi; but apart from kaboura and mosquitoes, it was completely deserted. We stripped and crossed hurriedly, wading close together. Over on the far side, a cluster of thorny cactus plants, contorted by the heat of the sun.

'You ever eat cactus fruit?' Andrew asked.

'No,' I replied, suspecting a hoax.

'Then you waste half your life,' he said, pulling off a large crimson fruit, which resembled a wrinkled apple. He broke it in half and passed me a piece. As I tasted its white flesh, dotted with tiny black pips, I was pleasantly surprised. It had a heavy, sweet taste, not unlike highly refined sugar.

We passed through another shallow swamp, with the pale reeds closing over our heads. As we emerged, we caught sight of the leaf roofs of Karasabai. A horse whinnied in front of us and a lone Indian rode by, with a cattle whip in his hand. Although we were still enclosed by the mountains, we had reached the high savannas at last, cattle-ranching Macusi country, our goal of the past few days.

The sun was already foundering in the clefts of the Pakaraimas. We could still see the Ireng River, winding its way between them, with the Brazilian hills behind it. The first houses which we passed had the same air of prosperity as those in the previous Macusi villages. Tobacco and skins were hung up to dry, with saddles and cattle whips beside them. Two more Indians passed on horseback, raising their hands in greeting as they broke into a canter. The dust settled slowly behind them. The atmosphere had a distant echo of old time Western country—in the figures of the two Indians, loping towards the village, followed by the tinkle of bells and the solemn lowing of the cattle, with their heads raised in silhouette against the blackcloth of the mountains. Perhaps, in this environment, the two savanna tribes had a future denied to the rest of the Indians.

The sun was still glinting weakly on the zinc roof of the District Officer's house. He turned out to be an old friend of Andrew's, an Arawak with some Portuguese blood, called Dennis Rodrigues. Like many of the Indians working in the Rupununi, he had been born in the Moruca. His brother was the teacher at Yurong Paru, whom we had met on the previous day, and his father held the same post at Tipuru. Even the local medical ranger was a cousin of his, while the school-teacher and his wife came from the same district. During the next two weeks I discovered that several savanna schools were staffed by Moruca Indians. Their obvious ability, which had carried them so far afield, suggested that they might emerge as leaders for the rest of their people.

Dennis took us over to the store, which had been built by the Government to provide inexpensive goods for the Indians. Peter and Simon came with us, to spend the wages they had earned. As we stepped inside the building, they whispered quietly to each other. They both bought new shirts and cigarettes for their fathers. As they stepped back to compare them, their nervousness made them seem abrupt.

They stayed with us on the next day, which we spent at Karasabai. But now that we had reached the Rupununi, their shyness had suddenly returned. That evening they changed their minds about coming farther south. By the following dawn they had vanished, back to the silent mountains.

8

The Disinherited Macusi

DUSK and a Saturday evening at Lethem, the little cattle-ranching town in the centre of the Rupununi. I was sitting on the steps of the rest house, waiting for Andrew to arrive. By now the gaunt Kanuku Mountains were almost lost in the darkness. Rising sheer from the savanna, they form a rugged barrier between the two Rupununi tribes, the Macusi and the Wapisiana. At the far end of the dusty street stood a vacant-looking hotel, a relic of a former attempt to encourage tourists from Georgetown. Nearby was an airstrip and an abattoir, where the cattle were slaughtered for the daily beef flight to the coast. Behind the rest house lay the Takutu, a tributary of the Rio Branco, which forms a highway to Bôa Vista, the nearest Brazilian town.

A few figures drifted down the street, which ran between Lethem's handful of houses. A pair of African porknockers, shouting a cheery greeting. Two silent Macusi boys, standing carefully aside as one of the town's half dozen jeeps bounced crazily over the ruts and skidded round a corner. Behind them, another Macusi family, walking with slightly bowed heads. All of them were wandering slowly in the same direction —towards the spasmodic flicker of lights in a rum shop at the end of the road. Owned by a Chinese called Ng-a-Fook, it was the scene of a Saturday spree which Andrew and I were intending to visit.

The past few days had been uneventful. After leaving Karasabai, we had crossed the last of the Pakaraimas, until the savannas stretched in front of us, down to the Kanuku Mountains, still forty miles away. Two days passed at Karanambo, where we stayed with the McTurks, an old Guianese family of Scottish descent. Their son Micky then drove us south, along the rough jeep trails, past the occasional ranch-house and a few Macusi villages. As soon as we reached Lethem, Andrew borrowed a bicycle and set out for the Moka-Moka, to visit his family. He had promised to be back in the evening. A Saturday night at Ng-a-Fook's was a part of Rupununi life which he felt I ought to see.

Meanwhile I had written my diary, using the scattered notes which survived from our last days on the trail. During the afternoon I had sorted out my plans for seeing the Rupununi. Two local figures provided me with all the information I needed—first Mr. Learmond, the District Commissioner, and then Ernie Hardy, a cheerful Northerner who had married a Rupununi girl. There was little to keep me in Lethem. I decided to spend the next few days with Andrew, at his home in Moka-Moka, where Ernie's wife worked as a teacher in the primary school. I also hoped to visit Nappi, a development scheme to the east of Lethem, where the local Agricultural Office was trying to resettle Macusi families. After that there might still be time to see a Wapisiana village, south of the Kanukus.

It was dark by the time Andrew arrived on his battered bicycle. I jumped on to the cross-bar and we set off down the road, weaving our way miraculously through the stray couples in front of us. We were greeted by an ancient gramophone, blaring out a Brazilian samba. Outside, in the semi-darkness, swaying figures and the shuffle of feet on the concrete floor beside the rum parlour.

We edged our way in through the smoke-laden atmosphere. After securing a drink, we both retired to a corner. The presidential Ng-a-Fook was leaning on the wooden bar, surveying the scene in front of him with an impassive air. The walls were lined with half stupefied figures, immersed in a hum of conversation, broken occasionally by the sound of raised voices. The faces round the dance floor outside were typical of the Rupununi. A crowd of coastal Guianese attached to the local Government station, and a few Brazilians, of mixed blood, who had crossed the Takutu in search of an evening's entertainment. Most of the others, especially the women, were partly or wholly Macusi.

A large, smart-looking station-wagon suddenly drew up nearby. A family of ranchers, of American descent, pushed their way into the rum parlour. Outside, in the shadows behind us, the opposite extreme of the Rupununi—a few Macusi families, perhaps on their first visit to Lethem, who were still too shy to come inside. Barefoot and roughly clothed. Children clutching their mothers' skirts, women huddled together in the background, and men with mute, expressionless faces, apart from their dark eyes, intent on the dancers. Afraid and yet fascinated by the colour and clamour before them.

There was still a suggestion of Indian custom on the rough wooden benches, where the men and women were sitting apart. At the beginning of each dance, there was a rush to the far side. Generally it ended up with half a dozen men clinging to the same girl in the hope of dancing with her. The samba gave way to a bolero, and then to the jerky rhythm of a Guianese steel band. Andrew pointed out a pair of attractive-looking girls, partly Indian with a trace of Scottish and Brazilian blood. They were members of the Melville clan, descendants of a Scottish cattle-rancher, who was almost the first European to settle in the savannas.

The expressions of the Indians varied—some timid, some diffident and others apparently at ease. Suddenly a tipsy Macusi lurched over in our direction, ignored by the people he stumbled against. Could we spare a cigarette? I gave him the remains of my packet. He looked up in vacant gratitude and staggered away again. It was after midnight by the time we left. As we pedalled down the road, we almost ran into another Indian. He was lying on the ground, with his shirt hanging out and an empty bottle beside him.

The scene in the rum shop was partly explained by the motley history of the Rupununi. Geographically the savannas are an offshoot of the Rio Branco grasslands, over in Brazil. During the past century Brazilian, rather than Guianese, culture has shaped their development. They attracted the interest of Europeans from as early as the sixteenth century, when rumour had it that El Dorado, the mythical Indian city of gold, lay in their direction. It was said to have been built by an Inca tribe, who fled eastwards, away from Chile, to escape the Spanish conquistadores. According to Sir Walter Raleigh, it was somewhere in Southern Guiana, between the Orinoco and the Amazon Rivers, beside a vast lake called Parima, whose shores were laden with gold. In his fairy-tale travelogue, *The Discoverie of the Large and Bewtiful Empyre of Guiana*, Raleigh described the city in exotic terms: 'Manoa, the imperiall Citie of Guiana, which the Spanyardes call El Dorado, that for the greatnes, for the riches and for the excellent seate, it farre exceedeth any of the world.'[1] Several early maps of Guiana actually mark lake Parima in the Rupununi area. Raleigh's hopes ended abruptly, in 1617, when his final expedition was beaten back from the Orinoco by the Spanish garrison of San Thomé; but the search continued long afterwards, leading to frequent clashes between Spanish, Portuguese and Dutch troops. It was not until the nineteenth century that the myth was finally dispelled by Alexander Von Humboldt, a well known German traveller, who traced its source to Lake Amuku, in the northern savanna. We had passed it in the jeep that morning, on the way from Karanambo, a barren expanse of reeds and water, half concealed by mist.

1. See Selected Bibliography.

In fact the Macusi and Wapisiana were similar to the other Guianese Indians. Farther south lay the Taruma, a large tribe which is now all but extinct. Occasionally they were attacked by the Caribs and subjected to descimentoes, or slave raids, conducted by the Brazilians, but otherwise they were undisturbed. During the seventeenth century the Dutch reached the Rupununi, and built a fort at a point called Arinda, to trade with the Indians and capture runaway slaves. But the British showed little interest until 1837, when an Anglican mission was set up in the Macusi village of Pirara. The teachings of its founder, the Reverend Youd, may have contributed to the birth of Hallelujah. His success was short-lived. Two years later a Brazilian detachment advanced from Fort São Joacquim, on the Rio Branco, and seized the mission, claiming that it was on Brazilian territory. When the news reached distant George-town, two lieutenants named Bingham and Bush set out with an army of twenty-seven coloured soldiers, to defend the integrity of the Empire. The incidents which followed were described by Richard Schomburgk,[1] one of the famous exploring brothers, who were in the Rupununi at the time. When the British troops arrived the Union Jack was promptly raised. They landed on the bank of the Rupununi River, all of them, according to Schomburgk, 'cursing and swearing at the uncustomary exertion'. On reaching Pirara they discovered that the Brazilians had retreated. A few days later envoys arrived, under a Captain Leal, the commandant of Fort São Joacquim, and a Dominican friar called Frater José dos Santos Innocentes. Seeing that the British were firmly en-trenched, they agreed to make a gentlemanly withdrawal. A final truce was arranged over the dinner table that night. A salvo of guns and rockets attracted the neighbouring Indians as bewildered spectators of the white man's strange behaviour. Toasts were drunk to the King of Prussia, the Schomburgk brothers' patron, and then to Queen Victoria and the Emperor of Brazil. Meanwhile the party grew merry, led by the jovial Friar José 'who became especially lively after the emptying of only a few bottles of champagne, which, as he attested, he had not tasted for thirty years'. Britain's only war with Brazil was over.

Youd died soon afterwards, and his mission was never revived. The modern history of the Rupununi began in the 1890s, with the arrival of H. P. C. Melville, a Scottish gold-prospector. He was found by a party of Wapisianas beside the Essequibo, where he had been left for dead while suffering from malaria. On reaching the southern savanna, he settled near Dadanawa, the Hill of the Macaw Spirit, and set up as a cattle-rancher, a step which prescribed the future of the Rupununi. He also

1. *Travels in British Guiana, 1840–44* (see Selected Bibliography).

adopted local custom by taking two Indian wives. Between them they bore him ten children who, along with their descendants, still form a local elite.

Melville was followed by other settlers, Brazilian, American and Scottish, including Andrew's grandfather and even a Russian emigré. Several of them eventually married into the Melville family. At first the cattle were sold in Brazil, where they found a steady market due to the rubber boom. Just after the turn of the century, there was talk of building a railway from Georgetown to Manãos, in Brazil, via the Rupununi. This plan was eventually dropped in favour of a cattle trail to the coast; completed in 1920, this brought the Rupununi under Guianese, instead of Brazilian, influence. The two hundred mile journey took several weeks, and starvation, stampedes and marauding jaguars caused heavy losses amongst the herds. But the cattle industry was expanding, and the private holdings in the south were now amalgamated into the Rupununi Development Company (R.D.C.). Then, at the end of the Second World War, Lethem was built as the district headquarters, with an airstrip and abattoir. The daily beef flight came into service, replacing the cattle trail.

These changes had their effect on the Macusi and Wapisiana. The presence of the ranchers suggested new standards. Their control of the land and offers of employment disturbed the Indians' old way of life. This was intensified by the Anglicans and Catholics, who founded missions and primary schools at points which were often unsuitable from an agricultural point of view. The leases held by the ranchers and the R.D.C. now cover more than four thousand square miles, or two-thirds of the savannas. The Indians' rights are limited to three small reservations, totalling less than five hundred square miles. Their numbers were once declining, but now they are on the increase again. The large younger generation needs a completely new outlet. While I was there, I hoped to discover if they were finding one.

A low mist over the Kanukus at dawn on the following day. According to a Brazilian proverb, the howler monkeys were making coffee, with the smoke from their fires concealing the mountain range. Andrew and I had been promised a lift to the agricultural station at nearby St. Ignatius; from there another jeep was going on to Moka-Moka.

We set out from Lethem with Bill Seggar, the Assistant District Commissioner who had done so much for the Akawaio in the Kamarang. The only expatriate officer in the Interior Department, he had been transferred to the Rupununi with his slim, attractive wife Daphne, who joined us in the jeep. We turned down the sun-parched road, past the deserted abattoir.

'Do you miss the Kamarang?' I asked, as the last houses slipped out of sight.

'Yes,' replied Bill. 'That's the pity of putting a lot of work into one place. You can't expect to be there for good. And it's very different down here.'

'I've had that impression already,' I said. 'We went to Ng-a-Fook's last night. It doesn't look as if Lethem is doing the Indians much good.'

'Yes,' he said, 'I know what you mean. Of course, that's not typical—but it's hard to know what's going to become of them. Although their way of life is changing, they're still being left behind. The other sections of Guianese society are developing much faster. The gulf's widening all the time.'

'But why do you think this is?' I asked.

'Well, it's mainly because all these changes are too haphazard. They're bound to occur, of course, but they ought to be gradual and selective, starting with their economy.'

'You mean that with economic development social changes would follow naturally?'

'Yes.'

'But how can this be done?'

'Well, you've got to consider the Indians themselves. They're a mainly agricultural people, so they'll have to develop this with products they can sell to the coast. And it's got to be arranged in a way which they themselves can understand. But it's not very easy to get new ideas like this accepted. I once had a plan for an Indian centre in Georgetown. I wanted them to build a new place for the Interior Department, with an Indian depôt and marketing centre beside it.'

'Did anything come of it?' I asked.

'No—the idea wasn't approved, so I just had to forget it. But there's one thing which would interest you here—Jack Dummett's resettlement scheme at Nappi. You must try and pay it a visit. I think it might provide a solution, at least for the Macusi.'

I wondered if this were possible, while the savannas were still dominated by the cattle industry. Then, as we rounded a bend in the road, St. Ignatius came into view. We drew up in front of a row of houses belonging to the local staff. I caught sight of a lean figure, tall and bespectacled—Jack Dummett, the Agricultural Officer, whose work Bill Seggar had mentioned. He smiled and shook me by the hand. He was going to Nappi in a few days' time—I would be welcome to come with him. He introduced me to Roy Hewson, the Superintendent of the station, who was taking us on to Moka-Moka.

We changed jeeps and set off again, down the rough, sand-surfaced track. The bare reaches of the savanna already had a skeletal look, now that the rains were almost over. The pale grass was yellowing beneath the unbending heat. Beside the track, the sun-scriven figures of cacti and sandpaper trees, and a scattering of large ants' nests, which lined the horizon like minature castles. A few cattle looked up as we passed. It was not hard to understand why this arid, relentless landscape could only support some ten or twelve head to every square mile.

As we drove along, Roy described the work they were doing at the agricultural station. Their main task was cattle breeding. They were trying to provide the savannas with a suitable, healthy stock.

'But is this any good to the Indians?' I asked. 'Aren't ninety per cent of the cattle owned by the ranchers and the R.D.C.?'

'Yes, that's true,' he said. 'But you see, our job's a technical one. We have to accept the situation and simply work from there.'

The initial cost of the scheme alone was nearly four hundred thousand dollars—ten times the annual sum then spent on Indian development. Yet almost the entire benefit would be going to the cattle-ranchers, rather than the Indians, who formed nine-tenths of the local population. This was not Roy Hewson's work, but that of the original planners, who had ignored the lop-sided situation in the Rupununi. The money could easily have been spent on Indian resettlement schemes in the more fertile areas, with model farms and communal herds. But even here a deadlock remained. Almost all the land was controlled by the ranchers and the R.D.C. Even if cattle were provided for the Indians, they would be short of pastures, under present circumstances.

In half an hour we had reached Moka-Moka. The houses were widely strung out beneath the forest-clad Kanuku Mountains. We stopped in front of the village school, a rough little adobe building which had been put up by the Indians on a self help basis. Ernie Hardy emerged to meet us, barefoot and clad in shorts. He introduced me to his wife Nita, one of the Melville family, with finely modelled Indian features, enlivened by her Scottish blood. Her work was entirely voluntary, as no other teacher had been available when the school was opened, two years before. Whenever Ernie had time he bicycled over from Lethem to help her.

Andrew's house was some way off, on the outskirts of the village. We drove into a neatly swept yard, where a handful of pigs and chickens were scratching for food beneath the mango trees. The house was built in traditional style, with a leaf roof and wooden walls, and two enclosed rooms at the back, where the family slept.

'Is my father-in-law's house,' said Andrew, as we carried our things inside. 'I was married in the old way. After they seen how I like their daughter, they persuade me to live in the house. Then they told me to go hunting and give me a cutlass to cut a new field. When they seen I could work well, everything was all right. Since then I been living here. But one day I going to build my own house.'

A little girl toddled in and laughed in delight at seeing him.

'She's the oldest one,' he explained. 'We call her Tung-Tung, a kind of a pet name. And this is my wife,' he added, as a girl appeared, with a child at her breast, carried in a sling. She smiled at me in greeting, a young face with high cheekbones and dark, reserved eyes, backed by a mass of jet-black hair. Andrew took the baby from her as she brought a bench forward. He seemed to be an affectionate father. As in every Indian home, his son was clearly the pride of the family.

His wife brought us some parakari. As we sat in the corner to drink it, she began grating cassava. Although she was only seventeen, her movements were already full of the deep patience common to all Indian women. My arrival seemed to have made her shy, but Tung-Tung was quite unabashed, clasping my knee and gazing at me with mischievous curiosity. After a while we wandered outside. The savanna was completely still beneath the midday sun. Almost half a mile away, the leaf roofs of the other houses, with the slate-blue mountains behind them.

'Those are we own,' said Andrew, pointing to a few cattle grazing outside the yard. 'We got thirty head in the family, between my father-in-law and myself and a next son-in-law.'

'Do all the people here have cattle?'

'No,' he said, 'we is the only family. The others all want some, but they got no money to buy them.'

We walked over to the school. Its atmosphere was pleasantly improvised. Apart from Ernie's occasional visits, Nita had only one assistant, a pupil teacher called Clara Rodrigues. She too was from the Moruca, where I had coached her for some exams just three years ago. Many of the fifty children were still in the process of learning English, while the ages in some classes varied from six to fourteen. It was often hard, Nita explained, to persuade their parents to send them to school. As soon as they were old enough, the girls were expected to help at home and the boys with hunting. Other aspects of Indian life still clashed with their new situation. Some of the older girls, aged thirteen or fourteen, were already virtually married. It was strange to think of them, here so child-like, as adults in their homes. They obviously loved the novelty and the affectionate guidance of Nita, who was a universal mother in the little world of the school.

The school-children's health was improving, through a U.N.I.C.E.F. school feeding programme and a campaign against malaria. The former was not entirely successful and shows how a scheme like this can fail, for want of explanation. The parents immediately assumed that they were no longer expected to feed their children. Until this was clarified, many of the children subsisted on the daily cup of milk and two biscuits provided by the scheme. But the anti-malaria campaign had spectacular results. Before it began, the savanna Indians were gradually declining; but since then they have increased and now their numbers are roughly six thousand. Judging by the number of children, their total could easily double within the next twenty years. This presented another problem. There was virtually no future for them without some far-reaching changes in the Rupununi. The first of these would have to be a suitable education and some form of independent employment. This meant a new school syllabus based on lessons in agriculture and home industries. Without this, the schools would merely bewilder the Indians, by cutting them off from their homes and their own way of life.

Ernie and Nita asked me to supper. As we sat outside their home in the last of the vanishing daylight, the Macusi were drifting back from their farms. They seemed friendly, as they greeted us, and yet they were more reserved than any tribe I had seen before.

Nita produced a photograph album which went back to the days of her Scottish grandfather, H. P. C. Melville. The pioneering cattle-rancher looked different from the man I had imagined. His stern, rather scholastic face seemed out of keeping with his rôle of virtual white chief of the Wapisiana. Then came the slim, becassocked figure of Father Cary-Elwes, the first Catholic missionary. Apparently he had been somewhat disturbed to find that Melville had two Indian wives, but the cattle-rancher's word was law and the situation was accepted. A minor clash soon occurred between Father Cary-Elwes and the local Anglican priest, the Rev. James Williams, over the question of who should baptize the ten Melville children. The agnostic Scotsman viewed the question democratically. He proposed that they should be divided. But the Xavier-like Cary-Elwes was not a man of compromise. When the Reverend Williams arrived, expecting to baptize his quota, he found that his spiritual rival had effected a *coup de grâce*. The tenth and last of the Melville clan had just become a Catholic. By the time we came to the pictures of Nita's generation, the family had begun to change. There were signs of Brazilian blood and a Georgetown education. But their favourite occupations were still those of the Rupununi—rodeos, sprees and the annual cattle round-ups. The freedom of savanna life had a stronger appeal than the lures of coastal society.

Ernie and I went down to bathe in a little pond at the edge of the village. His six year old son Paul came with us, a wild, intelligent imp, who shared the lives of the Indian children. Ernie began telling me how he had reached the savannas. He had been a bit apprehensive, he said, on hearing that I was writing a book. He and his long-standing partner, Geoff Lomas, another equally humorous Northerner, had once entertained an author in their store at Lethem. Finding him rather serious-minded, they amused themselves by posing as radical Empire Loyalists. For several hours, helped by the bottle, they preached hard-bitten beliefs in the white man's inherent superiority over the other Guianese races. Their guest never suspected a hoax. When his book finally appeared, they found the episode fully recorded. The two of them were described as hard drinking colonialists whose eyes blazed with racial hatred. Their success was amusing, but it worried them slightly. Although pseudonyms had been used, the setting made their identity obvious. Their friends had seen through the incident, but others might fail to do so.

The past which the two men had shared suggested a very different outlook. They had first met in the army during the Western Desert campaign. When they were demobbed, after the war, they satisfied their thirst for adventure by signing on as overseers on the Guianese sugar estates. But the harsh, domineering position in which they soon found themselves was far from their expectations. Both of them left the cane-fields in favour of the interior. For a while they prospected for diamonds, until they reached the Rupununi. Here Ernie married Nita and started his little store, with Geoff as his assistant. His wanderlust had almost ended. Life was peaceful here, he added, compared with the world of anxieties which he had left behind him.

After supper we sat and talked in a small room where the walls were hung with Indian ornaments and old photographs of the Melville clan. Nita's background had made her perceptive. I soon found that she knew a great deal about the Macusis' problems.

'You see,' she said, 'they find it hard to understand what's happening to them.'

'But don't you think the first thing they need is more land?' I asked.

'Yes,' she said quietly, 'that's true. I suppose the ranches will have to go. It was the Indians' land before, and now they need it again. But they're so independent, these people. They don't seem to mind being poor, as long as they're still free.'

'Do you think this development scheme at Nappi will work?'

'Perhaps, in the long run. But it's hard to get them interested. They accept things so easily. They scarcely believe that their lives can improve.'

'What about the children?' I asked. 'Is it going to be easier for them?'

'Well, I don't know,' she said. 'They're becoming a problem now. Most of the boys want to leave the village. They try to find work in Lethem, but of course they never get the chance. The trouble is the school syllabus—it's only now that they're talking of changing it. We ought to be teaching them things which they could do right here.'

She picked up a mandolin and began to play a Brazilian tune, watched by a sleepy-eyed Paul, who was sitting on Ernie's knee. The village was quiet when I left, an hour or two later, with Ernie leading the way. We were followed by an insistent Paul, who had now adopted me as 'uncle'. The half light of a full moon was sprawled across the savanna, enlarging the ants' nests which loomed out of the shadows. The mosquitoes were biting fiercely, a dark, straight-backed variety, quite different from those of the mountains. We said good night hurriedly and Ernie and Paul disappeared down the path. Andrew's house was completely silent. The family was asleep.

Well before dawn a wraith-like figure slipped out of the house—the other son-in-law, who was going to hunt. Andrew's wife was up soon afterwards, crouching beside the fire as she coaxed it into life. Then Andrew himself appeared, followed by his father-in-law, an Arawak known as Sonny. He went out to milk the cows, while a few stray piglets wandered inside and sniffled round the floor. Like most Indian pets, they seemed to be treated as members of the family.

Andrew was soon back with a bucketful of rich-looking milk. The yield of the local cattle was low, but a few head were clearly enough to satisfy a family's needs. Once more I realized the difference which a communal herd would make. The milk from the U.N.I.C.E.F. school feeding programme had improved the children's health beyond measure. Its effect would be more than doubled, given the means of providing milk for those who were not yet at school. This would also relieve the women, who tend to breast-feed their children until they are three or four years old.

Andrew and Sonny relaxed in a corner, smoking peacefully while their wives began cooking. Despite its lasting poverty, the life of a married Indian man is one of comparative ease. While, as in Andrew's case, he is living in his father-in-law's house, he is virtually the old man's servant; but already, as far as the women are concerned, he has a privileged male status. Breakfast consisted of the usual cassava bread and pepperpot, varied by coffee, for my benefit. The women ate in the far corner, hardly pausing at their work. Clearly, even in Andrew's mind, this situation was still unquestioned.

When we had finished eating, we walked over to the village. A grey jeep was drawn up by the school, with the United Nations insignia on its door. It belonged to the anti-malaria squad, whose work was financed mainly by the World Health Organization. Nita introduced me to the Medical Officer, a tall, dark East Indian, who had been working in the Rupununi for several years. During the past few weeks, he said, there had been a fresh outbreak of malaria. He was taking blood tests from the Indians and some coastal families who had settled nearby, and suggested my coming with him.

As we bounced along the track, he told me about his work. The anti-malaria campaign had begun in 1947, under the direction of Dr. Giglioli, an Italian specialist. Every building and stretch of water in Guiana was sprayed with D.D.T., and in the interior medicated salt and chloroquin tablets were given to the Indians. The results were completely successful. Malaria had almost vanished. The rate of increase in Guiana's population was now among the highest in the world. For the Indians, especially, this was the end of two or three centuries of steady decline.

We soon reached the nearby settlement. The people living there were mainly Portuguese and Africans, who had left the coast quite recently to farm in the Rupununi. Already they were making a living from the crops which they marketed. With the same enthusiasm and experience, the Indians could have been equally prosperous.

As we drove back to Moka-Moka, the Medical Officer described the problems of working among the Macusi. 'You see, their outlook is strange,' he said. 'They get so accustomed to illness that they don't worry with it. Even now they scarcely report their malaria cases. When a child gets sick they wouldn't tell you. They believe it's going to die, and so they just leave it.'

'Are you getting over this?' I asked.

'Yes,' he said, 'but it's hard work. You got to understand these people before you know how to move with them. A next thing, they don't really trust our medicine, because they scarcely seen it before. This house we're going to now will show you what I mean. They got a small boy with fever. I've got to take a blood test and leave some pills for him. I don't believe it's going to be easy. Last time we took some blood tests here, this family had a sick child and she died on the next day. The parents still think that the blood test caused it.'

We drew up outside a house on the edge of the village. It had a strangely deserted look. The Medical Officer smiled.

'They heard that we coming,' he said.

He knocked on the wooden post. After a long pause a wary Macusi face appeared. It was the father of the family. He looked at us guardedly.

'The family at home?' asked the officer.

'Yes,' he said reluctantly. 'They inside, all working.'

'I hear the boy getting fever.'

'No, is nothing. Is better now.'

'Well, I supposed to take a blood test. Otherwise he could get worse, and then all of you going to get fever.'

The man's face was obdurate. It was some time before he could speak. 'We don't like the thing,' he muttered, with his eyes fixed on the ground.

'But why you don't like it? Is the only thing can keep you from sickness.'

'The boy afraid. He afraid because his sister dead. And me and the wife afraid about it.'

'We could see the boy?'

He still looked doubtful. 'Yes, you could see him.'

The little boy was brought out. After a good deal of persuasion, blood tests were taken from the whole family. They came forward silently, watching the needle with suspicion. Ten minutes later, when it was over, they disappeared hurriedly. I realized what the officer had meant when he said how important it was to understand the Indians.

During the next two days, as Andrew and I went round the village, I felt that this vital understanding was missing from the rest of their lives. Karasabai, where we had stayed in the north, had seemed to be fairly well off. Living in a large reservation, most of the Indians owned a few cattle, and several community schemes were in progress. Given the opportunity, the Macusi need not be impoverished. But Moka-Moka was very different. The well-being of Andrew's family was exceptional. The other houses were poorly built and few of the Indians owned any livestock. The problems of permanent settlement had already set in. Game was getting scarce, they said, and the farms were far away from the village, due mainly to soil exhaustion. There was little chance of finding employment, apart from a few poorly paid jobs offered by the R.D.C.

The resignation of Ignacio, a typical middle-aged Macusi, seemed to speak for the whole of the village. As we approach the house, his wife is squatting by the entrance. She is cleaning a handful of small fish.

Ignacio is lying in his hammock. There is little reaction as we come in.
If anything, a trace of suspicion on his pinched, slightly moustached
face. Inside, it is half dark, apart from the sunlight which streams in
through a gap in the roof. Most of the space is taken up by five rather
shabby cotton hammocks. Some tattered clothes hang in a corner with
a bundle of dried tobacco beside them. Up on the rafters a rusty shotgun
and a few bows and arrows. Some pots by the fire. A pile of cassava
bread. Otherwise the house is empty.

We chat casually for a while, with Andrew as interpreter. At first
Ignacio seems uneasy, but slowly he becomes more talkative.

'Were you born in Moka-Moka?'

'No, over in Brazil.'

'But what made you come here?'

'I heard that things were better this side, so I come here, a long time
ago. My wife was born in Moka-Moka. We got three children now. Two
of them going to school.'

'And are things really better this side—like you thought they would
be?'

'Yes, some things all right. We ain't got so much sickness now, and the
children going to school.'

He is still hesitant. He turns to Andrew and makes an enquiry, which
is passed on to me. Why am I asking so many questions? I ask Andrew to
explain. Ignacio seems satisfied.

'But why were you worried about the questions?'

A long pause. He looks at Andrew. 'I was thinking you come about the
land story. We hear people going to come here to take away the land
and the house.'

'Which people?'

'Black people and East Indian people.'

'But who told you this?'

'Election people.[1] Is so they tell all the Indians.'

'I don't believe that would happen.'

Ignacio looks unconvinced. The rumour obviously worries him. It is
his turn to ask a question.

'Any Indian people in England?'

'No, no Indian people.'

'And black people and East Indian people?'

1. i.e. canvassers in the elections of July 1961. The 'black people and East Indian
people' are the followers of the P.P.P. and P.N.C. Hence if this indirectly racial pro-
paganda was in fact used, as many of the Indians claimed, it probably came from the
third party, the U.F.

'Yes, a few. But why do you ask?'

'Because here we got plenty. They coming to live by the village now.'

'Do you like them?'

'No. Black people going treat us bad.'

'But how do you know they going treat you bad? They ever treat you bad before?'

'Not directly. But we hear about it.'

'Who from?'

'These same election people. They say if we vote for black people they all going to come and live here. They say the black people going eat the babies and take away Indian women.'[1]

This piece of electioneering has clearly had its desired effect. The Indians' votes have been influenced, if not dictated, by the racial fears which this story has fostered. I try to change the subject.

'And school is a good thing?'

'Yes. But we don't know what's happening there.'

'But don't the children ever tell you?'

'No.'

'Why not?'

'We don't ask them. We don't know about school story.'

'And what about food. Is there plenty of game?'

'Not now. Once there was plenty, but now the game scarce. Sometimes we go fishing. But you can't find fish during the rains because the water is high. And when the rains finish, they're scarcely there. The cattle go in the creek and the fish get frighten.'

'So what do you do? Can you buy food?'

Ignacio almost laughs. 'How can we buy it? We got no money. Sometimes we only got cassava bread. And then the cattle destroy the farms and we can't get cassava.'

'But can't you earn any money?'

'No. We can't find no work.'

'But what about the tobacco?' I point to the bunch in the corner. 'Couldn't you grow some more and sell it?'

'One time outside people come here, and they tell me to grow it. They say I going to get plenty money. When I finish I got three bales. Then I

1. This story was also widespread. It encouraged the Indians in their opposition to the African P.N.C. candidate for the Rupununi. The P.N.C. then brought an action against the U.F. for using racialism. The case was dismissed on the grounds that the Indian witnesses were incompetent. Other canvassing methods used amongst the Indians included the distribution of sweets, tobacco and polaroid photographs, and trips in a light aeroplane.

couldn't sell it at all. They start to get rotten, so I had to burn them. I wouldn't grow anything more to sell—only what I need for myself.'

'What about cattle? You never had any?'

'One time I had a small cow. But we were hungry, so we eat it. We share it with the other people. I would like to get some cattle. But how can we get them? And the grazing land scarce.'

He has hardly moved as we talk. He is still recovering from fever. Something else occurs to me. 'You ever heard of the Nappi scheme? Couldn't you go there and start a new farm and grow things to sell, like peas and corn?'

'Yes, we heard something about it. But we don't know what they're doing. Sometime we might wait for a year and then they take away the crops without giving us money.'

He pauses again. After a moment, he points to the fire in the corner. 'We got to make a fire on the ground, because we poor and we got no money. In England everyone got a stove?'

'Yes. But couldn't you build a clay one?'

His eyes seem to shrug slightly. Then, in a low voice: 'We don't know about these things. We're only Indian people.'

By now we have been there for two or three hours. Suddenly a child appears—one of Ignacio's sons, seven years old and neatly dressed, with his school books in his hand. His father hardly seems to notice him. The boy glances round at us. After pulling off his shirt, he picks up a fishing line and scampers outside again. Ignacio watches him, now that he is disappearing. Will it be any different for him?

The feelings expressed by the other Macusi were very similar. Only the young people seemed to have any confidence, and unless radical changes occurred, even this would be lost. Two things were uppermost in the minds of the older generation—their suspicion of the other Guianese races and a sense of complete defeat at their new status as a land-hungry serf population.

This racial attitude is common to most of the Indians. They feel that Guiana's independence will threaten their few remaining rights. Their suspicion dates from the eighteenth century, when the Dutch paid the Caribs to capture runaway African slaves. This created amongst the Indians a sense of dependence on Europeans and a dislike of the Africans. Being entirely European, the missionaries increased this feeling. The Indian reservation system, set up in 1910, had much the same effect; although it failed to protect them, it taught them to look on the other Guianese as a people from whom they needed protection. Finally the Constitution kept them under British control long after most Government departments were run by Guianese ministers. By the time this arrangement was changed, in August 1961, the gulf was almost complete. Through no fault of their own, the coastal Guianese had little connection with the Indians, who, in their turn, now dreaded the prospect of being controlled by them. In the 1961 elections, this apprehension was selfishly used by the right wing party, the U.F., as a means of winning Indian votes. Now there is fear in every village—a fear which may undermine the Indians, once Guiana is independent.

But basically the Macusi were suffering from a feeling of tribal despair. Change had destroyed their way of life and their sense of identity. The land was their only livelihood. It was now controlled by a handful of ranchers, whose presence also made them aware of their relative poverty. They were a disinherited people, and, with their Indian fatalism, they accepted their situation.

Land reform was the only remedy. Even within the reservations, the Indians have no legal title to the land which they occupy. They can be dispossessed overnight. There has often been talk of redistribution in the Rupununi, but little has ever come of it. In 1948, for example, a newly appointed Welfare Officer suggested that the private ranchers' leases should be allowed to lapse. The whole of the northern savanna could then be thrown open to communal grazing. The holdings of the R.D.C., which dominated the southern savanna, would be transferred to the Wapisiana for the purpose of raising cattle. The committee which reviewed these proposals included members of the ranching élite. Within a matter of months, they were dropped in favour of another scheme. The Macusi could move to Karasabai, where development schemes would take place, while eight hundred square miles would be set aside for the Wapisiana in the southern savanna. Even these revised proposals were of little benefit. The Macusi, quite understandably, were unwilling to leave their homes. The Wapisiana scheme was delayed until 1958, when the area was reduced to four hundred and fifty square miles.

Nothing further was ever done. Now that the Indians' numbers are increasing, the problem is more acute than ever. The arrival of new coastal settlers need not conflict with their interests. The land could be divided between them on a basis of guaranteed tenure. If the settlers were carefully selected, the Indians would soon lose their suspicion. With a new, mixed economy, based on cattle-raising and farming, they could still have a prosperous future. Only a reform of this kind can overcome their racial suspicion and land hunger.

There had been only one attempt to find a long-term solution to the Macusi problem—at Nappi, the resettlement project pioneered by Jack Dummett, the Agricultural Officer for the Rupununi. A message arrived at Moka-Moka late one afternoon—meet him at St. Ignatius, for Nappi, early on the following day.

Sullen skies and a passing shower, the tail end of the rainy season, as I left the village on a bicycle which Andrew had borrowed for me. After a while, a pale wave of sunlight washing over the bare savanna. Mist rising out of the hollows and shrouding the lonely cattle. An hour later, near St. Ignatius, a handful of Macusi children, already on their way to school. They were less shy here, almost children of Lethem. A shout from one of the little boys, with tousled hair and an old school satchel half as big as himself.

'Where you go on the bicycle, mister?'

'Georgetown.'

'He far. That bicycle got to fly.'

'Is a flying bicycle.'

'Then we all coming with you.'

They laughed and ran in pursuit for a moment, until they vanished round a bend in the rain-swept, sandy road. A pattern of white roofs appeared over the brow of a low hill—the agricultural station.

Five minutes later I was sitting in Jack Dummett's verandah, drinking a welcome cup of coffee brought by Joan, his attractive Canadian wife. We chatted about Moka-Moka. Jack's views on the Macusi seemed to be similar to mine. At Nappi he was trying to find an answer to their dilemma. His dark, rather hawk-like features grew quietly enthusiastic as he talked about his work. The Indians' first needs, he explained, were the use of new farming methods and the cultivation of crops which could be sold on the coast. The easiest way to achieve this was on a co-operative basis. This meant agricultural training and, above all, resettlement in a productive area. Nappi was an ideal site. Some thirty miles from St. Ignatius, in a belt of forest below the mountains, it was surrounded by a stretch of highly fertile land. If this were fully developed, it could eventually provide for several hundred families. Up to this point it seemed quite simple. It was hard to see how the scheme could fail.

'But it's not so easy as it sounds,' said Jack, sipping his coffee thoughtfully. 'We started just over a year ago. The whole idea was fairly new, so I couldn't get the authorities to approve it right away. We had to improvise completely, scratching about for funds and equipment wherever we could get them. I suppose it wasn't a bad thing—I wanted to see how the Indians would react, before we made the scheme official.'

'And have they responded all right?'

'Well, you know the problems we're up against—the psychological ones, I mean. To start with, they're resigned and distrustful, mainly because of the rough deal which they've had in the past. It's hard to raise their enthusiasm to the extent of getting them to leave their villages. But the young people are interested. We cut a road last year, from the savanna through to the site, and cleared about twenty acres. The first crops should be ready soon and I'm hoping that that will encourage them.'

'But how many people are involved?'

He smiled. 'At first there were only three—but now we've got about twenty. They're already building permanent houses. Anyway, you'll see for yourself.'

The jeep was standing at the gate. A moment later we were off, with a large grass-cutting machine roped in at the back. Jack's assistant came with us, a silent young Macusi with the exotic name of Olympia—a moment of nostalgia, perhaps, on the part of the priest who baptized him, remembering a classical education. Jack was obviously not in the habit of dallying. The little jeep flew along the track, leaping over the pot-holes and swerving dizzily round the corners. Conversation was impossible. I sat back and thought about Nappi. The whole idea corresponded closely with the conclusions I had drawn from my brief experience of the Macusi.

An hour later we passed through the village which gave the project its name. Formerly a single Catholic mission, it was now carefully divided. In one half lived the remaining Catholics and in the other the followers of the new evangelical sect, the Unevangelized Fields Mission. For a moment I almost expected to see a line of clerical frontier guards, stationed amongst the ants' nests to watch for renegade Indian souls. I had heard that this sectarian rivalry was confusing the Macusi. But apparently the U.F.M. considered this a worthwhile price for conversion to the strict, puritanical creed which Andrew had so resented. They were also campaigning back at Moka-Moka. The Catholic Indians there had been lent a hand-wound gramophone, with records encouraging them to follow the real Christian faith—the one offered by the U.F.M., as opposed to Catholicism.

A little way beyond the village, the forest rose up in front of us. We churned our way along the half swamped track which had been cut by the Indians. At first we passed through low secondary growth, a sign of previous cultivation, perhaps a generation before. Then it began surging up into the lofty virgin forest, where the soil had been naturally fertilized by an endless cycle of decay. Suddenly we came to a wide clearing, enclosed by a sheer grey wall of trees, with the dusty-blue Kanukus just visible behind them. The soil had obviously been well chosen. The fresh green clusters of maize almost concealed the view, growing to a height I had never seen before.

Just beyond the first field stood a new Macusi house, with its sun-baked adobe walls reinforced with wattles. A crop of peas was drying outside, and a young woman was roasting farine from freshly grated cassava. Both of these articles could be sold if produced in sufficient quantity. Half a dozen men gathered round, as we drew up in front of a rough little shed. Their leader was a young Macusi called Manuel, who had once lived in Moka-Moka. As we climbed out and stretched our legs, he told Jack the local news—a pig had been mauled by a jaguar, the rice was almost starting to bear, and one of the men had fever. His confident tone was very different from the resignation of most of the Indians in his home village.

Jack showed me a little machine which had been rigged up inside the shed. It was used for grating cassava, he explained, which was then made into farine. The design was his own, while the engine had been salvaged from a disused water pump. The idea was simple, but effective. Several hours of manual work could now be reduced to some fifteen minutes.

'A change like this can make a big difference,' said Jack. 'Out in the villages they sometimes get up at two or three in the morning to start making farine. They won't be so overworked now. I'm hoping that it will give them some time to try and improve their homes.'

'And how have they taken to this idea of grating cassava mechanically? It's a big change for them, isn't it?'

He laughed. 'Yes, you'd be surprised. In spite of all the time it saves, the women were pretty indifferent at first. They're so used to hard work that they almost depend on it. And the hours they spend at cassava grating have a social importance for them—it's their main gossiping time, which they don't like to miss. But of course they'll find a substitute, once they're used to the change. The younger ones soon accept it, when they see how much difference it makes.'

Despite the technical side of his job, he had obviously recognized the essential human factors involved in working with the Indians. As we walked round the clearing, he pointed out the crops they were growing—rice, soya-beans and peas, all of which were new to them. We stopped to talk to a group of men. Jack was obviously far more than a mere agricultural officer. He discussed their every interest. Were they missing their home village? Was there any fever about and how was the hunting going? He seemed to be aware of everything which was important to them.

'Of course it's all pretty makeshift,' he said. He pointed to a ramshackle combination of old pipes and petrol drums, beside the nearby creek. 'We had to use anything we could find to build that water pump. But it works pretty well, and the water's healthy.'

The new grass-cutting machine had just been unloaded. Jack went back to the shed to explain its mysteries to the Indians. I watched them as they gathered round, listening carefully. A few minutes later, Manuel was driving it independently. As I walked on through the settlement, I stopped to talk to one of the men who was working outside his home. Unlike most of the older Macusi, he had already learnt English. I pointed to a heap of dried peas, lying in a corner.

'You grew the peas?'

He nodded. 'Yes, I grow them. We ain't know about these things before.'

'And you had hard work to grow them?'

'Hard work, yes. Some people get vexed and gone away. But more people coming all the time. They waiting to see how we making out. Then all of them going to come.'

'And Mr. Dummett is helping you?'

'Yes, he helping plenty. The people does like him here.' He pointed to an improvised chimney in the corner of his house. 'Is he make that thing for me. Stop the smoke getting in me eye. He got a mind to how we feeling.'

A simple remark like this could be decisive for a scheme like Nappi. However much the Indian changes, material factors always come second to his awareness of personalities. In this case they were depending on someone who both knew and respected them; hence their unusual enthusiasm.

We left late in the afternoon, with Olympia and another Macusi who was suffering from fever and needed a lift to Lethem. A brief breakdown a few miles from Nappi—the cooling-fan had come adrift. Olympia produced a piece of wire and delved inside the engine. A moment later we were off again, with the jeep still rattling doubtfully.

It was dark by the time we reached St. Ignatius. Jack was already looking tired. He was still supposed to be convalescing from a recent illness. But after supper we sat and talked until late that night.

'All this work you've done on the scheme—do you feel it's been worthwhile?' I asked.

'Well, it's been quite a strain,' he said. 'The main thing is that it's so

187

slow. These ideas are new to the Indians. You've got to win their confidence and bring them round gradually. They won't be pushed into anything. You have to allow for their pace, for example. They can't work full time—they still spend three or four days a week hunting and fishing for their families. You have to accept this kind of delay.'

'Do you think that your plans have fitted in with their traditions?'

'Yes, I believe so, as far as they can. Of course, some traditions have to go—their method of cassava grating, for example. That's why the young people are important. They're really the only ones who can accept these changes. Anyway, I expected these problems. The real difficulty lies in working in this remote spot, with practically no communications. And it's not always easy to convince the authorities of the value of a scheme like this. But at least I'm sure of one thing—we have proved that the scheme can work, even on this improvised level.'

Nappi justified his claim. For the younger Macusi, at least, the distance between collapse and recovery now seemed to be much less than Moka-Moka suggested. Given some ten years, a dozen or so Guianese of Jack's perception and technical ability could transform the Indian situation.

The next morning slipped by unnoticed, as I browsed through Jack's bookshelves, which were stocked with everything from Proust to Mittelholzer. I thought about the next few days. I would soon have to be back in Georgetown. Meanwhile there was just time to visit the Wapisiana. I had seen a few of them at Lethem, a strong-featured, well built people. They were said to be changing rapidly; but, living well away from the town and the influence of border society, they were apparently less disturbed than the neighbouring Macusi.

That afternoon Jack and I drove back to Lethem. A cheque to cash, and a seat to be booked on the next week's plane to Georgetown. I dropped in to see Bill Seggar at the Administration Office. As luck would have it, one of their jeeps was heading south the next day, round the foot of the Kanuku Mountains into Wapisiana country. It was going as far as Wichabai, an old ranching outpost on the Rupununi River. From there I could make my way to Sand Creek, a nearby Wapisiana village.

We went on to Moka-Moka to collect my hammock from Andrew's home. Now that he was back in the village, he was anxious to do some work on the farm. As he spoke no Wapisiana, there was little point in his joining me on my journey south.

He came back to Lethem with us. When I had said goodbye to Jack, we sat and talked on the steps of the rest house where I was spending the night. Dusk was shifting down the street. A few people ambled by, with

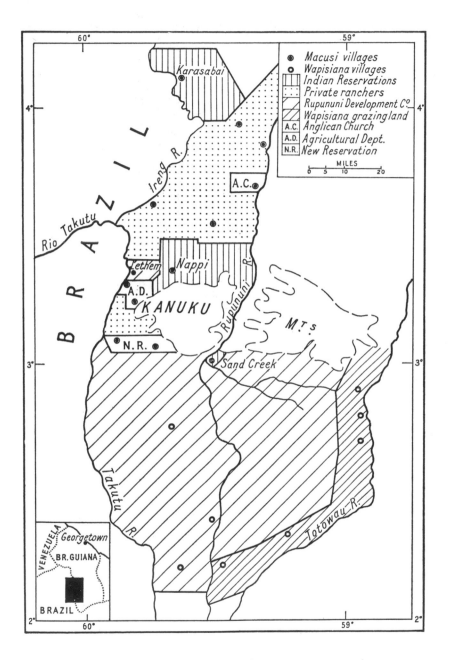

LAND TENURE IN THE RUPUNUNI SAVANNAS

an air that suggested how slowly time passed in the unhurried frontier town. It seemed much more than a week since I had first sat there, waiting for Andrew. It was easier now to understand why he had been so unpredictable, sometimes diffident and at others quite easy-going. Lethem and the Rupununi were a strangely ambiguous setting—inert and dozing on the surface, knockabout and happy-go-lucky. But beneath this there always lingered the silent presence of the Macusi—a presence to which he still belonged.

We chatted intermittently. For the first time since we had met, Andrew seemed reticent. Perhaps he was suddenly aware that we were going two different ways—ways whose distinctions had been forgotten as we travelled together. He was thinking of going back, he said—back through the mountains to Tawailing to try his luck in the diamond fields.

A light suddenly flickered behind us. Reflections dancing on the black waters of the Takutu River. Andrew stood up to go. We shook hands and then both laughed at each other's formality. He paused at the bottom of the steps, grinned and offered a mock salute. A moment later his stocky figure vanished into the cloistering darkness, down the road that led towards Ng-a-Fook's.

9

The Teacher Boys

T<small>HE</small> sound of a jeep outside the rest house, followed by a sharp rap on the door. It was Stanley, the partly Indian driver, with a lazy-grinning, good-natured face, who was taking me to Wichabai. He had to be there in time to meet the mail plane, he explained—we must leave in a quarter of an hour. Outside, it was still pitch dark, perhaps just five o'clock. It seemed only a few minutes since I had fallen asleep. I fumbled in the corner for my clothes. As I picked up my shirt, I noticed a slight movement. A russet-brown scorpion was clinging on to it, waving its tail suspiciously. I disposed of it with a sandal and finished dressing rather more cautiously.

Ten minutes later Stanley was back, with a young Guianese called Ivan, who wore a picturesque sombrero, curling up high at the edges, a trophy from Bôa Vista. A ghostly Lethem slid through the headlights as we turned towards the savanna. A bewildered owl caught in the glare, hypnotized, then suddenly rising and drifting away on motionless wings. The hunch-backed figures of the sandpaper trees, crouching by the pot-holed road that shook away the last trace of sleep. The heavy clouds were beginning to pale; behind them, a cold streak of light, filtering slowly through the darkness. The Kanukus on the horizon, transformed from a faint silhouette into a massive, watchful silence.

The jeep trail followed the line of the mountains, past the deep stretches of forest which scrambled up their lower slopes. Some of this was fertile land, which could be used for resettlement if Nappi was successful. After an hour's driving, we passed through Macusi village, the last outpost of the tribe before Wapisiana country. The sun glared down on the breathless savanna, throttling the sandpaper trees and hardening the mud-built ants' nests. A long, low swamp, a flight of duck and occasionally a herd of cattle, turning to watch us solemnly. By mid-morning we were at Wichabai. The Rupununi River was in flood and the jeep was unable to ford it. I would have to find some other means of reaching Sand Creek, still ten miles away.

Just beyond the airstrip stood a large wooden house, stern and aristo-cratic-looking, which reminded me of the managers' quarters on the sugar estates. We pulled up below it, in the shade of a mango tree. A well built, slightly bent figure was standing at the foot of the steps. It was John Melville, one of the sons of the pioneering Scotsman. He had once been the largest rancher in the southern savanna. Though the R.D.C. had now taken over, he still lived in the old ranch-house which he had built for himself. True to the cosmopolitan outlook of the Melville clan, he had married a Brazilian girl. As he led us up the steps into a large, bare room, two of his daughters, dressed in colourful Georgetown fashion, retired modestly.

The mail plane was delayed, he said, as he plied us with Brazilian coffee, thick and black, in small cups; it would not be arriving till mid-afternoon. As we talked, a Quixote-like rider loped into the dusty yard. He dismounted and came up the steps. It turned out to be Nash Atkin-son, another Indian from the Moruca, whose family I knew well. They had often told me about him, describing his work as a medical ranger in the southern savanna.

'And where you heading now?' he asked, after we had been introduced.

'Sand Creek,' I replied. 'But I don't yet know how I'm getting there.'

'That's easy,' he said. 'I'm going that way. You could take a ride in my bullock cart. But I got to wait on this mail plane. A teacher from Sand Creek is coming on it. I promise to meet her and take her back.'

As the morning drifted by, he told me more about himself. The wanderlust of the Moruca Indians, which had scattered so many of them over different parts of the interior, began in the 1930's. A large group of them left the north-west to work on a tripartite boundary commission between Guiana, Venezuela and Brazil. The three years for which it lasted are full of legends for the men who survived them, both Indians and coastal Guianese. The Brazilians soon retired from the wind-swept plateau of Mount Roraima, unable to bear the cold. Three hundred droughers were permanently employed in bringing supplies from the coast. Men and stores were lost in the rapids, and others died through beri-beri and malaria. There was hardly a man amongst them who was not invalided out at one point or another.

'When this thing finish,' Nash added, 'I stayed here in the Rupununi and marry a Wapisiana girl. That was a good time ago, about twenty years now.'

'And how did you start this medical work?'

'Well,' he said, 'after I come here they had a new scheme. They wanted to find a medical ranger for every Indian tribe. They couldn't get coast people to work up here in the bush, so they choose me and a next Indian. After they give us six months training, they send us back here to work. Then they find it was going all right, so they take another four boys and train them in the same way. They got about six of us now, working all about in the bush, taking medicine to the Indians.'

'And what's the work like?' I asked.

'It's going all right—but it's hard too.' He pushed a battered old blue cap on to the back of his head. Beneath it a crop of curly hair, which, as his uncle had once told me, came from a Portuguese ancestor. 'You see, this place so big,' he added. 'I only got the horse for travelling, and all this savanna to cover, with three or four thousand Wapisiana. I really need a next man to help. I scarcely got enough medicine, too—but I still trying.'

He gave me a broad grin from his sun-tanned and time-gnarled face. He seemed a cheerful character. Like many others from the Moruca, he had shown that the Indians were capable of providing for their own needs, if given the opportunity.

Morning passed into afternoon. The heat was already waning by the time we heard the plane, a distant speck of sound in the stillness outside. A handful of curious Wapisianas had gathered at the end of the airstrip, pointing to a silver dot over the blue-grey mountains. It swooped down and came to a halt in a cloud of red dust. A few passengers stepped out. One of them was a manager of the local balata company. I watched him talking to an old Wapisiana who was standing nearby.

'How's the balata going?'

'He going all right. But I got worries. This foot cut, and he paining me.' He pointed at his foot, which was swollen and septic. The manager glanced down at it.

'And when do you think you're going to be ready?'

The old man hesitated. 'Can't say. Maybe December time.'

'You must try and finish by October. We need the balata right away.'

The Indian made no reply. The manager turned away. He looked taken aback as he recognized me. I had once clashed with the company's director over their treatment of some Indians at Orealla. We shook hands and talked for a moment, in a slightly monosyllabic style.

Suddenly Nash waved to me. He introduced me to Linnette, the young coloured teacher from Sand Creek, and we walked over to the bank of the Rupununi River. Nash had found a canoe for us. Five minutes later we were across, with our belongings loaded up on to his bullock cart. He himself went on ahead, leaving us in the hands of the tushau from Sand Creek. We set off hurriedly, anxious to escape the kaboura that haunted the river banks. The ramshackle wooden cart lurched down the deeply rutted track. Linnette and I were perched in front, with the tushau standing up behind us, cracking his whip and hallooing indignantly at the reluctant bullocks. Each time we came to a creek, he goaded them into a brisk trot, whooping triumphantly as the cart leapt over the pot-holes and plunged into the shallow crossing.

'How long have you been teaching at Sand Creek?' I asked Linnette.

'About a year now,' she said.

'And you like it there?'

She smiled. 'Oh, yes. It's different from the coast, of course, but the village is nice and peaceful. And the Indian children are so quiet, I really like being with them. The other teachers are young, too, so we all enjoy it. Does anybody know you're coming?'

'No, I only decided yesterday.'

'Well, that doesn't matter. You could stay with the teacher boys—is so they call them in the village. Three of them are Indians. The other one, Noel, he's from Georgetown. They'll be glad to have you there.'

The hills were framed by the bullocks' horns, as they ambled on, with heads bent between the creaking shafts. The shadows were beginning to lengthen over the green-brown savanna. A pair of tiny scarlet birds followed us for a while, cheeping indignantly, flitting between the sand-paper trees, flashes of sudden brilliance against the passive colours behind them. The crickets were still humming all round us, pausing in silent enquiry as we trundled by. A flock of quail rose up from the path with a startled flurry of wings, gliding over the grass and dropping down to safety.

A little way from the track, I could see the first Indian farms, still two or three miles from the village. Ahead of us, two Wapisiana women, perched gracefully on their bullocks, riding in slow procession towards the jagged horizon. By now the last of the sunset was dying in a gap in the hills. A hint of dusk, gathering speed as it closed down over the shrinking savanna. A lone bat flipped past our heads. The fireflies were glimmering through the darkness. Somewhere beyond us, in the forest, the distant call of the howler monkeys, lamenting the long night ahead.

We stopped briefly at Nash's house. As we continued, a new moon was rising slowly behind us. A moment later we reached the creek which gave the village its name. A steep descent and, just beyond it, water foaming through the rocks. The tushau whooped in encouragement. The cart swayed and rattled hysterically, as the bullocks heaved their way across, struggling for a foothold on the rocks, until they emerged on the far side and scrambled up the bank.

Five minutes later we reached the village. A large semicircle of houses stretched round on either side of us. A swarm of children greeted Linnette, looking up at me shyly, as if to enquire if she were responsible. Over on the far side, the sound of guitars and banjoes, and a pressure lamp, flickering weakly. Most of the village seemed to be there, dancing and drinking parakari after a masromani at which a new field had been cut.

Linnette pointed to a large, dilapidated building, where the other teachers lived. Two little boys shouldered my baggage and led me over to it. I was met by Noel, the teacher from the coast, a Portuguese of about twenty, with a pinched face and a pleasant smile. Inside, the twang of another guitar. As it came to an end, the other three teachers emerged. They all looked much the same age as Noel, who introduced me to them. The first was Vauji, a slight Macusi, who was running a spinning course for the girls. The other two, Dionysio and Oliver, had heavier, rather dark features. They were both Wapisianas.

They were glad to see me, Noel said—it wasn't often that they had visitors. As they led me up the steps, a crowd of school-children gathered round in friendly curiosity. A moment later they were slinging my hammock, bringing me water for a much needed wash, and making coffee for me. The teachers' rugged quarters, converted from an old Indian house, had an atmosphere of dishevelled comfort. Their hammocks were slung from side to side, with guitars and books piled up in the corners and an open fire burning in the mud-floored kitchen. My arrival was accepted without question. Time would explain why I had come. Meanwhile they simply welcomed me in traditional Indian fashion.

Noel took me to meet Mrs. Vieira, the half Portuguese, half Indian head-teacher. She was the daughter of Stephen Campbell, who was a father-figure to the Indians. Although I had never been able to meet him,[1] I had often heard his name. Coming from a Moruca family, he was the only Indian who had ever held a seat on the Guianese Legislative Council. He had recently joined the U.F., carrying most of the Indians' votes with him. He was now pressing for legislation for their future security, especially in terms of land tenure. As we chatted, Mrs.

1. Two months later we met in London, when he was attending the Guianese Independence Conference.

Vieira told me that she and her Portuguese husband, Johnny, had been running the school for nearly eight years. When they first arrived in the village, there were hardly more than a hundred children. Now there were almost twice as many. Their numbers seemed to be increasing even more rapidly than those of the Macusi.

Johnny walked back with us. The lilting tune of a bolero came from the house where the party was being held. Mandolin backed by a shuffling maraccas, the half sad rhythms of Brazil, falling, then surging up again. The savanna tribes were once famous for the traditional palishara, the dance of the red-headed finch. But the Wapisiana are skilled musicians, and can pick up new tunes and instruments almost instinctively. Since their contacts with Brazil and the coast, their own music has almost died out.

'What did you think of the north?' asked Johnny, as we sat outside the teachers' house. I told him my impressions of the Macusi. 'Yes,' he said, 'they've had a rough time. The Wapisiana are better off—they're less resigned than the Macusi.'

'But why are they so different?' I asked.

'Well, things aren't so hard here. The Company holds most of the land, but it treats them better than the ranchers. And of course they're farther away from Lethem, which keeps them out of trouble.'

'But haven't they got the Macusis' problems—land shortage and no employment?'

He nodded. 'It wasn't so bad before—but now their numbers are going up and they're starting to get uneasy. The young boys want to earn money, but of course there's no work for them here. But otherwise they've been pretty lucky. They've had a good priest here, Father McKenna—it's a pity he's away right now—he's really helped them a lot.'

'In what way?'

Johnny hesitated. 'Well, he's done all kinds of things outside his church work. His first idea was a village field. The Indians worked on it together, growing maize and cotton. They made a bit of money from it and started a village herd. They've got about forty head now and plenty of milk for the children. That worked pretty well, and when they saw it was going all right, they started on other schemes—they built their own co-operative shop and put up the new school. You see, just one man's encouragement makes a big difference to the Indians—it explains things to them, reassures them.' He paused again for a moment. 'They can make out all right these people, if only they get the chance—the trouble is, they don't often get it.'

By the time we had finished talking, it was after midnight. The party on the far side of the village showed no sign of flagging. Suddenly one of the Indians appeared and offered us some parakari. The ghostly figures of the village cattle stirred in front of us. Beside them an ancient mango tree, with its gnarled, gesticulating fingers clutching at the stars. One or two Indians drifted by, offering a tipsy greeting, with the children close behind them.

I said goodnight to Noel and Johnny and stood at the window for a moment, listening to the sounds outside. Snatches of Wapisiana gaiety, freed by the flow of parakari, with the night-long chorus of crickets forming a ceaseless background. An Indian suddenly passed on horseback, moving slowly into a canter. A wild shadow and the drumming of hooves, frescoed across the darkness.

A Sunday. The brief nirvana of lying, half dozing, in a hammock. Noel and the other teachers obviously felt the same way; a sympathetic inertia reigned long after we had woken. A few stray guitar chords came stumbling through the morning air—left-overs from the festivity of the previous evening.

Despite its being a Catholic mission, the life of the village seemed hardly affected by the fact that it was Sunday. The morning service was already over. The women were heading for the farms, seated astride their bullocks with an air of independence. Wareshis and baskets hung beside them and hunting dogs followed close behind. A girl passed with a gourd in her hand, on her way to fetch water. Then two boys with bows and arrows, going in search of fish. They were changing—this was inevitable, with the presence of the Church. But the changes were inconspicuous. Somehow they had blended with their Indian surroundings.

This impression grew on me as I walked round the village with Johnny. The houses were much less scattered than those at Moka-Moka. Built round the open space where the cattle slept at night, they still had a village atmosphere. This was strengthened by the women, as they worked together at home and left for their farms in small groups. Unlike the Macusi, they were a closely knit people. Their sense of identity had survived. Even their expressions were different. The will to live was still alight in their often strikingly handsome features.

The standard of living seemed fairly high. Most of the houses were large and clean-swept. Tobacco was hanging from the rafters and several of the women were working on the heavily woven hammocks for which the Wapisiana are famous. Many families owned a few steers and some of the men had found employment as vaqueiros, or cowboys, for the

R.D.C. Others were still bleeding balata, despite their meagre wages.[1]

But these outlets made life hard, one of the women told me shyly. By taking the men away from the village, they clashed with their day to day economy. Their cassava crops were neglected and families were left to fend for themselves, without a man to look after them. Wages were usually too low to bring any real compensation. The only solution was to create an outlet within the village. This would not have been difficult. Many of them had already sold a few cattle and hammocks in Lethem. If they were helped to develop these products, they could make a living from them.

But on the whole Sand Creek was much better off than Moka-Moka. Change had been reconciled with their customs. There was little real poverty, and even a chance of prosperity. Why was there such a difference between the two villages? Tribal temperament played its part, but the main explanation was deeper. It seemed to lie in the different ways in which change had taken place. At Sand Creek it was gradual and consistent, but among the Macusi it was haphazard. They were influenced from outside, by the rum shops and stores of Lethem and the presence of the cattle-ranchers, while here the novelties came from inside, through the Church and the teachers, who shared their lives with the Indians and understood their customs and temperament. This alone had been decisive. It created a positive link between the old world and the new. The Indians had not simply been faced with the choice of surrender or withdrawal. Their trust had been won, and change was accepted and fitted into their way of life. Given the same advantage, the other tribes could have shared their confidence.

Yet this was only the first step towards a complete readjustment. For most of the following afternoon I talked to the village tushau, a grave, middle-aged Wapisiana who spoke very little English. We were sitting in the shade of a mango tree outside the Vieiras' house, with Oliver, one of the teachers, acting as interpreter. He had had eight children, the tushau said; all but two of them had died, mainly from malaria. But that was a long time ago—they scarcely had malaria now. One of his children was still at school; the other was teaching in a neighbouring village. They could both speak English, he added proudly. Life would be better for them.

1. The British Guiana Balata Company, a subsidiary of Booker Bros., has a monopoly of the industry. Hence they can prescribe wages, which are generally thirty-eight cents per pound of balata. This is less than half the price paid in Dutch Guiana and Brazil, the other balata producing countries. There are heavy penalties for smuggling balata across the border, and most of the company's employees are Indians, who are unable to form a Union.

'So you like the school here?' I asked.

'Yes, we like it. Things changing up. We old people never knew about these outside things.'

'What about food and money—can the people get enough?'

'Most people, yes. Only sometimes we punish.[1] But new children coming all the time, and the land is getting scarce.' He paused for a moment and looked around him. A heavy, rather solemn face, not unlike that of Oliver, with his strong, confident eyes and mouth. The two of them seemed less far apart than the young and older generations in most Indian villages. The tushau nodded thoughtfully. 'We really need some money. That's not so easy for us. Even if we find work, we got to leave the village for it. And sometimes, when we finish, we scarcely got any money.'

'But can't you get it by selling cattle?'

'Yes.' He hesitated slightly. 'But we ain't got so much cattle, and only this small reservation. All about here is Company land.

The reservation covered twenty-eight of the southern savanna's three thousand square miles. It was the only one in Wapisiana country. Most of the surrounding land was held by the R.D.C. But then I remembered the grazing area which had been transferred to the Indians.

'What about the grazing scheme—doesn't that help you out?'

'Not so much. Is far from here. If we keep cattle there, we can't tell what's happening to them. And now is getting hard for us—more people living here all the time.' He pointed to the village around us. There were some thirty or forty houses. The reservation would be far too small to support a village cattle industry.

'So what about the young people? What are they going to do?'

The tushau looked doubtful. 'We can't tell. Maybe they going to stay at home and live like the old people. Some might go to Lethem or Georgetown. I hear that plenty want to leave.'

A long pause; then, from the tushau, the inevitable question. 'What about this politics? Election people been here. We didn't understand what they say, but they promise plenty good things. But since then nothing happen. We didn't hear anything from them. They tell us this P.P.P. is going to take away the land.'

I offered a lame reassurance—none of the Guianese politicians were hostile to the Indians. But the tushau still looked apprehensive. Words alone would not convince him. He was worried by the future, rather than the present. So far change had been beneficial, but this alone was not enough. External factors also mattered and here there was still

1. Suffer.

uncertainty. Potentially they could be peasant farmers, selling their products to the coast and living much as they had always done. But this depended on three things—land, agricultural training and marketing facilities. Beyond the point which they had reached, help could only come from above—from a Guianese Government with a new Indian policy; and although it needed a human basis, practical issues like this were important.

The teacher boys were amusing company. I had hardly been with them for twenty-four hours before they were treating me as one of themselves. Although they were all close friends, they were very different in character. The Portuguese Noel, open and friendly; then the two Wapisianas—Oliver, stocky and shy, and the good-looking Dionysio, who was hoping for a place in the teacher-training college in George-town; and finally Vauji, a Brazilian Macusi, the group comedian, with a puckish face and a boisterous sense of humour. The three Indians were completely at ease with Noel and the two girl teachers, who also came from Georgetown. On a personal level, at least, the older Indians' apprehensions about the coastal Guianese were easily forgotten.

Noel and Vauji were mysteriously busy on the day before I left. When evening came, their secret was out—they were preparing a chicken curry for a farewell party. As we sat round the rough wooden table that night, I realized how different they were from any other group I had met in an Indian community. They were a typical cross-section of the Guianese in the interior—Noel, the Vieiras, the three Indian teachers, and the two girls from the coast, one African and one Portuguese. There was no sense of distinction between them; they simply shared the same situation. The turmoil of coastal politics, with all its racial implications, suddenly seemed remote and meaningless—as if it could hardly have been a part of the country to which they belonged.

'You know,' said Mrs. Vieira wistfully, looking round at the others, 'at first there was only three of us here—Johnny and myself and one pupil teacher. And now all these others with us, and twice the number of children. And this year we had two boys who got scholarships for Georgetown. They're going to secondary school there.'

The others smiled at her motherly pride. Meanwhile Vauji, sitting beside me, had been unusually silent. Suddenly he came to life and started bombarding me with questions. Was it true that the teachers wore wigs at Oxford? How many books did I read in a week? Why did I spend so much time scribbling in an old notebook? And what was I writing about Vauji?

'I'd like to go to England,' he added, grinning impishly. 'They got any Indians living there?'

'No,' I said, 'but that wouldn't matter.'

'Then one day I coming. You think I would like it?'

'Perhaps, for a short time. I don't believe you would want to stay there.'

Suddenly, as we finished eating, a rending clap of thunder outside. The rain began pouring through the holes in the roof. The teacher boys picked up their guitars and sang in wild defiance to the storm. Ten minutes later, when it was over, the others said good-night and left. The teachers went on strumming gaily. Their repertoire ranged from West Indian favourites to Brazilian tunes which still had a trace of Indian melody in them. Occasionally Vauji got up to dance, reducing us to fits of laughter, as he wriggled his way satirically through a coastal style calypso.

Noel produced a pack of cards. We decided to play a few rounds before going to sleep. A handful of schoolboys appeared from nowhere and gathered round, watching us closely. Coffee was made and cigarettes were placed reassuringly on the table. One round stretched into another. Our intended half hour became an hour, still varied by Vauji's antics. By the time the cocks began crowing, we were all weak with laughter. The first streak of dawn at the window, snuffling over the jagged grey mountains. Outside in the village, stillness. The soft creaking of hammock ropes, followed by an empty silence.

A few hours later they were making breakfast and hurrying off to school. I had meant to leave early. Stanley, the driver, had promised to meet me back at Wichabai. Johnny decided to come with me. Soon after the boys had left, he appeared with two ancient bicycles. We tied our belongings on to the back and rode over to the school to say goodbye to the others. The children were crowded close together on the rickety wooden benches. Dark Wapisiana faces, shy, eager, some coy, some mischievous, poring over their slates and glancing up at the teachers. Noel, with the five year olds, who were still learning English, and Dionysio, watchful and patient, with one of the older classes. There was something of the previous evening in the atmosphere.

By the time we left, it was overcast. We were soon caught by a burst of rain. Nash appeared as we passed his house, and ushered us in sympathetically. We must have some parakari, he said—the only way to prevent a cold. He seemed to be in party mood, chatting incessantly— the Boundary Commission, the Rupununi and finally his birthplace, the Moruca. In a few days time, I would be there, on the last stage of my journey. Over two hours passed, with the parakari flowing steadily. The rain had only lasted briefly. I pictured an indignant Stanley, waiting at Wichabai. At last we waved goodbye to Nash and pedalled on again.

We struggled on, labouring slightly, thanks to the parakari and the rain-steeped, muddy sand. Wearily through a stretch of swamp, pursued by a pair of marsh birds, which keened anxiously overhead, swooping down and swerving away from within a few feet of us. A herd of cattle, watching suspiciously, fidgeting, then stampeding wildly across the open savanna. The rolling of hooves, strangely muted by the surrounding dampness.

An hour later we reached the bank of the Rupununi River. Johnny whooped and shouted for a boat. A mocking echo in reply. Then suddenly two Wapisiana boys appeared on the far bank and paddled over to us. Back at John Melville's house, Stanley was waiting expectantly. He greeted us with an injured expression.

'It's late. We got to hustle,' he said.

'The wind was against us,' I explained, 'and some parakari in it.'

He nodded sympathetically. We piled into the jeep, together with four policemen from Lethem and Olga, one of John Melville's daughters, who was returning to Georgetown. Stanley banged the door and set off at a rapid pace. Half an hour later we suddenly stopped. The policemen jumped out and walked over to a nearby house. The Indian who lived there had been charged with cattle-stealing. A young Wapisiana appeared and lounged by the jeep, staring at us in mild curiosity.

'You help to kill the cow?' asked Johnny.

A long pause. 'No,' said the Indian curtly, in a voice half mocking and half defensive. 'But maybe I help with eating it.'

'Does this often happen?' I asked Olga.

'Yes, quite often,' she said. 'But it's natural—the Indians are poor, they have nothing to eat. They see a cow and no one in sight, so of course they kill it.'

I remembered another explanation, which I had heard from an Indian. The Macusi were often surprised when charged with cattle-stealing. The ranchers who employed them had taught them to rustle—so why shouldn't they try it for themselves? There was also their old scale of values. What could one man possibly want with thousands of head of cattle? It would hardly affect him if you took one when you happened to be hungry. But new concepts were in force. Colonial law had made a distinction between the Crown's removal of the Indians' land and the Indians' removal of the ranchers' cattle.

Silence in the heavily laden jeep, as we drove on again. We churned our way across the savanna and through long pools of water left by the morning's rain. A brief pause at Macusi village, where I talked to the school-teacher, another Moruca Indian. But Stanley wanted to press on. By dusk we were back at Lethem.

Before the plane arrived the next day, I chatted to Mr. Learmond, the District Commissioner. 'What do you think will become of them here?' I asked, as we talked about the Indians.

He hesitated. 'It's hard to tell. We've got to bring them to the point where they can live on equal terms with settlers from the coast.'

'But how's this going to be done?'

'Well,' he said, 'it's got to be gradual—Jack Dummett's scheme is important, it might give us some ideas.'

'Are there any alternatives?'

He raised his hands. 'There's Lethem, of course, it's bound to expand. There may be new industries and even secondary schools. I suppose they'll affect the Indians.'

It seemed unnecessary to ask just how they would affect them. We said goodbye and I wandered outside to join Ernie for a drink in his store. A few minutes later we heard the plane. There was quite a crowd beside the runway—the Seggars, Jack, Ernie and Geoff, Olga and also Andrew's brother, who was in the police force. Apparently he had taken to it more easily than Andrew. He came over and talked to me.

'So you going back to Georgetown now?'

'Yes, then on to the Moruca.'

He looked at me. 'Andrew's a wild boy. I hope he didn't give you any worries?'

'No. We had some problems at first—but then we got on well together.'

The others were clambering on to the plane. We shook hands and said goodbye. Safety belts and metal seats, the practical informality of the Guianese airways again. Suddenly I felt halfway back to the almost forgotten world of the coast. I had only one more district to visit—the Moruca, in north-western Guiana. Here, perhaps, I could judge the outcome of all that I had seen of the Indians.

Through Indian Eyes

THE atmosphere of Georgetown had changed. There was less political tension. But it felt like a lull before the storm. The long awaited report on the February riots would soon be published. Speculation was returning to every political forum—to the rum shops and street-corners and the balconies of Bel Air Gardens, the city's only modern quarter, occupied mainly by Booker's European staff. The ghosts of Black Friday were being revived. Would there be any evidence of planned right wing subversion? Or were the riots simply due to existing poverty and the Marxist phobia let loose by the budget? In much of Georgetown it was rumoured that the report would strike a final blow at Dr. Jagan's waning popularity. But the opposition was negative. Although it included some of the Unions, it was mainly inspired by small groups who feared for their vested interests. If the Premier fell from power, there seemed to be no one to replace him.

I was leaving for the Moruca before the report was due. I had met up with an old friend—McAlistair Ashley, known as 'Mac', a Guianese District Commissioner, with whom I had often stayed at Springlands during my first visit to Guiana. He had just been transferred to the North-West District. In a couple of days he was going there with Mr. Cassou, the Commissioner of the Interior. As the Moruca lay on their route, they had offered to take me with them.

I was looking forward to the trip. The journey would be a repetition of the first one I had made in Guiana, three years ago. Before going to Orealla, I had spent some time in the Moruca, working with the young people, who had built a community centre. During the past two years some of them had written to me, especially Benson, an Arawak who worked at the local Government Station. But, in addition to these personal connections, the Moruca Indians might provide an answer to some of the questions which had emerged from my travels. Because of their history, and their location near the coast, they are the most advanced group in Guiana. If their transition had been successful it could easily be the same for the other tribes.

I rang Mr. Cassou at his office. 'Mac's gone back to Leguan,' he said—the island in the Essequibo River, from which he was being transferred. 'He had a few things to clear up. We can meet him on the way. We'll have to catch the north-west steamer.'

'When does it leave?' I asked.

'Three o'clock tomorrow morning.'

Georgetown was still and deserted as I made my way to the docks. Silence on the waterfront. A row of warehouses gleaming silver beneath the arc-lights. A greeting from the night-watchman, an old East Indian, lame, with a grizzled face.

'She leaving just now,' he said. He pointed to the *Arawana*, the little steamer on which we were travelling. 'You searching for diamonds, Chief?'

'No, I'm studying the Indians.'

He looked at me expectantly. I fumbled for a coin.

'Thank you, Chief. Take care in the bush. They got tiger and snake and thing.' He saluted and faded back into the shadows.

I caught sight of Mr. Cassou and joined him on the cramped little deck. Muffled activity below us. The last of the cargo was being secured in the open hold; drums of petrol, bales of wire and a tractor for the paddy fields of the Essequibo Islands. The heavy, sweet smell of mud and molasses hung round the wharves; a smell that follows you through Guiana, like a description of the past—the bitter and sweet, the hardship and glamour, the sweat and poverty of the cane-fields that belie the European's usual conception of the West Indies. Like the face of the old night watchman; picturesque and broken.

But here, too, the past was receding. The life of the Demerara docks was now shared by Cuban and Russian boats, loading rice for Havana and the Communist bloc. Two battered hulks were moored beside us. I could just make out the names on their bows, *Queen of Berbice* and *Canje Pheasant*—old channel-steamers, Mr. Cassou explained, banished to spend the last of their days in the mud-brown estuaries of Guiana.

The dark faces of the crew were caught in the half light, as we slid away from the massive greenheart timbers that lined the wharf. The engines shuddered into life, churning the water, chocolate coloured. The lights of the docks were soon dwindling, like a dying firework display. The pin-point lanterns of fishing boats, as we crossed the bar of the Demerara towards the open sea. A warm breeze. Mr. Cassou was dozing.

Suddenly, after two hours of sleep filled with the throb of the engines, it was cold and dawn. A colourless light that seemed to expand the flat, empty horizon. We had reached the mouth of the Essequibo, over twenty miles wide and barely discernible from the sea, until you notice the silent mudflats turning slowly inwards. In front of us lay the islands which I had often seen from the air. The nearest of them was Leguan, where Mac was meeting us. The skeleton of an old barge, stogged in the mud which was patterned by wind and water. A pair of goats browsing despairingly off a lone mangrove tree. A small church came into sight, rounded and squat, with a stone tower. It was one of the few buildings which survive from the days of the Dutch. Their settlers favoured the Essequibo, whose islands and low coastline form a South American Holland. The ruins of an old fort can still be seen on a nearby promontory, built to defend their tobacco plantations from the marauding Spaniards.

As we drew in to Leguan, a handful of figures appeared on the stelling, summoned by the siren of the *Arawana*. I recognized Mac, a tall, spruce figure, mainly African, with a trace of Scots blood. He was wearing a white cork hat, as he always did on these occasions, half in acceptance and half in satire of all that it symbolized.

The little crowd was watching us, curious about an arrival which had an official air. Every aspect of Guiana is crammed on to the riverside stellings of a coastal journey. In the very word stelling, the Dutch past. Slavery still, in black-ivory shoulders, stooping to unload the cargo. Indenture in East Indian faces, with bright kerchiefs round their heads and meagre wealth displayed in their ornaments, bangles, bracelets and golden ear-rings. Poverty in the helpless cripples. The clamour of beggars and the jostling of people who have always lived shoulder to shoulder. Easy nature in flashing smiles and suspicion in casually watching eyes. The cloying, jumbled confusion of smells. The colour and strangeness of the fruit spread out in front of the vendors, purple aubergine, bananas, pineapples, plantains, mangoes and water-melons, with a pink gash displaying a centre filled with shining black seeds. Gold-panning equipment stacked in a corner—the dreams of countless porknockers in the interior. Politics splashed across the walls, 'P.P.P., Jagan our leader.' Change and a glimmer of new prosperity in a pile of rice bags and the blue and white uniformed school-children. Vivid, ambiguous and rootless; Guiana's identity.

We breakfasted in a wooden rest house overlooking the river. Mac said goodbye to his office staff, who were obviously sad to see him go. A taxi had just arrived, and we set off down the narrow road that cut through the paddy fields. A launch was waiting on the far side to take us on to Wakenaam, the next island. Here the road twisted and turned, leaving a cloud of dust behind us. Another boat at the end of a decrepit stelling. A flock of sandpipers rose from the mudflats, a twitter of fear and a flash of white, as they flew zig-zag along the bank. Beyond them, a roughly cut brown sail drifting across the horizon.

The East Indian who owned the launch was pleading insistently with Mac. 'Chief, this boat is all me living. And now me hear people say the Government going to put a launch here.' He threw up his hands in despair. 'So wha' me going do, Chief? Me got wife and pikaninny, and no rice land at all.'

Mac did his best to pacify him. Had he still been stationed at Leguan, the man might have appeared at his office with a chicken or a basket of fruit. A refusal would probably have led to mutters of racialism. The task of administration is never easy in Guiana.

At Supenaam, on the far bank, a cluster of houses and a timber yard. A carpet of sawdust on the landing, full of the tang of freshly cut boards, greenheart, mora and silverbali. Mac and Mr. Cassou went on to arrange for a jeep to Charity, some thirty miles away. From there a launch would be taking us right to the Moruca.

A couple of Indians came into sight, Arawaks from up river, poling a raft of logs down to the sawmill. I stopped to take a picture of them.

'Smile, buck-man,' shouted the East Indian launch-owner derisively. Two minutes ago, humility—now all arrogance. Incidents like this are not common, but the Indians are the only people on whom the coastal Guianese can inflict the treatment which they themselves have often received in the past. The two men made no reply. But their eyes smouldered and they watched closely to see if I would laugh.

The jeep was already waiting. As we sped down the road, we wound the windows up hurriedly whenever another car appeared, to protect ourselves from the choking dust. School-children turned to stare as we passed. A handful of women washing clothes in the brackish trench-water. The settlements were little townships, with rum shops and battered cars, more casual and less progressive than those of the east coast.

The north-west has a distinctive character. Known as the Forgotten Province, it has a crowded past. First there was the Dutch occupation, still echoed by its names and the crumbling ruins on its river banks, now overgrown with forest. When Guiana became British, at the close of the eighteenth century, the centre of settlement moved eastwards, to Georgetown and beyond. The land in the north-west was hardly used for sugar. After emancipation African families came to live there, well away from the ugly memories of the sugar estates. Disinherited and exhausted by generations of slavery, they did little to develop the region. For almost a century it was unnoticed. Then, in the 1890's, gold was suddenly discovered near the Venezuelan border. The north-west became the gateway to dreams of a new El Dorado. Gold fever swept through the country. Its symptoms, according to the *Colonial Gazette*, were 'a quickened pulse, increased vigour of the organs of respiration and a high degree of excitement pervading the whole nervous system'. Those afflicted were advised to visit the gold fields, which would 'either kill or cure the patient'. Over 10,000 porknockers rushed to the area. New townships sprang up—Better Hope, Charity, Land of Promise and Enterprise, transit points to the mining centres of Arakaka and Golden City. By 1894 Guiana was one of the world's main gold-producing countries. It was rumoured that sugar would soon be ousted from the economy. The Venezuelans showed their interest by laying a claim, which was promptly rejected, to the whole of the north-west. As it turned out, they had little to lose. The pay-dirt, as the gold was called, soon began to dwindle. By the turn of the century the shout was over. The north-west settled back into a torpor from which it has never recovered.

Charity is a ghost town of the prosperous nineties; a large administration office, rum shops and a few wooden houses, straggling along the end of the road beside the Pomeroon River. The Moruca launch was waiting for us, but the two Indians who had brought it down were nowhere to be seen. I wandered into the market to look for them. Here and there an Indian face, but none that I recognized.

Suddenly I felt a hand on my arm. I turned round and saw an old Portuguese, sitting on a packing case.

'You looking for someone, Skip?'

'Yes,' I said. 'You know an Indian called Solomon? He's from the Moruca.'

He shook his head. 'Never seen him. I don't believe you'd find him here. Why don't you take a rest, Skip?' He made room on the packing case.

I was glad to escape the heat for a moment and sat down beside him. He pulled out a bottle of rum and passed it over to me. His face was rugged and unshaven. One of his legs had been amputated.

Blood tests being taken among the Macusi by a member of the anti-malaria squad. During the past fifteen years the disease has been almost eradicated throughout Guiana

The Nappi resettlement scheme. Jack Dummett, the local agricultural officer, instructs one of the Macusi settlers in the use of a new piece of equipment

Macusi children learning English in the new school at Moka-Moka village. (Flash)

Aibilibing's house at Amokokopai. A traditional round-house providing for fifteen or twenty people

The last traditional house in a Seventh Day Adventist mission being abandoned in favour of a more modern style

An Akawaio village in which housing methods have been transformed mainly through missionary influence. The new style is incompatible with the Indians' way of life and the houses are rarely used except when the missionary is present

A modernized home in an Arawak village where the Indians have not learnt to be ashamed of traditional methods. While providing perfect standards of hygiene, it is built entirely of local materials and still allows for the Indians' way of life

'Auntie Bella' Atkinson, a Spanish Arawak of the Moruca district, wearing a pañuelo, the traditional Catholic head-dress

'Where you come from?' he asked. 'British?'

I nodded.

'Skip,' he said, 'I'm a British subject, an old British soldier. Born under the British flag and there I'm going to die.' He hiccuped and thrust his stubbled jaw forward. 'I fought in the First War, you know, West Indian Regiment, down in Egypt. The British are fine people— God sent them to rule the world.'

'Did you lose your leg in the war?' I asked, thinking that it might seem ungracious to offer an exchange of opinions on his last remark.

'No,' he said. 'I lost it right here, when I was hunting for diamonds. A sting-ray catch me, the wicked old bastard.' He took another swig of rum. 'But, Skip, I'm an educated man, a very historical man. Rooke, God save him, the British admiral—you know what year he captured Gibraltar?'

'1704,' I replied.

He roared in approval and slapped my knee. 'And you know who was the youngest general in the British Army?'

I was nonplussed. 'No, I forget.'

'Wolfe,' he said, with a bellow of triumph, 'Wolfe, at the siege of Quebec.' Suddenly his face lengthened. 'At Quebec those soldiers was rejoicing, but back in England, his poor mother, her only son. . . .' His eyes filled with distant tears. I almost felt a lump in my throat.

'But, Skip, I going to fight again.' He leant forward and whispered hoarsely. 'These coolies[1] don't like we Patagee. Is only this leg stopping me now from going to Georgetown to fight for the British. That old bastard sting-ray destroy me—and this thing,' he added, glancing reproachfully at the bottle. He paused. 'You could help me out, Skip?'

I felt in my pocket. He checked me suddenly.

'Don't let those coolies see,' he said, with an air of conspiracy. I slipped a coin into a cigarette packet, pulled it out and offered him one. He took it stealthily and looked at me with approval. 'Good British boy,' he said.

Suddenly I caught sight of Solomon, the Indian who was in charge of the launch. By now he must have been looking for me. I said goodbye to the old Portuguese.

'I glad to see you,' said Solomon. He grinned. 'Benson tell me you was coming.'

We hurried down to the launch, where Mac and Mr. Cassou were waiting. Charity slid away behind us. The green banks of the Pomeroon were dotted with small settlements and coconut plantations. Solomon

1. East Indians.

209

was sitting quietly in the engine room. I chatted to Mr. Cassou, hoping to learn something more about Indian policy. But he seemed reticent. His predecessor had made an official protest about one of my articles on the Indian situation. Although it had only discussed the period of British administration, which ended in 1961, I could sense that Mr. Cassou was uneasy. Yes, he said, in the past the Indians had been over-looked. The main trouble had been financial—there had never been enough money or staff in the Interior Department. An application for assistance had now been made to the United Nations; but Guiana had many major problems and this one had been relegated to a position of least priority. There were bound to be changes of policy, he added, but as yet they were undecided.

An hour or two later we reached the mouth of the Pomeroon. The launch rocked from side to side as we headed across an open bay towards the Moruca River. A pelican flew past the bow. Beyond us two large birds like cormorants folded their wings and plummeted down, vanishing in a cloud of spray, then mounting slowly upwards. We turned into a narrow gap in the mangrove swamp; a tangle of roots on either side, plunging into the dark mud. As we passed the Moruca sawmill, an Indian family waved to us from a corial.

The mangroves soon gave way to the swamp savanna which stretches for some twenty miles behind the coastal strip. An endless, water-logged solitude, broken by ité palms and occasional patches of dry land. The narrow river twisted onwards, edged with tall moka-moka reeds, whose constant swaying has lent their name to a popular Indian dance. The Moruca Indians arrived here in August 1817, during the bloodthirsty war of independence in neighbouring Venezuela. Before this they lived in the Orinoco, as members of the Catholic missions which kept them loyal to the Spanish crown. Encouraged by the Capuchin priests, they resisted the rebels fiercely. The outcome was described in a rousing funeral oration delivered at Barcelona in 1818. A translation of it survives in the archives of the Moruca mission:

'When the rebellion against Spain reached Venezuelan Guyana, in the Lower Orinoco, there were twenty-nine flourishing Catholic missions in that district, with a population of over 21,000; and, be it said to their glory, they remained faithful to their King and defended themselves right manfully. . . . The insurgent rebels tried every year to invade the villages, but always in vain, for the Fathers took the best and most efficacious means to withstand them, calling their Indians to arms. In consequence the community incurred the resentment of the rebels to such an extreme that they were threatened with the terrible expression that of the beards of the Capuchin Fathers they would make halters for their horses. At last they succeeded in their wicked design, God, in his inscrutable purpose, permitting them. At the end of January 1817, they seized the villages by surprise, an event which was followed by the cruel massacre of thirty Capuchin Missionary Fathers. . . .'

Meanwhile the Indians had fled. Most of them vanished into the forest, but a small band crossed the border, paddling through a network of creeks which were unknown to their pursuers. When they reached British soil, they appealed to Governor Murray, who allowed them to settle on a group of islands beside the Moruca River. A few years later they were visited by Hilhouse, the Indian Quartermaster. 'The Spanish refugees are about a hundred in number,' he reported. 'These Indians are very industrious and expert in the use of firearms. Their cultivation is very extensive and their houses of a much superior description to those of the coastal tribes.'[1]

Gradually they intermarried with the local Arawaks and Warraus. To distinguish them from the other Indians, they became known as the Spanish Arawaks. Their old loyalties survived and in 1840 a Catholic mission called Santa Rosa was founded on Kabukali, the largest of their islands. Later a school was started. Spanish was still spoken until the end of the nineteenth century, when English was introduced. Since then they have made rapid progress. Their district was singled out for some of the earliest and most important Indian development schemes. It is also the birth-place of Stephen Campbell, the Indian politician. Many of the younger people have been to secondary school in Georgetown. During the past few weeks I had met several of them, teaching among the other tribes. They seemed to have reached the point towards which the other Indians were struggling. But had this really been successful? And how did they feel about a future which they could now assess?

We were held up for a while—the engine was giving trouble. By the time Solomon had repaired it, dusk was settling down. Stillness in the space around us, save for the lonely cries of the marsh birds and the occasional plop of a fish. Two hours later we saw the lights of Akwero, the first large island, with the officer's quarters, a rest house and a few Indian homes.

One or two figures came down to meet us. The first was old Mrs. Atkinson, Nash's aunt, who was known to all simply as 'Auntie Bella'. She was still in charge of the rest house where I had stayed three years ago. She greeted me in surprise and bustled round as we unpacked. Outside, the familiar silhouette of the palm trees and the nearby houses.

1. William Hilhouse, *Indian Notices* (Georgetown, 1825).

We had been travelling for eighteen hours. We chatted for a while and then retired to sleep.

'The old man asking to see you,' said Auntie Bella, early the next morning, as she pattered round the rest house, removing imaginary specks of dust from the spotless tables and chairs. 'He heard how you come back. He say is a long time he ain't talk to you.'

I leant on the balcony for a moment. A stone's throw away, the narrow Moruca, winding towards Kabukali Island. I could just see the mission of Santa Rosa with the white-roofed primary school beside it, enclosed by coconut palms. A corial drifted by, laden with school-children. I recognized George and Elaine, two of the Indian teachers, both born in the Moruca. They were smartly dressed, almost as if they were setting out to work in Georgetown; but like the children they still travelled in a corial.

I went over to see Eugene, Auntie Bella's husband. When I was first in the Moruca, we had spent many evenings together, as he taught me Indian basket-work and described his days with the Boundary Commission in the 1930's. I peered into their dark little house. He gave me a twinkling smile and pulled out a gnarled old pipe as I sat down beside him.

'I hear you been travelling about,' he said. 'And you seen the boy Nash, too?'

'Yes,' I replied, 'he sent you good wishes.' We chatted about the Rupununi.

'That fan I teach you to make—you still got it?' he asked with a chuckle.

'Yes,' I said, 'I still got it.'

'You should have stayed more long,' he added. 'You was learning all right.'

Auntie Bella had been busy. She placed a breakfast of eggs, cassava bread and local coffee in front of me. Their background had given the Moruca people a standard of living and ease of manner unknown to the rest of the Indians.

'Things change since you been here,' she said. 'Some of my grand-children gone away, working in Georgetown and teaching in school. And you scarcely hear the old music now, with shak-shak and mando-lin.'

'Yes,' said Eugene, 'they forgetting it.'

'But we staying peaceful,' said Auntie Bella. 'I been to Georgetown last year and as soon as I meet I want to come back. We old people like this place.'

A face appeared in the narrow doorway. 'Is you, Colin?' said a familiar voice. For a moment I was dazzled by the sunlight, streaming in from outside. Then I suddenly recognized Benson, with whom I had worked on my previous visit. He laughed as we shook hands. 'I been waiting for you all this time,' he said. 'So how's the travel going?'

I told him about the past three months.

'I'm still working in the office,' he said. 'I got to hustle over there now. But we going to get plenty of time to talk. You coming over with me?'

Mac and Mr. Cassou were there. I sat in a corner while they went through the files on a nearby resettlement scheme known as the Kumaka Road. Its scale and expense made it the most important development project among the Indians. It was one of the main things which I hoped to see while I was in the Moruca.

Half an hour later we set out to see John Ferreira, the local Captain. Solomon gave me a subdued grin as we stepped into the open boat. Being an employee of the Interior Department, he was slightly over-awed by the presence of the others. The spray curtained up on either side of us as we swept round the narrow bends, slowing down each time we passed a corial. I recognized some of the Indians' faces, less passive than those of the other tribes. Many of the women wore golden orna-ments, a legacy from the Spanish days of their ancestors. We passed Kabukali on our right. A cluster of corials at the landing, with well built houses behind them and a path leading to the nearby school and the mission.

Two minutes later we reached Kumaka, where John Ferreira lived. We turned into a narrow inlet beside his wooden store. With a streak of Portuguese blood, he was the most ambitious of the Moruca Indians. Three years ago he had been the up-and-coming politician of the district, with sound ideas on local development and Indian policy. Since then he had been elected Captain. He was also an astute business man. The store had made him prosperous. He had his own launch and a large new house was being built for him. We found him supervising the men who were working on it. He had aged. A touch of grey at his temples, over a rather long face.

'What are the main problems here?' asked Mac, after a brief round of introductions.

The Indian mind tends to withdraw when faced with authority. Even John was no exception. He seemed nervous as he replied. 'Well, there's the road scheme. The people finding it hard to settle. They got so much heavy forest to clear. And then there's a long time to wait before the crops are ready.'

'What crops are you planting?' asked Mac.

'We starting with cassava,' he said. 'Then we go on to cocoa and coconuts. But we still finding it hard. The Government tells us to grow these new crops and then sometimes we can't sell them.'

We chatted on for a few minutes. Mac seemed dissatisfied when we left. He felt that John had nothing concrete to say. Yet I knew from my own acquaintance with him that he was one of the most advanced thinkers among the Indians. Neither side was responsible for this lack of communication. It was simply a matter of temperament. The Indians themselves were shy, while officialdom has a formality which makes them uneasy.

We crossed the river to Kabukali, where we were met by Ruben Stoby. For many years he had been Captain of the Moruca, with the only shop in the district. His word was law until he was ousted by his younger rival, John Ferreira. Local politics were still a good-natured battle between them, with their shops on either side of the river serving as debating centres. There was no inhibition about the burly, tempestuous figure of Uncle Ben, as the Indians called him. Always joking and out-spoken, he had publicly rebuked a succession of Governors for their neglect of the Indians.

He led us inside his shop, a long building where the shelves were stacked with sweets, tinned foods, coloured cloth and locally made baskets. Two attractive looking girls stood behind the counter. A few women were buying food. They watched us with curiosity.

Ruben always enjoyed an audience. He opened three bottles of coca-cola and banged them down on the counter. 'What about the bridge?' he asked, with a look of good-humoured aggression, directed straight at Mr. Cassou.

'The bridge?' asked Mr. Cassou.

'Yes,' said Ruben, 'the bridge we wanting, to cross the river from here to Kumaka. That way the children can get to school easy and the people can reach the farms.'

'It's a good idea,' said Mr. Cassou, 'but the funds aren't available now.'

'But is not the first time we ask,' said Ruben. 'I tell the Governor when he been here. Then I tell the Minister and the last Interior Commissioner. Now I tell you, and like nothing going happen.' He looked at me with a broad grin. No one was ever left out of his game. 'Ask Mr. Henfrey. He been here and living with us. He knows we Indians. Is not true we need a bridge?'

Ruben was in command. I nodded.

214

'Next year we should have funds,' Mr. Cassou assured him. 'We'll see what we can do about it.'

A sceptical grunt from Ruben. But he grinned again as we said good-bye, knowing that he had at least entertained us. I promised to come back and see him later. Now that the Moruca was almost caught up in the mainstream of Guianese affairs, he might easily have become a political figure, had he been ten years younger.

That afternoon we returned to Kumaka for a meeting of the Producers' Co-operative Society. It had been founded some ten years before, to encourage the Indians' agriculture by arranging the sale of their crops —cassava, coffee and copra. For a while it seemed to be creating a new economy. But the market for cassava soon dwindled and the cost of transport to the coast made it hard for the Indians to gain a profit. They had never really grasped the complex design of the society. As soon as it began to fail, suspicion set in. They felt that they had been exploited by yet another confusing aspect of the coastal world. There had been too wide a gap between the plans and the people involved. Had they been carefully consulted, the society could have been given a form which they understood and trusted.

The Moruca Indians were not yet inflicted with a sense of time. When we reached the Co-operative building, only a few people were there. Ruben, sitting defiantly in the middle of the front bench, as if challenging the world to remove him; an old man called Bernardo, who was one of the keenest local farmers, and two or three women at the back, whispering to each other. Gradually the others arrived in their corials. By the time the meeting began, some thirty people had come; faces that were usually alert, now passive in response to the official atmosphere.

The proceedings were supervised by an officer from the Guianese Co-operative Department. The local secretary began by reading the minutes of the previous meeting. His audience showed little reaction. The Co-operative Officer then stood up and delivered a long report on the results of his last visit. Production was low, he said. Share capital was going down and their machinery was lying idle. The Indians had ignored the Government's 'goodwill and solicitude'; their indifference was 'a classic form of ingratitude'. I felt that this would hardly encourage them, but when the report came to an end, there were murmurs of assent. Clearly very little of it had been understood.

Its details suggested that the society was still on the decline. But it scarcely touched on the reasons for this. With a large area to cover, the officer could only pay occasional visits to the Moruca. When he was there, he was taken up with administrative questions. He had little chance to examine the human factors behind them.

A few other points were raised. 'I see that a lot of people are leaving the society,' said the officer gravely. 'Does anyone know the reason for this?'

The Indians glanced at each other. A pause. Eventually Ruben spoke up. 'We hear this new Government going to take away the society money. So the people want to take back their share before a next man get it. Is that making them leave the society.'

The others whispered in agreement. It was typical of the way in which rumour could spread, simply for want of someone to explain an issue to them. The officer tried to reassure them, but they still looked suspicious.

Eventually he changed the subject. 'I think you should try some new crops,' he said. 'And livestock too—you could start keeping goats.'

Giggles amongst the women—the usual reaction to novelty. 'We don't know about that,' said a man's voice. 'If we get these goats, they going stray about and drink the cassava water. That would surely poison them.'

This time the officer looked unconvinced. 'What about new crops?' he asked.

'I been trying some,' said Bernardo. 'I grow some fine peanuts and sell them. But next time they all fail. I didn't know the right way to plant them. We don't see the Agricultural Officer, to get advice about how to work. Since then I ain't try again.'

'Yes,' said a voice from the back, 'we ain't see the man at all. He ain't talk to nobody, only sit and listen to radio. We frighten to go to him, because he only get vexed with us.'

At last the discussion seemed to be reaching a productive level. The Indians themselves were the only people who knew the real reasons why their development was going so slowly. By now they had almost lost their restraint. Their genuine feelings were emerging. But suddenly the issue was cut short.

'Are there any more questions?' asked the officer curtly. The meeting slipped back into a startled silence. But Ruben was not so easily subdued.

'This politics is the trouble,' he said. 'Look how it got we people confused. One person say one thing, a next person say another—we can't trust any of them. We Indians need more education, someone to explain these things.'

The officer made no further comment. Perhaps this was simply regarded as Ruben's inevitable parting grumble. The meeting was brought to an end. The Indians drifted away again, still betraying no reaction. But once they were in their corials and paddling back home together, all their feelings would emerge.

'You see how lazy they are?' said the officer, when we were back at Akwero. 'That idea of keeping goats—the cassava water was just an excuse. The trouble is they're too lazy.'

The sun was stooping over the islands. The children were bathing together, leaping off the top of the launch and tumbling each other out of their corials. It reminded me of countless evenings three years ago: but then I had never quite known the complexities which lay beneath this laughter and sunshine surface.

The next day Mac and Mr. Cassou were continuing to the north-west. Thanks to the Kumaka Road scheme, the Moruca was now linked with the Waini River, some twenty miles away. A launch was due to meet them there, at a settlement called Quebana.

We left Kumaka landing by jeep. We were joined by a couple of Indian families who were on the way to their farms. The 'road' was simply a dirt track which cut through the heavy forest, with clearings on either side. It was started in 1955, as the basis of a scheme which is similar to the Nappi project. Ever since the gold rush days, the Indians of the north-west, consisting of Arawaks, Warraus and Caribs, have been declining steadily. Resettlement seems to be the only way of providing for them. The land stretching behind Kumaka, from the Moruca to the Waini, is all fertile virgin forest. Like the Nappi region, it could support several hundred families. In view of this, the Kumaka road was backed with a hundred and fifty thousand dollars, by far the largest sum ever spent on an Indian project. It would stretch for twenty-two miles, from the Moruca to the Waini, with ten acre lots on either side. The Indians would leave their scattered homes, amongst the swamp lands of the north-west, in order to settle there. Potentially, this offered an outlet for dozens of dwindling communities. A few families were already there. It was hoped that they would support themselves by growing new crops for sale to the coast.

The rough sand road dipped over a hill and past a few scattered clearings, planted with young cassava. But the pace of settlement seemed to be slow. There was little sign of new crops, and cultivation was spas-modic after the first few miles; the forest soon towered up unbroken on either side of us. We drove on for almost an hour. I was surprised that we hadn't stopped at any of the farms. Then I remembered the last four miles, which we would have to cover by foot. There were also a few Indian settlers there. Perhaps we would have a chance to talk to them.

Mac had shared my observations. 'There's not much settlement yet, is there?' he said, as we stepped out of the jeep. 'And they don't seem to be growing anything but the usual cassava. It must have been almost the same when you were here, eh, Colin?'

'Yes,' I replied, 'but maybe it's because of the problem they raised at yesterday's meeting—when they said they needed advice from the Agricultural Officer.'

'Yes,' said Mac, 'but one man can't possibly visit all these farms. And he hasn't any means of transport.'

'But why not?'

'There's no money for it.'

'But they've managed to build him a large house,' I said, remembering a new building which we had seen at Kumaka. 'I'd have thought it was more important for him to have some means of visiting the people.'

Mac shrugged. 'Maybe. But a man from Georgetown wouldn't live in any other conditions. You've got to remember that. The trouble is, Colin, you see everything through Indian eyes.'

We stopped to talk to Eugene Stoby, Ruben's oldest son, who was in charge of a group of men working on the road. He answered a few brief questions from Mac and Mr. Cassou. They seemed to be mainly concerned with technical aspects of the scheme—the surfacing of the road and the design of a wooden bridge which was being built nearby.

Five minutes later we walked on. The farms soon began again. Here they were being opened up mainly by settlers from the Waini. One or two families were at work, pausing to watch us shyly from behind the tall stems of cassava. But the others seemed to be in a hurry. They showed no sign of turning aside to talk to the Indians.

I dropped back to join the local officer, who was just behind me. 'Aren't we going to stop at any of the farms?' I asked.

'Well,' he said, 'you'd see the same things at each one of them.'

'But what kind of things?'

'The crops—just cassava and bananas.'

'But what about the people themselves? Aren't we going to talk to them?'

'I don't believe there's much point,' he said. 'Their complaints are always the same.'

'Always the same? But doesn't that suggest that nothing's been done about them?'

He hesitated. 'Well, I'm not sure,' he replied. 'It's the first time I've been up here. But it's hard to get these people to change.'

'But there seem to be so few of them here, considering the money spent on the scheme. Wouldn't you find out the reasons for this, if you talked to them?'

'Perhaps,' he said. 'But it's not so easy to get their confidence. Sometimes they're afraid of officials. There's not much we can do really.'

The launch was waiting at Quebana, a little village beside the broad-flowing Waini. We had lunch together before they set out. 'You're not saying much,' Mac commented. 'Anything wrong?' I felt churlish. It would be some time before I saw him again. We shook hands and said goodbye. A group of children came and joined me in the shade of a cashew tree, as I watched the launch disappearing.

I started back down the road, in the hope of getting time to talk to some of the Indians. I soon caught up with some children on their way back from school.

'How far you going?' I asked.

'Till at Yarrow Creek,' they replied. It was not far from the point where we had left the jeep—an eight mile walk every day.

'What are your names?'

'Gabriel,' said a little boy, round-faced, sturdy and dark. He pointed to his two companions. 'And this one Francis and he Daniell.'

'Where you come from?'

'Manawarin.'

I had once been to the Manawarin region. Its inhabitants are mainly Caribs, descendants of the warlike tribe, who have now retreated up the creeks, broken by their contact with civilization.

The children were whispering to each other. 'You been to Manawarin,' said Gabriel shyly. 'You stop and play games with we all.' I was touched. It was nearly three years ago. The school-children there had made me a basket, which I still had, back in England.

'Is here we living now,' said Gabriel. He turned aside to a little camp on the edge of a clearing. His father met us, stocky and ragged. The camp was almost empty.

'How long have you been here?' I asked.

'Three or four months we come from Manawarin.'

'And the farm going all right now?'

He looked doubtful. 'Is hard work clearing this forest. And we scarcely get food here. This creek got no fish. Things was better at Manawarin.'

'But you're growing new crops?'

'No, only this cassava. We ain't know about new crops. Nobody tell us nothing. And we got to pay for the coconut plants. We got no money, so we can't buy.'

I said goodbye and carried on. I stopped to talk to Eugene again, a burly younger version of his father, genial but with a serious expression.

'Yes,' he said, 'the road's coming on since you was first here. We expect to finish next year.'

'But it doesn't look as if people are using the land,' I said.

'Yes,' he replied, 'they getting discouraged. They find it hard to clear the forest. When they come here, they got no food and they got to work for a couple of months, cutting down the trees. Then they got to wait again before the cassava is ready. And you know how we Indians live— no money, no savings, just what we get each day. Is that making it hard for them. They need someone to move among them, and find out about these things.'

By the time I reached the jeep I had kept the others waiting. We bounced down the road back to Kumaka, with a crowd of children clinging on to the back. Their faces reminded me of Mac's comment. But how else could one view the scheme, except through Indian eyes? The personality of the Indians was its raw material. They still lived from day to day. Having no source of food nearby, they naturally found it hard to provide for the early stages of settlement. There was no allowance for this. And the idea of permanent crops was new and essentially long term. No one had managed, or perhaps even tried, to convince them of its value. These were the results of a system, not of the individuals concerned;[1] development was still treated as a part of administration. Eugene had realized what was wanted—someone in close touch with the Indians, who could adapt the scheme to their needs, as Jack Dummett had done at Nappi. This was the only basis on which it could succeed.

A fiery sunset between the ité palms, signature of the dry season, which was approaching at last. The sound of bare feet on the steps of the rest house. Benson's nine year old twin sisters, the spitting image of each other, nicknamed Piggy and Buck.

'Look, we bring whitey for you.' They pile their present on to the table, a handful of green pods with sweet white seeds inside them. 'Is what you writing?' They press forward. 'Piggy, look how he writing funny.' Suddenly they remember their mission. 'Benson say you must eat with us, now them people gone. We mummy cook supper. They waiting now.'

1. The plans for this particular scheme were drawn up well before Mr. Cassou became Commissioner of the Interior.

They seize me, one by each hand, and lead me through the lantern-lit darkness to where they live at the back of the island. A wooden house, small but well built. The light falls on hibiscus blooms, deep scarlet, out in the yard. Inside, it is similar to homes in the coastal villages. Two or three rough chairs, hammocks for the children, but beds in the inner room, where their parents sleep. A stove burning in the kitchen, with only a pile of cassava bread to make it an Indian setting.

Benson's father, Bertie, appeared, a well built, patriarchal figure, now stooping slightly. Like many of the Moruca Indians, he was widely travelled. He had worked with the Boundary Commission, and then on the local dispenser's launch. He had since retired and opened a shop at Akwero. He was justly proud of his family, which was one of the most talented in the Moruca. All his eight children had striking looks, due partly to a trace of Spanish blood in their ancestry. Bertie had been ambitious for them. His three eldest sons, including Benson, had been to secondary schools in Georgetown. But this imposed a difficult choice. They could either stay in the interior, which offered them no real outlet, or else they could go to Georgetown, where they tended to feel out of place. Only Benson had found a job within the Moruca itself. The next son, Leon, had been a cartographer; but now, growing tired of the coast, he had come back to help his father in the family shop. Kenneth, aged seventeen, was working as a Post Office clerk in Georgetown. I had met him there not long ago, half urbanized and lonely. Had local outlets been developed, this gulf could have been bridged. With an agricultural training centre for instance, their temperament and ability could both have been satisfied.

'You heard how we worried with this politics?' said Bertie, as his wife appeared with our supper. 'We don't know what this new Government is doing. It looks like the mother country is deserting the Indians.'

The Moruca people's conservatism is a legacy from the days when they fought for the Spanish Crown in the Venezuelan war of independence. Now that the British are leaving Guiana, their descendants feel that the crisis is being repeated.

I tried to persuade Bertie that his fears were probably groundless. 'I think it's just that the people on the coast never had a chance to know the Indians. If they get the chance now, I don't believe they'll be unfriendly.'

But Bertie still looked perplexed. 'So you been up the road today?' said Benson.

'Yes,' I replied, 'right to Quebana.'

'And how you think it's making out?'

'I'm not so sure. The people seem to be finding it hard.'

'Yes,' he said, 'they scarcely settling there. And if one man says he finding it hard, the others wouldn't come in a hurry. If this scheme's going to work out, I believe these development people got to see it in a different way.'

'How? By explaining it to the Indians?'

'Yes,' said Benson, 'just so. And by knowing what they feel about it. That would encourage them.'

As we talked, Leon arrived with some beer from the family shop. Piggy and Buck were sitting in a corner, whispering to each other. Eugene was looking through a heap of postcards, sent to him by a pen-friend in Germany. But Bertie was watching us, grave-faced. He had hardly said a word since his first anxious enquiry.

'You know,' said Benson the next day, as we sat in the open boat-house, 'the things we were talking about last night, they got me interested. I've been thinking about it since you were here—about the things we young people could be doing in the Moruca.'

Outside, the landscape was fading into a toneless grey. A flicker of lightning and a roll of thunder. The wind rose, lashing the roof and driving a blanket of rain across the level horizon.

'What about the road scheme?' I asked. 'Wouldn't they take part in that?'

'I don't believe so,' he said. 'They don't feel it's going to work out.' He paused. 'There's one thing I'd like to do—I want to learn something more about this community development. You must send me some books about it. I hear they got a place in America where you can study it. I'd like to try for a scholarship there and come back to work in the Moruca.'

I knew there was little chance of this. Most of the scholarships for Guianese were going to members of the P.P.P. and its junior branch, the Progressive Youth Organization. Yet, with the necessary training, Benson's enthusiasm could have been vital to the Moruca.

The rain had almost died down. I decided to visit the school, up at Kabukali. Benson shouted to a little boy who was passing in a corial. 'You could take Mr. Henfrey to Kabukali?'

'No school today?' I asked, as we paddled down river.

The little boy looked at me cautiously and then grinned. 'No, I got a bad cold'—and a profitable one, too, judging by the pile of fish in the bottom of his corial. Nor had it spoiled his appetite; as soon as we reached Kabukali, he scampered off to Ruben's shop to buy himself some sweets.

I walked over to the school. Past a grove of citrus trees and along a path through a narrow swamp. The chanting sound of children's voices, echoing out of a large wooden building on a slight hill. Like all denominational schools, it had now been taken over by the Government. But the nuns, who had previously run it, still played an important part. Most of the teachers were recruited from amongst their former pupils. I sat at the back and watched them for a while—Elaine, with one of the junior classes and George, who had been trained in Georgetown, with a group of older children. They both had the patience and understanding which were harder for a coastal teacher to acquire. Beyond them stood one of the nuns, dressed in flowing white robes. The school was the centre of the children's lives, even if they sometimes played truant when the fish were jumping. A few of them, mainly orphans, were still cared for by the nuns in the nearby convent.

The Catholic mission had done a great deal for the Moruca people. Its only weakness was its conservatism. The local priest and most of the nuns were still Europeans. The new left wing Government made them uneasy, and their feelings had spread to the Indians. Here, as in other colonial territories, the Church had become identified with colonial rule. In failing to change this identity, it had lost much of its influence.

But the secularization of the school gave the Moruca its first real taste of politics. It was not a pleasant one. The Government's aims were understandable, but their methods proved alarming. The local priest told me that he was not informed of their plans. The nun who acted as headteacher was abruptly dismissed. A substitute was sent from the coast, but as he did very little the Indians felt that his appointment was political. Their protests were ignored, and the children then went on strike, refusing to attend school. The situation was now a stalemate; the new head-teacher was away 'on leave', and one of the nuns was acting for him. The Indian teachers also suffered. At the end of the year the best qualified pupils always applied for teaching posts. Recently most of their applications had been unanswered or rejected. The vacancies were filled by teachers from the coast. This was also interpreted as a political move.

All these changes had increased the Indians' inherent suspicion. As I walked back through Kabukali, I found that it was still strong in Ruben Stoby's mind. He was sitting in the open parlour behind his shop, sharing a bottle of rum with two Indians whose faces I knew. Liquor was forbidden on the reservation, but Ruben had drunk it for years, largely on principle.

'Mr. Henfrey'—he raised a hand in lordly greeting. It was an ines-capable summons. He pointed to the bottle with a mischievous look, by way of invitation. One of the men brought forward a chair, as I came to join them.

Ruben glanced round at the others. 'Mr. Henfrey, what you think of this Government? Is a cockroach Government, no?'

'Why so?'

'Because they don't like we Indians. I feel we was happy all these years. Now the Government changing up, we coming into politics and getting kind of embarrassed.'

'What sort of embarrassment?'

His quizzical face grew serious. An audience was gathering outside. A few schoolboys and a couple of women; then, for a moment, Auntie Bella, on her way to the mission, wearing a pañuelo, the traditional Catholic head-dress, made of a white kerchief.

Ruben was aware of them. He banged the table emphatically. 'The main object is our lands. We're afraid our lands will be taken from us. Where you born, there is your birth-place. We feel that this land of Guiana is we Indians' land.'

'So what do you think about Independence?'

'Well, Independence means to say that you must have what is yours. But we Indians aren't certain of nothing. We aren't the people who making the laws. That is the people in the cities. We got no word in it.'

'True,' said one of the others, 'is so. And we don't trust those people.'

Ruben leant forward again. 'If the Queen had thought for we Indians, no one would get no Independence in this country now. You see, when the white people come here, they find we Indians, they treat us good and everything was all right. But now things changing, and change got us worried. Is only one thing we Indians want, and that is to live peaceful. We ain't want no race story. Black man and East Indian is we friend. We only want to live peaceful. That is the whole story.'

Ruben's conservative views expressed the anxiety of many of the Indians. British rule and the reservations had given them a sense of security. Few of them realized that this system had actually caused their anxiety, by suggesting a need for protection. For Ruben it remained an ideal. But in fact it could never last. Contacts with the coast were increasing and the reservations were bound to be opened some time after Independence. With a careful policy, designed to build confidence on both sides, this need not threaten the Indians' welfare.

Being a much younger man, John Ferreira had different views. I talked to him on several occasions, over the counter of his shop. Benson took me to see him again on the day before I was due to leave. It was almost dusk by the time we arrived. The sound of a wireless from the back room and a murmur of voices behind us, as his daughter gossiped with a bevy of girls who were buying food and cloth.

'You see, we got so many problems,' said John. 'The biggest one is the economy, like we was talking about with the other two gentlemen. We need agricultural development and more help with the road scheme. But the thing that really got us worried is this politics.'

'But what do you feel about them?'

'Well, I think it's hard for us. The people got used to the old ways and so they don't want to change. They're frightened of losing the reservation. But I feel the British have done a great harm by keeping this reservation—it learned us to live in dependency. They thought we was just a Cinderella people. They feel the Indians are primitive, it doesn't matter how they live. But that wasn't right. It made us like children. We've got no experience of outside affairs. They should have changed the reservation, allowing it to develop for the benefit of our children.'

'But how do you think they should have changed it?'

He thought for a moment. 'Well, I would have liked it to be the same as the reservations in Canada, where outside people can come and live with the Indians. In that way we could learn from them. This road scheme, for example—the outside people could have shown us what to do in our farming. The new Government should study that. They should let outsiders come here, to get the people accustomed.'

'But when·Independence comes, how do you think it will affect the Indians?'

'Well,' he said, 'you know how most of us been voting for the U.F. We hoping now that Stephen Campbell would make the Government do something for us. If we get consideration, we could make out all right. But politics makes life hard for the Indians, especially the most primitive ones. They're frightened about this Independence and about people from the coast. It might make them flee to the forest, over to Brazil and Venezuela.'

John's views were well thought out. But no one had ever consulted the Indians about the policy applied to them. He had suggested the possible outcome. Changes would now alarm them, by creating a situation for which they were not prepared.

'I got a machine like that,' he said, indicating my tape-recorder. 'I'll play something for you.' He delved underneath the counter and brought out a new-looking tape-recorder. 'Is a little talk I gave,' he explained.

225

'When we was voting for the council[1] here, I had to describe things to the people.'

He switched the tape-recorder on. The others were suddenly quiet, as his voice came through, slow and solemn, reading a carefully prepared speech. 'As your Captain, I am bound to explain what your council is doing for you. First we must understand that we are not living the lives of our foreparents. We must now give up the old ways. As you know already, most of us have adopted the English way of living. We have clothing, stores, lamps, outboard motors and radios, etc. So you see we are going ahead steadily. So also rules and laws has to go together with our development. Another thing your council is doing is to defend you before the Government about your land, your health and your rights. So I ask you to come and vote for your council. Put someone there who will fight your case before the Government.'

He turned the tape-recorder off. There was a moment's silence. The others had been listening closely, although they must have heard it before. Politics were nothing new, but now, for the first time, they had realized how they might be affected by them. Their future, as John's speech had shown, was seen as a fight for recognition.

Benson was waiting for me outside. I was leaving with John at two in the morning—his launch was going down river to meet the steamer from Georgetown. Meanwhile, Benson and his friends had arranged a farewell party over at Kabukali. We paddled round the bend and across the river to Ruben's landing. A corial passed slowly by. From the depths of the moka-moka reeds, the intermittent croaking of frogs. Fireflies dotting the darkness and the sound of music as we reached the island. The party had already begun.

Most of the young people were there—Elaine, George and the other teachers, Eloise, a relation of Stephen Campbell, Benson's brother Leon and a dozen others. All the girls wore colourful dresses and some of them were in high heels, with their hair up. John Ferreira had been right. There was no time to look back to the past. And here there seemed to be little need. There was none of the ragged uncertainty which I had seen elsewhere. Instead, a group of young people who were virtually Westernized and quite able to live on equal terms with the coastal Guianese.

The gramophone was playing a calypso. George came over and sat beside us. Benson found three bottles of beer—there was no sign of cassiri.

1. Several of the more advanced Indian districts now have councils which meet regularly and deal mainly with aspects of local development schemes (see Appendix B).

'Colin, man, why you go back to England?' asked Benson. 'Stop here and work with us again.'

'Yes,' said George. 'But you know, Benson, we've got to work for ourselves now. And look'—he pointed to the others—'there's nothing stopping us.' He turned to me. 'I'd like to start a study group here,' he said, 'to find out what's happening and see what we could do in the future. I've been discussing it with the others. When you get back to England, I'll write to you about it.'

I watched them dancing for a moment. High heels tapping to the rhythm of calypso and laughter on their faces. They had some positive quality, perhaps just confidence, which the other Indians had not yet acquired. They had shown that they could not only survive, but also make good their complete adaptation; and despite its being so complete, they still enjoyed the Moruca. Change had not cut them off from their own community or the rest of their people. In many cases, such as Benson and George, it had created a genuine interest in the problems which faced them. Their mixed blood and Catholic background had given them a certain advantage; but apart from this there was no reason why the same should not be achieved among all the Indians.

I got up to dance with Eloise, a slight figure in a pale orange dress, with her dark hair swept up behind her head; eyes that had little of the nervous shyness of Indian girls elsewhere. As the music came to an end, George stood up in front of the others. It was a farewell party, he said— but only half one of farewell. In the old days there had been a ceremony of initiation into the tribe. Now it was forgotten and instead they could only give a party—but this was what they meant by it. As he sat down, Elaine came forward and gave me a bunch of flowers. I thanked them all. There was more to be said, but it seemed unnecessary. Benson looked round at me. He laughed and turned the music on again. Gaiety came back easily.

The hours passed rapidly. We suddenly realized that it was nearly two o'clock. Benson and I decided to leave unobtrusively. But the others protested. We linked arms and danced our way down the path, with the music fading behind us. We reached the landing breathless and laughing. Then, unmistakably, the sound of John Ferreira's launch from over at Kumaka.

We said goodbye for the last time. They laughed again, as Benson and I wobbled out on to the river in his corial. Then, as we left them behind, there was silence, still silence of the savanna, broken by the sound of our paddles and the putter of the launch, growing steadily closer. We reached Akwero just ahead of it and packed my belongings hurriedly.

'You left the flowers,' said Benson suddenly, as we went down to the launch. He ran back to fetch them for me. 'Write to me when you reach England,' he said. 'I'll come and see you there one day.'

Akwero vanished into the darkness. 'You could sleep,' said John, with a smile. I slung my hammock inside the launch. Three hours later, the Pomeroon mouth, covered with mist and strangely empty. And a bunch of pale savanna flowers; reminder of Moruca faces.

II

Orealla: the End of a Journey

GEORGETOWN again. Jostling crowds and city smells. The slow clatter of donkey carts, pierced by the blaring of horns. A matter of days before I must leave. There was just time to revisit Orealla and say goodbye to the Indians.

Nine o'clock at the wooden station, its green paint peeled by the blinding sun. The platform was almost deserted. I had just missed the morning train. The guard looked at me sleepily. 'Next train? About twelve o'clock. And a hot journey, man.'

Three hours to wait. I left my bag and walked down Main Street, cool and shadowed beneath the plane trees. At the far end the crowds were gathering, lining the pavement and blocking the road, chattering, arguing restlessly as they waited for the report on the riots, which was about to be published.[1] I crossed over to the museum to see Vincent Roth, the curator. Now in his seventies, he is the most knowledgeable person alive on almost every Guianese topic, especially the Indians.

'Where are you off to now?' he asked, as he shuffled across his office.

'Back to Orealla,' I replied.

'Going home again, eh?' he chuckled. 'I hear it's a nice spot up there. And when are you leaving B.G.?'

'On Wednesday.' Just five days time. It was hard to believe that the Oxford term began in just a week.

'I wonder what they'll be up to next,' he said, pointing down at the queues below us. They were pushing their way towards Bookers Stores, where copies of the official report were now on sale. Agitated groups were forming, waving their arms and discussing its contents, regardless of the traffic. Faces with suspicion on them; others casual, carefree and grinning. A crowd which would laugh or riot again at a moment's

1. Its findings are discussed in Appendix A.

notice—unwitting neighbours of the Indians, whom they could easily save or destroy.

Two hours later, the familiar landscape of palm trees and paddy fields. The Berbice train was unusually peaceful. Unlike my journey of three months ago, this one provided no James to entertain me. Only two motherly African women, all frills and floppy hats, protesting weakly at the heat. They smiled and sighed, offered me peanuts and fell asleep soon after we left Georgetown.

The sun poured in through the rickety window, making me drowsy. I nodded. The rattling of the train grew misty. I was back in the Moruca. Night time, a party, old Ruben Stoby dancing a wild calypso. Flowers, dark hair and the sound of cicadas. Benson was shaking me by the arm, I must hurry, the launch was leaving. I opened my eyes and came face to face with my genial travelling companions. 'Mister, you was sleepin' hard. Sometime you dreamin' about you gal.' Two broad smiles, and they shook with laughter. 'We meet Rosignol.'

The light was already softening over New Amsterdam, as the ferry swung slowly across the Berbice River. The bumpy, cattle-strewn Corentyne road, in an overloaded taxi. It was dark by the time we reached Springlands.

The flicker of a lantern from the Indian depôt behind the gas station. I wondered who was there. The whisper of voices died away as I tapped on the wooden door. Solomon, a boy from Orealla, and three or four people from Siparuta, a small village farther up river. Among them was Morris, the Indian boat-hand who worked for the Forestry Department. The launch was going up the next day, he said. There would be plenty of room for me. We talked for a while and shared cigarettes. Murmurs of good-night as I left. And from Morris, 'Good sleep. Until in the morning.'

Engine trouble. A late start and then the slow stretch of the Corentyne River. The Indians from Siparuta were laughing and chattering to each other. They had been silent at Springlands. Morris on his own at the stern. Dark face watching the tangled forest; muttering occasionally, still disgruntled at the engine.

The sun was glinting on the red and white sand of the hill at Orealla. Two corials, motionless on the mirror-like water. I recognized Alan in one of them. He waved as we passed by. A little crowd gathered on the bank, with Nelly and Henry in front. A moment later the warped door of the shack was opened. The children followed me inside, putting my bag down in a corner and sweeping the dust and cobwebs away.

I left them playing on the steps and wandered through the village. Past the mango tree and the school and under the tall bamboos. The children were bathing at the water's edge. Old Nelly Herman, sitting in a doorway, spinning cotton in the last of the daylight. A large, half finished house on the corner. It belonged to Harry, one of the men who had worked on the housing scheme. He was sitting outside with his family and friends. Beside them lay several bags of rice which had just been harvested—a new crop for the Indians. They had recognized their potential share in the sudden prosperity which rice had brought to the coast.

They waved and I went over to join them. We chatted—nothing had changed, they said, the village was the same as ever.

'And how was the travelling?' asked Louis, one of the boys from up the hill. 'Worse than when we been to Kaieteur?' He grinned, remembering our journey together.

'Kaieteur was nothing,' I said, true to the cult of hyperbole which is part of travel in the interior.

Louis laughed, suspecting the joke. He pressed me for more details. It grew dark as we talked on. Over in Uncle Charlie's house, firelight and a murmur of voices. But by now it was getting late. I could see him in the morning.

Albert and his family were waiting for me by the time I got back; Juliana, his doe-eyed wife, with Nelly and Henry beside her. They sat on the bench and watched me unpack. Albert tied my hammock for me, helped by an insistent Henry. Yes, he said, the men were returning from their working grounds—the water had fallen in the creeks. There would be no more logging now, until the new rains began.

'And where you been since you gone?' he asked.

I told them about it all—Hallelujah, Tawailing, and the Rupununi. The children listened, wide-eyed.

'You must be weary now,' said Albert. 'You could come and eat with us in the morning. The children going call you.'

A trail of figures filing out, barefoot, into the darkness. The water was lapping at the river bank. Suddenly the breeze rose, running through the leaves in the roof and knocking the corials together, softly, a conversational sound. Otherwise it was quiet and timeless. Familiar faces, a relaxation. The stillness of Oreälla again, after the continual movement of the last three months.

The sun was creeping over the river, when I was woken by a tap on the door—a little boy, with some eggs from his grandmother. Outside, the

231

familiar signs of the village coming to life. Parrot calls, the splash of water and corials stranded on the mudflats, where the tide had fallen. Then a patter of feet behind me; Nelly and Henry—breakfast was ready.

They led me to their home, round the corner, where Albert and Juliana were waiting. The children had already eaten their fish and cassava bread. They sat and watched us for a while, combing each other's hair and laughing quietly. Then they disappeared down the path, with their slates and school books under their arms.

Uncle Charlie was at home, weaving a matapee. He looked up as I appeared, and patted the rough bench.

'So you come back again,' he said, as I sat down beside him. 'They tell me you was here last night. I say you must be waiting till morning to come and visit me.'

His wife was squatting on the floor, scraping cassava. She fetched us a calabash of paiwari. Uncle Charlie handed it to me.

'Like you going back to England now, and you can't drink no more paiwari? We Indian people would punish without it. You does miss it when you there in England?'

'Yes,' I said, 'I can't get it.' I had often remembered its thin, bitter taste, which was different from any other I knew. 'So what have you been doing?' I asked.

'Well,' he said, 'same like before. I been at the farm and doing this straw-work. And a couple days back I been fishing up Mapenna Creek.' He pointed down river, a wrinkled hand, to a creek mouth below the hill. 'I ain't find no fish at first. People been pulling logs there and all the fish gone away. But I does know them, where they go. They got a next creek, side by Mapenna. I follow them up there and make a good catch.'

His teenage son, Franklin, appeared, with a transistor radio in his hand Uncle Charlie shook his head. 'You see how this boy got radio? We old people never had such things. We don't know about it. But these youngsters got different ideas—they ain't worry with fishing and so.' He paused. 'But this travelling—you been all about in Indian country?'

'Yes,' I said, 'all about—Kamarang, Orinduik, Rupununi, Moruca.'

Uncle Charlie nodded gravely. As I went on to describe my journey he was full of questions. What did the people look like there? Did they still wear loin-cloths? And what about this Hallelujah? I could see him noting every detail.

'Yes,' he said, 'these distant nations, Patamona, Akawaio, they got a nice way of living—is so all we people was living before the white man come. The Indians was powerful people then—Puerto Rico, Cuba, Trinidad, Venezuela, this same Guiana, all was Indian country. We was

232

different from other races. But now we all coming together, getting new ways.' He picked up a little girl, his grandchild, and sat her down beside him. 'Even me, I getting old, but I get accustomed to these ways. We meeting outside people now, here at Orealla. And they seen how we Indians living.' He looked at me with a twinkle in his eye. 'They even drinking we drink, this paiwari—they getting civilized.'

'Are you glad about these new ways?' I asked.

He paused, with his head on one side. 'Well, I glad about it,' he said, 'and sometimes I not so glad. People was telling us things would change. And change coming quickly now, things we never expect to see—radio, engines, different races. You know, we people was always free, like to govern weselves. We like to be going here and there, and nobody can't stop we from going—that is Indian people. And we shy too. We can't talk so much until we drink paiwari. Outside people don't understand how we got we own ways.'

'And what about this straw-work? Like the young people forgetting it?'

'Yes,' he said, 'they forgetting it all.' He pointed at Franklin, who was sitting outside with a couple of friends. 'They got no interest in it now. They say is a tedious job. The same thing with we Arawak language—they scarcely know to speak it. You see, when I was a small boy, nobody teach me this straw-work. I only watching at old people and putting my hand to it. Is so these youngsters should do now. In days of old we was Indian people and up to now we is Indians. We supposed to practise these things.'

He seemed to have much the same feelings as other intelligent Indians. Change itself was not resented, so much as the way in which it occurred—a sudden gulf between young and old, the death of a culture and the presence of a world which hardly understood them.

He sipped his paiwari thoughtfully. 'Yes,' he said, 'we like to be quiet, living all alone. But that can't happen no more now. Sometime, when you come back here, you might not see Orealla—the place going to come like Georgetown.' He paused. 'But when you going back to England?'

'In a few days.'

'In the flying machine?'

'Yes, in the flying machine.'

He looked at me. 'You young and yet you travelling far, over sea and forest. I was wanting to go to England when I was a boy. I might have seen some wonderful things. But now I only dreaming about it.'

He stood up and limped over to the corner. I heard him rummaging in a basket. 'Look,' he said, 'I make this for you.' He handed me a small

233

pegall, a straw container, beautifully made with the traditional snake skin pattern. 'When you meet England, you must show them this pegall. Sometime, when you coming back, I might be low in the grave—and all these things going with me.'

I had to be leaving the next day. The last time, two years ago, the Indians had made an occasion of it—an all-night party, with the band still playing, as I set off down river. This time it would be quieter. Only a few people knew that I was going down with the mail boat, at one o'clock in the morning. It would be simpler that way. I wanted to leave Orealla as I had always known it.

That afternoon I walked through the village to take a last look at the Corentyne from the crest of the hill. As I passed, the sound of laughter from a house on the corner—Indian laughter, unrestrained, reckless, from deep inside them, a sound which is hardly ever heard when strangers are about. I was summoned by Japhet, a grizzled old Warrau, with a cloth cap on the back of his head.

'Mr. Colin, come take a sip.' He waved an unsteady hand. 'We been keeping masromani. And now we taking a little something.'

Inside the open house, the usual signs of paiwari. Japhet himself, in a jovial mood, a circle of people sitting on the floor and several large jars in the centre. As I sat down next to Japhet, I realized how conscious they still were of their tribal distinctions. There was hardly an Arawak among them. They were mainly Warraus from up on the hill, with sharper, more foxy features. Once swamp-dwellers, they are often described simply as the dirtiest tribe. In fact they are just the least conformist, unpredictable, hard to approach and always happy-go-lucky.

A little old man came and sat beside me—Wilson, the owner of the house. He offered me a brimming calabash. A moment's silence, as I drained it, followed by murmurs of approval. The Indians seem to gain as much pleasure from another man's drinking as from their own.

'Mr. Colin,' said Japhet loudly, 'I seen how you like this paiwari. You drinking over mark.' The others laughed at his mock reproach. 'But outside people don't like it,' he added. 'They say we is ignorant and we got to leave off paiwari. But we is not so ignorant.' He looked round at the others. A circle of faces watching him, men with half smiles, the women impassive. 'Yes,' he added, 'we Indians got science. We was the first people who learn to make this paiwari. Long ago we had proper science-man, piai-man, who was prophet and doctor. All that finish now, because we changing up. But one thing we can never change is this paiwari. We is Indians, this is we drink. If they stop we making it here,

234

we going in the forest and make it. And if they follow we into the forest, we going up in the mountains. Nobody can't stop this paiwari.'

Roars of laughter and applause at Japhet's tipsy oratory. The calabash was promptly filled and passed over to him.

'Yes,' said Sebastien, a younger Warrau, 'outside people don't like it at all.' A little boy stumbled towards him and landed in his lap. Sebastien looked up as if to say something. Then he seemed to decide against it. Instead he gave the child a sip from the calabash.

The others began chatting again. 'So you going away soon?' asked Wilson.

'Yes,' I said, 'I got to go back.'

'Stay here a little time,' said Japhet. 'If you stay in this Orealla, you wouldn't have any worries. You only got to grow some cassava and catch a little fish. And we going find you a nice girl to help you in the house and so.'

The others laughed in glee. 'But, Mr. Colin,' said Wilson solemnly, 'I don't believe you's a proper white man. To how you drinking so much paiwari and always gaffing with the people, you must be some kind of an Indian—a buck-man like we all.'

The banter was still in full swing when I left them and carried on up the hill. Japhet and a young man called Kenneth came with me.

'You know if Lillian's at home?' I asked.

'Yes,' said Kenneth, 'I believe so, and she got paiwari. Everybody sporting today—after they been at work,' he added.

He was right. Old Lillian was in voluble form. She greeted me with arms outstretched. 'Sonny Boy,' she said reproachfully, 'you going away again. And you going tonight. Is so I hear.'

'And how do you know?' I asked.

She winked, as much as if to say—which was very often true—that Lillian knows everything. Then she gave me a wistful look, paused and suddenly broke into an improvised version of 'Tipperary'. She held out her arm and we danced round together, with the others clapping in time. When it was over, a round of paiwari, while the hillside still echoed with laughter.

Japhet and Kenneth had disappeared. I wandered back on my own. Below the hill, the village dozed. Roofs half hidden by coconut fronds, with the purple forest beyond, and the slow bend of the Corentyne, forming a vast, sun-glinting lagoon. The heat-muffled thud of wooden beaters, as the women washed their clothes. Laughter from the paiwari spree and children wild at the water's edge, where the bamboos dipped over the river. Five, ten, twenty years time. I wondered how it would be. Perhaps, if I ever had the chance to find out, I would be reluctant to take it.

Dusk was gathering over the village as Albert and I sat on the stelling. The watch-fires were being lit in the houses behind us. The plash of a paddle—one of the men, back from his fishing-line. The mail launch, moored at the end of the stelling, waiting for the tide.

We were joined by Vin, Captain and Harry and a few others who knew I was leaving—Juliana, Nelly and Henry, Ellen and Clifton, the schoolteachers, and Bertie, the village comedian, with his two sons, Victor and Austin. They had brought a jar of paiwari. One of the boys strummed a guitar; between the calypsoes, a mari-mari, the last of the traditional dances. Bertie's feet began tapping. Overhead, the moon was rising, criss-crossed by the intricate pattern of the bamboo stems. Out on the river a few corials still drifted quietly by.

We talked very little. I felt drugged by the stillness and the hum of cicadas. We must have been there for almost an hour when Captain put a hand on my shoulder and pointed down the stelling. A little crowd of people had appeared. Somehow, perhaps through Lillian, they had heard that I was going. They had come to say goodbye. Some of them had brought presents—an elegant tibisiri basket and a model corial, a straw fan and a bottle of cane juice. When was I coming back? they asked. And then, from one of the old ladies, 'You got to remember Orealla.'

They sat round, whispering to each other, beneath the arched bamboos. A slight breeze ruffled the water and lifted the leaves overhead. Once or twice a shooting star plummetted into the darkness. Albert and I chatted, while Henry fell asleep in my lap.

'You would reach home soon? Two or three days from now?'

'Yes,' I replied, 'in three days.'

'You must tell you family about us. Tell them we is a poor people who only got the place where we living—but we still trying. We ain't know what going to happen. But God ain't worry with rich and poor. So say how we is a next people, just the same like them.'

The figures beneath the bamboos had vanished. There was less than an hour till the boat was leaving. Only a handful of people remained. Two of the boys were asleep. We drank the last of the paiwari and said goodbye to each other. Ellen, subdued and silent, Bertie still full of jokes; Captain looking rather solemn, and Vin, tired and smiling.

Albert and I walked back slowly. He seemed to know what I was thinking. As we reached the end of the path, he looked at me, held out his hand and simply said goodbye.

I watched him disappear into the shadows. The little shack was silhouetted in the pale moonlight. I packed my bag automatically. Tape-recorder, hammock, camera, notebooks and then the presents they had given me.

I looked out over the river. A moment later, the sound of a hooter. The boat was about to leave. It was chugging impatiently by the time I got back to the stelling. Glitter-black swirl of water below us, as we cast off. Along the bank, past the houses. The outline of the hill behind them, capped with coconut palms. Corials moored at the water's edge, rocking gently in our wake. I looked back as we reached the point. I could still just see the Indians' fires, glimmering through the darkness.

I knew I would be unable to sleep. Instead I lay on the roof of the launch, watching the forest slip by. Somehow, at times like this, one has a defence mechanism which makes it hard to believe that one is really leaving. I wondered what would become of them, the Indians with whom I had talked and travelled, danced, eaten and stayed. The more I had seen, the more uncertain their future seemed to be.

First of all, why should they change? Is it just a Western assumption to expect them to do so? Perhaps assumptions are often involved; but the age-old noble savage theme and the issue of which way of life is better are no longer relevant. They ignore the human reality, the people and their situation. All the Guianese Indians are changing; they simply cannot avoid it. So are most South American tribes and other similar groups—the Dyaks, Papuans and Eskimoes, the Bushmen of Australia and even the gypsies in Europe. Other societies are expanding into their territory. Most of these are Westernized and whenever primitive people meet them they lose faith in their own way of life. They try to adopt Western culture because, quite apart from anything else, they want to share its material standards. This may be for better or worse. But once it starts, there is no going back. The past has vanished, beyond recall, as soon as they cease to accept it.

The Indians have clearly reached this stage. Their problem is no longer a question of whether change should be allowed, but of how it should be effected. Depending on Guianese policy, they have two possible futures. They could easily go on declining, as they have under British rule, imitating and yet ignored by the rest of the Guianese people; or else they could be integrated, in a cultural and economic sense, by coming to understand and accept some positive solution.

I had seen the first alternative in several different forms. At Orealla, suspicion and collapse, because change had been haphazard, at Para-makatoi, a sense of futility, because it had been enforced, and amongst the Hallelujah Indians, resistance, for the same reason. But Sand Creek and the Moruca were entirely different. Here, instead of a sense of decline, there was something positive—change of a kind which fitted into the lives they lived as Indians. In both places it had occurred in a very similar way. It had been gradual rather than sudden, and also it had come from inside, instead of being imposed. Consistency and personal contact had made a vital difference. The people working among the Indians—the Vieiras, for instance, and the teachers—knew and were trusted by them. They had seen them as human beings and realized that, like any others, they have certain permanent features—their independence and sense of environment being the most important. Change must be adapted to these, and to their surviving traditions, if it is to have any meaning.

But what does 'integration' amount to? What future can the Indians have, in purely practical terms? And how can it be brought about on this internal, human basis? Their best prospect seems to lie in becoming a farming community, selling crops to the coast. This would give them a regular income to satisfy their new ambitions, and, being self-employed and rural, it would suit their personality and environment. But it clearly requires three things—the gradual, rather than the sudden, opening of the reservations; the granting of freehold titles to the land they already occupy; and finally, development schemes with an agricultural basis.

But this, though important, would not complete the Indians' integration. They are faced with two levels of change—the acquisition of a new way of life, through planned development, and membership of a new society, a virtually independent Guiana. The second is a problem of relationships. Indian suspicion and Guianese indifference, like other colonial relics, must somehow be overcome.

These two levels are closely connected. A new way of life and a new society both require the same thing—confidence between the Indians and the other Guianese. The older Indians are conservative, too conservative, perhaps, to ever belong to this; and all of them, both young and old, suspect authority. This means that the only answer lies in fairly informal methods among the younger people. A team of young village workers, both Indians and coastal Guianese, might easily sway the balance. Assisting experts like Jack Dummett, they could provide for the human aspects of schemes such as Nappi. They would also learn to trust each other. The problems of change and relationship would then be solved together.

Informal, unorthodox methods are not a part of colonial tradition. But this factor no longer limits Guianese horizons. The Indian problem can only be solved by a plan which treats it as a human issue. In terms of all that I saw, both on the coast and among the Indians, a plan of this kind is possible, if only the need is acknowledged. The Indians are just a handful of people—a little known minority in a restless, unpredictable country. But they are people like Uncle Charlie, Captain, Vin, old Lillian and Albert, with children like Nelly and Henry. Perhaps, in a new Guiana, they will be recognized.

APPENDIX A

The Guianese Background

(i) 1580–1796. Early settlement and Dutch Rule

Guiana has always been the neglected child of the New World. From the outset of the European conquest, early in the sixteenth century, there were few realistic attractions in the swampy, malarial coast between the Orinoco and the Amazon. Guiana was a land of fable, the home of half the fairy tales woven by early explorers. First came the myth of El Dorado, thought to lie farther west until Raleigh assigned it to Guiana. Keymis found this insufficient and added stories of 'men who had eminent heads like dogs and live all day in the sea and speak the Carib language'.[1] In the south lay the Crystal Mountains, which glittered from a great distance; there were mermaids, dragons, two-headed snakes, men with heads beneath their shoulders and the Gouvingas, an Indian tribe with claws on their hands and feet. It is hardly surprising that the country was known to the Dutch as 'the Wild Coast', and to others as De Mirara—the land of countless wonders.

The Spanish conquistadores were engrossed with the more tangible wealth to the west, in the Aztec and Inca empires. Guiana was a poor man's portion, settled and squabbled over by the British, Dutch and French, until it was finally pieced out into the three modern colonies. By the end of the sixteenth century all three powers were trading with the Indians, who welcomed them as allies against the rapacious Spaniards. English interest at this stage was more romantic than commercial. It began in 1594, when Raleigh, fired by rumours of gold, sent his men up the Orinoco. Their samples of ore convinced him that El Dorado was situated in his 'large and bewtiful empyre of Guiana'. He was followed by his two lieutenants, Keymis and Berry, who sailed along the coast and up most of the bigger rivers, including the Corentyne. But Raleigh never gained much support for his dream of an English Empire to rival

1. Laurence Keymis, *The Second Voyage to Guiana, 1596* (see Selected Bibliography).

the Spanish Main, and in 1617 it vanished, when he and Keymis were defeated by the Spaniards in the Orinoco. Keymis promptly hanged himself, while Raleigh returned to be executed, as the price of his failure.

This was the end of English influence for nearly two centuries. Guiana was left to the Dutch, whose perseverance was better suited to the Wild Coast. Well before Raleigh's time, they began trading with the Indians, exchanging knives, axes and beads for tobacco, dyes and hemp. Their first permanent settlement was founded on the Pomeroon River in 1580, and during the next thirty years several others followed. Many of these were wiped out by disease and parties of Caribs, who still dominated Guiana and the Lesser Antilles. The turning-point came in 1621, when the Dutch West India Company was formed. Its charter from the States-General entailed a monopoly of the African slave trade and the right to settle the Essequibo. A fort called Kyk-Over-Al was built, on an island some fifty miles up river, where settlement had already begun. With its strong commercial backing, early Dutch colonialism was a persistent force; for over a century, Kyk-Over-Al was the focal point of expansion.

The Dutch were soon firmly entrenched, with neighbouring settlements in the Pomeroon and Berbice. Gradually their trade with the Indians took second place to the plantations which sprang up on the banks of the Essequibo. Cotton, tobacco and sugar were grown, both by the company and by private settlers. The slave trade, on which they depended, created a new society where a small white oligarchy was vastly outnumbered by Africans. Without the active support of the Indians, who controlled the country behind them, the Dutch were caught between two fires. This made them diplomatic towards the Caribs and Arawaks, who were said to number over a hundred thousand. The employees of the company were obliged to treat them with respect. No Indian could be enslaved, except for those from remote tribes, whom the Caribs sold as prisoners of war. Though expedient, rather than enlightened, this policy compared well with that of the Spanish conquistadores, who had already exterminated most of the Indians elsewhere.

The hey-day of Dutch rule was largely the work of a single man—Laurens Storm van's Gravesande, who became Commandeur of Essequibo in 1742. His methods of consolidation were clear-cut and decisive. Soil exhaustion was forcing the planters to move down river. His first act as Commandeur was to build a new fort, named Zeelandia, at the mouth of the Essequibo. This change was significant; it dictated the future pattern of settlement on the narrow coastal strip, which is several feet below sea-level. The need for a highly centralized system of drainage and irrigation encouraged the growth of large scale plantations, which have always formed the background, both social and economic, of Guiana's development.

The interior was still important. The runaway slaves and neighbouring Spaniards were a serious threat to the handful of settlers. Van's Gravesande used the Caribs as a virtual police force, by posting them behind the plantations, where they could capture absconding slaves and help to suppress their revolts against the tyranny of the planters. The Carib chiefs were won over with staves of office and regular gifts, while the Arawaks and Akawaio were also conciliated. Van's Gravesande dealt severely with anyone who ill-treated the Indians. But otherwise his policy was hardly beneficial. Whenever their power looked dangerous, he played them off against each other. The system of gifts and slave-hunting, which destroyed their self-sufficiency and introduced racial feeling, was the beginning of their decline.

Van's Gravesande also encouraged expansion in the interior. Forts were built on the Rupununi, Moruca and Cuyuni rivers. The boundaries which he laid down were close to those of modern Guiana. He even seems to have recognized the future importance of Demerara, where settlers, both Dutch and British, were increasing rapidly. A separate Commandeur was appointed for the Demerara region. Berbice was still in private hands, but already settlement followed a pattern of three closely knit colonies, based on the three main rivers. By the time the old Commandeur retired, in 1772, the previously scattered settlements had become a political entity.

The slave trade was now at its zenith, providing the large plantations with a steady flow of cheap labour. The price of a sturdy African averaged one thousand two hundred guilders, or one hundred pounds. A large number died on the journey or soon after their arrival, but the morality of the system was as yet unquestioned. Few slaves obtained their freedom. Those who escaped were killed by starvation, disease or the Caribs. Contemporary records have left descriptions of the harshness with which they were treated:

'In July of the same year, 1783,' writes Rodway,[1] 'the Negro Cato was convicted of attempting to steal a bag of coffee, and ordered to be publicly flogged to bleeding, to be branded, to have both ears cut off, and finally to work in chains for life. In March previous the Negro Louis, having been convicted of murder, was sentenced to be broken on the wheel, where he was to remain from 10 am to 4 pm, after which

1. J. Rodway, *History of British Guiana 1688-1893* (see Selected Bibliography).

his head was to be cut off and stuck on a post as a warning. Elizabeth de Wever, having cruelly flogged her mulatto woman Mashy, and poured melted sealing-wax into the wounds, was fined eighty guilders and severely reprimanded . . .'

Revolts were frequent and cruelly suppressed. The most notorious occurred in 1763, when the four thousand slaves in Berbice, owned by some three hundred European planters, virtually controlled the colony for eleven months. Under a leader named Coffy, who proclaimed himself Governor of Berbice, they offered to share the country with the Dutch, providing that they were freed. Reinforcements arrived from the Netherlands and the British West Indies, and Indian levies were brought across from the Corentyne and the Essequibo. Eventually hundreds of slaves were killed and the rest recaptured. The luckier ringleaders were hanged; others were broken on the wheel or burnt over a slow fire.

Despite these outbreaks, which continued until well into the nineteenth century, the planters flourished on the export of coffee, cotton, tobacco and sugar. Foremost among them was John Gladstone, the father of the future Prime Minister, and another Englishman called Boode, who owned five plantations (one of them aptly named Boode's Lust) and over two thousand slaves. His annual income was fifty thousand pounds—roughly a quarter of a million by modern standards. Rodway has left an amusing, if slightly lenient, description of the daily life of a planter, the key-stone of early Guianese society:

'The Massa was a very great personage, everyone in his little kingdom treating him with the most servile respect. He rose with the sun and came down to the gallery in dressing-gown and slippers, then taking a little silver whistle from his pocket, blew it as a signal to the house-boy, who brought his coffee, pipes, tobacco and the indispensable gin-flask. With these the planter made himself comfortable until about nine o'clock. . . . At eleven o'clock came a heavy breakfast of pepperpot, salt fish and beef steaks, with plenty of roast plantains and other vegetables, being precluded by an appetizer and closed by a digester from the inevitable flask, while in the course of the meal a few glasses of claret, beer, or 'London Particular Madeira' were taken'. . . .

And so the day drifted on, divided, it seems, between eating, sleeping, drinking and being paddled round his estate in a gilt barge. Finally, when evening came:

'If the Massa was in a benevolent mood, he would order the slaves to be supplied with schnaps of rum in the yard, while he sat in the gallery, receiving their homage and thanks. About eight or nine o'clock he went to bed, very rarely incapacitated by his numerous drinks, but what may be called well-soaked'. . . .[1]

(ii) *1796–1947. British Guiana: the development of a multi-racial colonial society*

The Anglo-Dutch war of 1781 was the beginning of fifteen years turmoil, during which Guiana changed hands no less than six times. First it was taken by the British and then by the French, who built a new city at the mouth of the Demerara. When the Dutch regained control, in 1783, they named the French settlement Stabroek and made it their capital. But the British recaptured the territory in 1796, and although it was briefly surrendered once more, they were now the effective rulers. The planters were undisturbed by these rapid changes. Being cosmopolitan and virtually autonomous, they simply transferred their loyalties to the British Crown. Local affairs went on as before until, in 1831, the three colonies were combined into a single British Guiana, with Georgetown, the former Stabroek, as its capital. The constitution was almost unchanged until the end of the nineteenth century; it was based on a Court of Policy, which was heavily influenced by the planters on all fiscal questions.

By the end of the eighteenth century, Guiana's slave population numbered seventy-five thousand. Another five thousand arrived each year, to be purchased by the planters, whose production was increasing. The early years of British rule saw extensive development. Roads, bridges and schools were built, while Georgetown grew rapidly. Its suburbs, inhabited mainly by half-castes, were forerunners of the present day shanty-towns on its outer fringe. But the centre of the capital was close to Europe in its sense of fashion; with a circulating library, coffee-houses, cockpits, a theatre and 'all other manly amusements tending to promote health, dissipate spleen and abate scandal',[2] Georgetown was a confirmed outpost of the early Victorian world.

But the planters' crest of the wave was short-lived. It was based on a system of cheap labour without which it could hardly survive. The planters were aware of this and protested loudly at the growing opposition to the slave trade. But in 1807 it was abolished, mainly through Wilberforce and Fox. Although the institution survived for another thirty years, Guiana was now on the brink of radical social changes.

The leaders of the Anti-Slavery Society were not content with their

1. J. Rodway, op. cit.
2. J. Rodway, op. cit.

245

gains. They continued to press for total emancipation, mainly through the missionary movement, which had just reached Guiana. The conversion and education of slaves was fiercely opposed by the planters. When a missionary called John Smith arrived, in 1817, he was warned by Governor Murray that, if he taught the slaves to read, he would immediately be banished. Whether he did so is still uncertain, but in 1823 several members of his slave congregation knew that Parliament had passed a bill to improve their conditions. Women could no longer be flogged, and their stint was now limited to nine hours a day. But the Court of Policy, backed by the planters, delayed announcing these measures. The slaves soon began to suspect that their masters were trying to conceal an order for full emancipation. Disturbances broke out, led by members of Smith's congregation. Although they used little violence, the slaves gradually took control of the East coast estates. Martial law was declared in Georgetown, and the movement was savagely suppressed. The leaders were shot and hung in chains, and their heads were nailed on wooden spikes as a warning to their fellows. Smith was charged with complicity and sentenced to be hanged; although reprieved by the British Government, he died in prison before the news arrived.

The case of the Demerara Martyr, as John Smith came to be known, reinforced the movement for emancipation. Finally, in 1834, slavery was abolished throughout the British Empire. The majority of Guiana's Africans moved to Georgetown and the rural districts, where they lived in shanty-towns and communal villages. Their former owners received compensation, but during the next decade three-quarters of the plantations were abandoned or amalgamated, for want of labour. Sugar production fell and the planters' market dwindled, through competition with slave-owning countries, such as Cuba and Brazil. Unless they could find a new source of cheap labour, they faced a total collapse.

In order to fill this gap, they scoured the Empire for indentured labourers, who came to work for a minimal wage, with the option of a passage home at the end of five years. The Portuguese and Chinese were followed by Jews, Maltese, Irish and Assyrians; ex-slaves were also brought over from the West Indies. But, apart from the first two groups, few of them survived the conditions. It was only in 1838 that a long term solution was found, when John Gladstone imported a batch of labourers from India. The system was temporarily suspended, through pressure from the Anti-Slavery Society, who recognized it as little more than a disguised return to the past. But in 1845 it was renewed under Government supervision. The East Indians now formed the bulk of the immigrant population. Few of them returned to their homes and, by 1917, when indenture was abolished, they numbered a hundred and twenty-six thousand. The Africans were a few thousand less while the Portuguese, Chinese, Indians (Amerindians) and British formed small minorities.[1]

By this time Guiana's rapidly growing population of over three hundred thousand was one of the most multi-racial societies in the world. Any analysis of it purely in terms of racial groups tends to be oversimplified. Despite their very different backgrounds, its people have long since begun to develop a common indentity. Seeing that Guianese society is little more than a century old, this degree of assimilation is much more remarkable than the limited survival of racial consciousness. There are two main factors behind it. The immigrants were completely cut off from their various home countries; and also they all passed through the grist-mill of the plantations, which disinherited and gave them a uniform situation.

But this alone is hardly enough to create a single people within the course of a century. Each of the indentured groups reacted in different ways to its new situation. The Africans were already diffused into the various social strata open to non-Europeans. Their obvious distinctions from the East Indians are largely historical. Long before the latter arrived, the literate Africans had adopted the European values and culture which symbolized their emancipation. Hence their movement to the towns, where they are still a majority, especially in the Public Service and the teaching profession. Nor do the African villages suggest any real separatism; they are simply a legacy of the days when the Africans grouped together after emancipation.

The East Indians have a much closer identity; their numbers are larger and their culture stronger, while they have had less time to be assimilated. Up to 1917, fresh immigrants were still arriving—a stage

1. At the last official census, taken in April 1960, the provisional figures were:

East Indians ..	..	..	..	279,460
Africans	..	..	..	190,380
Mixed descent	..	..	..	66,180
Chinese	..	..	..	3,550
Portuguese ..	..	..	..	7,610
Other Europeans ..	..	..	5,230
Amerindians	..	..	..	22,860

Total 575,270

(From The Report on British Guiana for 1960, H.M.S.O., London, 1962.)

which ended a century earlier for the Africans. They have hardly married outside their race and many of them are still Hindus; but otherwise they too are turning towards a Guianese culture pattern. The survival of their peasant traditions gives an impression of solidarity. The typical East Indian is a rice farmer with three or four acres of land, who also does occasional wage-work on a sugar estate. But within a short while there may not be a 'typical East Indian', just as there is now no longer a 'typical African'. The prosperity brought by rice is a springboard for the young generation, whose education has carried them into business, the professions and the Public Service. Rapid economic growth is now creating a class structure which hardly corresponds to race; the somewhat facile tendency of British and American journalists to analyse Guianese politics simply in terms of Africans versus East Indians is dangerously unrealistic.

The minority groups are also diffused. The Portuguese labourers, who came from Madeira and the Azores, were immediately distinguished by their keen business sense. They soon owned most of the shops, both in the towns and the country districts. This made them unpopular, and in 1856 there were serious riots against them, instigated by an African who called himself Angel Gabriel; summoning his followers with a trumpet, he led them through the Portuguese shops on a looting spree. But these differences have decreased. Although they have come to form a mainly commercial middle class, the Portuguese have intermarried and regard themselves entirely as Guianese.

The Chinese were much more reserved. They too invested mainly in stores and groceries. Their former aloofness has now declined, through their adoption of Christianity and the motley local culture. Although they often speak Chinese, they rarely wear traditional dress, and they have also intermarried, especially with the coloured people centred on the towns.

There are few British expatriates left, now that the Guianese Public Service is entirely localized. The transfer of the sugar estates to company ownership has prevented a white settler problem of the African type. Most of the Europeans in the country are now of local birth and accepted by the other races. For mainly geographical reasons, the Indians (Amerindians) are the only group which has remained almost distinct. The pattern of coastal settlement excluded them from the melting-pot developments of the nineteenth century. After emancipation, the British had no more use for a people who loved their freedom too much to conform to colonialism. Their welfare was left to the missionaries, who tended to detribalize them, but hardly reduced their isolation.

Even in 1962, a modern sociologist dismissed them in a single page, concluding that 'the Amerindians do not constitute anything more than a minor problem in British Guiana today, and since they are mainly resident in the interior lands, they scarcely impinge upon the coastal population or enter into the discussion of social or economic policy'.[1]

Taken together, even these distinctions hardly imply a society which lives in racial compartments. Every tenth Guianese is of mixed origin. Differences of occupation have made for racial interdependence, rather than rivalry, while economic development and the trend towards a single culture are still reducing race consciousness. Surviving cultural differences can widen rather than restrict the growth of a central identity. Only political tension, caused by external policy or subversive local opposition, is likely to make racialism a threat to Guiana's future.

The country's economy is still dominated by sugar. Improved techniques and organization have compensated for the increased cost of labour, mainly through the enterprise of a single London company, Booker Bros. McConnell and Co., which now owns almost every estate, along with holdings in other local industries. Despite a recent policy of relative liberalism in staff recruitment and workers' welfare, the company's moral position is complex. It hinges largely on whether this policy —of better housing and social security, etc.—is designed to do more than simply appease political pressure; and whether, in longer terms, it is to be a preliminary to the integration of sugar into a wider economy. On the official level the schemes seem sincerely motivated; but the long-term issue, by definition, indicates the divided loyalties of an organization depending largely on overseas shareholders. Even if Bookers is a stimulant to the Guianese economy, some of its profits, despite re-investment, are necessarily sent overseas. Also it is likely to maintain sugar's dominance of the economy, partly at the expense of other more beneficial sectors of the economy. The support of Commonwealth sugar preferences disguises the fact that rice, for example, is more viable in terms of local conditions and available markets. Though the economy would be weaker, but for the presence of Bookers, diversion of profits and competition with potential local ventures seem indefensible as permanent principles.

Welfare schemes, while improving conditions, do little to increase the individual's or the society's resources. They simply alleviate the pressure, but not the need, for such changes. The primary-producing countries formed by colonialism need rapid diversification and

1. R. T. Smith. *British Guiana* (see Selected Bibliography).

the transfer of resources to local ownership. The traditional expatriate companies are, in their original form, an immediate obstacle to these needs—and yet, if sincerely liberal, a potential channel for their fulfilment. It will be hard to judge their contribution to economic independence until this transition is actually over.

Meanwhile Guianese poverty continues, partly because of the survival of this colonial economic structure, but also for want of capital and exploitable natural resources. Sugar and bauxite, also foreign owned, comprise 75 per cent of exports; only rice, amongst local products, features high on the export list with 13.6 per cent. Recent development schemes, financed mainly by the Colonial Development and Welfare Corporation, have concealed, rather than solved, the roots of the problem.

Aimed largely at social welfare, they were designed primarily to reduce political pressure. Land reclamation schemes have helped to establish rice farmers, but little more has been done for agricultural diversification or the opening of the interior. The current development plan is inadequate, mainly for want of capital, and hamstrung by political trouble and the lack of technical experts. The future depends on several factors—increased investment and low interest loans, the training of experts, new fields of production and the willingness of foreign companies to liberalize their economic, as well as their social policies.

This economic stagnation was made possible by the lack of constitutional development until the late 1940's. Throughout the nineteenth century, the Court of Policy was controlled by an official majority, with an elective minority which simply represented the planters. Only in 1927 did the new middle class gain an effective minority role in legislation. Fifteen years later provisions were made for a wide extension of the franchise, and, for the first time, an elective majority in the Legislative Council. It was not until 1947 that elections were held under this new constitution. They revealed a new political consciousness which pointed ultimately to Guianese independence.

(iii) *1947–62. The Rise of the People's Progressive Party and the Problems of Independence*

Among those elected to the Legislative Council in 1947 was Dr. Cheddi Jagan, a twenty-nine year old East Indian. He had just finished his dental training in the U.S.A., where he had married Janet Rosenberg, an avowed Marxist. Their formation of the Political Affairs Committee, a small radical movement, was Guiana's introduction to party politics. Although the Legislative Council rejected most of Dr. Jagan's early proposals, including higher taxes on sugar estate land, and a reduction in the salaries of expatriate officials, they were a taste of things to come. In 1950 the P.A.C. was turned into the People's Progressive Party, in which Forbes Burnham, a young African lawyer, was Dr. Jagan's main colleague. Their programme was based on demands for rapid independence and economic reform.

British officials were already anxious about the P.P.P. But in 1953 a new constitution was introduced, as the first step in a gradual approach towards independence. It entailed universal adult suffrage and a bi-cameral legislature. The lower half was mainly elective and the upper controlled by the choice of the Governor, who had an absolute veto. The executive included six ministers from the majority party, while the Governor retained emergency powers and the control of law and order. This embodied a misunderstanding which was never fully acknowledged in the subsequent crisis. The P.P.P. made it perfectly clear that they thought the constitution inadequate. This was their election platform when, in April 1953, they won an overwhelming victory with eighteen of the twenty-four seats in the lower House of Assembly. They regarded further constitutional changes as a vital part of their promise 'to bring a new socialist deal to the lives of the working people of our country'.[1] But the British Government had implied that it meant to protect all vested interests.[2] Obviously these two attitudes were bound to clash.

The P.P.P immediately launched their reform programme with measures for the secularisation of schools, improved drainage and irrigation, more direct taxes and a Labour Relations Bill, providing for the recognition of Unions by a workers' poll. The Government soon split into the two camps of the P.P.P. versus the rest. Discontent was widespread and the P.P.P. ministers encouraged strikes as a means of exerting pressure for a more liberal constitution. But suddenly, on October 7th, the existing one was suspended. The Governor declared a state of emergency and troops were flown in from Jamaica 'to prevent Communist subversion of the Government and a dangerous crisis both in public order and in economic affairs'.[3] Guiana's new deal was over.

This was widely recognized as a panic decision. The only shot fired in the 'crisis' was aimed at the lock on the P.P.P. office, when British

1. Dr. Cheddi Jagan, *Forbidden Freedom* (see Selected Bibliography).
2. *Report of the British Guiana Constitutional Commission, 1950–1* (Colonial No. 280, H.M.S.O., 1951).
3. *British Guiana, Suspension of the Constitution, 1953* (Command 8980, H.M.S.O., 1953).

troops broke in and rifled Dr. Jagan's desk. 'I flew into this crisis city of palms and wooden houses late last night,' wrote a British reporter, 'and this afternoon, eighteen hours later, I am still looking for the crisis.'[1]

Meanwhile Janet Jagan was in prison, for holding an illegal meeting. On the same day as the British Government extended the Declaration of Human Rights to all its colonies, five P.P.P. leaders were detained and political meetings were banned. There was an immediate return to a nominated Government. When Dr. Jagan and Mr. Burnham tried to reach England to plead their case, British and American airlines refused to take them, and Trinidad, Dutch Guiana and the U.S.A. withheld transit visas. Eventually they were forced to charter a plane for their sole use. The subsequent Command Paper provided a thin collage of excuses for the suspension. It emphasized that the acting Government had encouraged strikes; but with ultimate legislative control still in nominated hands, the P.P.P lacked the status of a responsible Government. Dr. Jagan's vague Marxism was inflated into a red terror whose intended victims included the local Girl Guides and Boy Scouts. His aim of secularizing the schools (previously suggested by a British Colonial Development and Welfare Corporation official) was condemned as Marxist. The P.P.P.'s organization, modelled on that of the Labour Party, was described by the Governor as 'a well-developed cell system' with 'a hard core of some four hundred to five hundred party members, concentrated mainly in Georgetown, who are ready to do violence at the bidding of the leaders'.[2] This statement can be judged by the fact that, during the crisis, copies of Nehru's *Towards Freedom* were seized as Communist literature. Several other charges followed, without any adequate evidence. In the words of Mr. James Griffiths, M.P., the report was obviously 'scraping the barrel'. The Colonial Secretary, Mr. Lyttelton, stuck to the charge of Communism—a technique strangely similar to South Africa's all-excusing Suppression of 'Communism' Act.

There were certainly two sides to the case. Dr. Jagan felt that Marxist theories gave his nationalism the support of a world-wide context. It was this which formed his views, rather than any intention of thrusting Guiana into the cold war orbit. But the British Government, foreseeing this as a possibility, depicted it as Dr. Jagan's intention. It was feared that he would nationalize sugar, thus refusing to compromise, in the way expected of nationalist leaders, with the existing status quo and all its vested interests. Yet the governor never used his veto, by way of warning

1. *Daily Herald*, October 9th, 1953.
2. *British Guiana, Suspension of the Constitution, 1953.*

the P.P.P.; it was also rumoured that American views contributed to the British decision. At the time it seemed unlikely; but in view of the fact that, ten years later, Mr. Dean Rusk was pressing the British Government to renew direct colonial rule,[1] it may well have been true.

The Robertson Commission of 1954 recommended 'a period of marking time in the progress towards self-government'.[2] This was maintained for four years, with disastrous results. The nationalism behind the P.P.P. was a completely new entity, powerful and yet composed of different classes and races. It had welded the Guianese together with a single political aim which overrode their internal distinctions. Had independence been rapidly granted—and in terms of political consciousness, the country was almost ready for it—full responsibility might have made this unity permanent. But now a brick wall was placed in front of it; the impact simply broke it apart. Their loss of responsibility encouraged the new leaders to discover their differences. In 1955 they came out. Mr. Burnham left the P.P.P., taking the moderates with him, on the grounds of Dr. Jagan's superfluous Marxism.

It was not until 1956 that the emergency measures were relaxed. The next year saw a limited return to elective government, through a new constitution with a single chamber legislature. By now the political split was complete. The P.P.P. won nine seats, while three went to Mr. Burnham's People's National Congress. After a period of peaceful government, both parties asked for further progress towards independence. The result was a plan for internal self-government in August 1961. With an elective majority in the lower House of Assembly and an executive consisting mainly of ministers from the majority party, this amounted to a qualified form of complete independence. The Governor retained emergency powers, with control of the police, foreign affairs and Public Service appointments.

Independence was now in sight. The only critical problems were the country's economy and the superficially racial appearance of political loyalties—Dr. Jagan's followers being mainly East Indian and Mr. Burnham's African. But this was not a stereotype and, in so far as it was true, it was due to differences of occupation rather than overt racial sentiment. Meanwhile a new group had emerged—the small, right wing United Force party, led by Mr. Peter D'Aguiar. His followers consisted mainly of business men like himself, and the upper strata of the professional and Public Service classes. The policy of the U.F. was to attract foreign investment

1. *The Times*, June 29th, 1963 ('U.S. Wants British Guiana Constitution Suspended').
2. *Report of the British Guiana Constitutional Commission, 1954* (Command 9274, H.M.S.O., 1954).

by encouraging private enterprise; but its principal aim was negative—to bring the P.P.P. to its knees.

The polls of August 1961, with a record ballot of ninety per cent, showed that political interest had widened. The P.P.P. regained power with nineteen seats in the House of Assembly, while eleven went to the P.N.C. and four to the U.F. There were mutters from the U.S.A., where the excitable Senator Dodds, of the Foreign Relations Committee, declared that 'international Communism has established its first beach-head on the South American Continent'.[1] But, as the new Premier, Dr. Jagan remained cautious. He denied any intention of nationalizing the major industries. Guiana's immediate needs were rapid independence and, above all, economic progress, with aid from every available source.

Shortly after the elections, Dr. Jagan visited the U.S.A. Here he stressed Guiana's need for capital for her development schemes, existing funds being inadequate; but he made it quite clear that his policy was socialist. Guiana would remain neutral. Commitment to any prescribed ideology or political pressure-group would be fatal for his country, which needed a radical, but empirical, programme of reform. Dr. Jagan went on to say that American democracy was on trial. Would they refuse the aid he needed, merely because of his socialism? 'Will she (the U.S.A.) withhold her aid at the very real risk of that (the Guianese) democracy being overthrown by a dictatorial uprising based on the people's poverty?'[2] There was an uncanny prescience in this particular question. Unfortunately the answer was 'yes'. The U.S.A. refused any aid. So did West Germany, France and Italy. Britain increased hers by a negligible amount, and declined to reduce the rate of interest on her loans to Guiana. The only concrete offers came from Poland, Czechoslovakia and Cuba. Subsequent events must be seen in terms of this total lack of sympathy from the Western powers.

This apparent lack of confidence lowered the Government's prestige. Foreign investments dwindled, while local capital left the country at an alarming rate. By January 1962, despite an exchange control system, the Government needed fifteen million dollars for immediate expenditure. The fatal budget of February aimed to redress this balance. It included a capital gains and annual property tax, another on advertising and a Compulsory Savings Bill for the higher income brackets. Obviously these measures would affect only big business and the middle class, most of which is centred on Georgetown and aligned with the U.F.

1. *New York Times*, August 4th, 1961.
2. 'Towards Understanding'. An Address to the National Press Club, Washington, 1962, by Dr. Cheddi Jagan.

A whirlwind attack was immediately launched by the Georgetown press. It was led by Mr. D'Aguiar's *Daily Chronicle*, which announced in a single edition that the budget was both Marxist and anti-working-class! But the Premier had failed to assess the hold of big business on Georgetown opinion. He also underestimated the forces he was aligning. Even the lower middle class would be tangibly, though not greatly, affected by the Compulsory Savings Bill. The Public Service and Government workers were restless about a wage dispute, while the leader of the T.U.C. was strongly opposed to the P.P.P. For Mr. D'Aguiar and his followers there were vested interests to protect; for Mr. Burnham it was a Government risk which the opposition was bound to exploit. The two leaders promptly joined forces to encourage the demonstrations and strikes which swept through the capital during budget week. Local business concerns combined to encourage their own workers to strike, although sugar interests were not involved and Booker Bros. took no part. Although Mr. D'Aguiar denied any part in inciting the riots which finally broke out on Black Friday, February 16th, the subsequent Commission of Enquiry[1] clearly disbelieved him. Certainly both he and Mr. Burnham refused the Governor's request for help in calming the mob. By the time the troops had restored order, the damage stood at eleven million dollars, with five people killed and eighty injured.

The Commission concluded that the riots were neither planned nor intentionally racial; but, at least in effect, they had emphasized racial differences. Above all, they had shaken national unity and economy, the two main factors in any prospect of stable independence. In the subsequent motion of censure, Mr. Burnham was curiously unaggressive. It looked as if he recognized that his influence had been used against the national interest.

The West, of course, could now wag its finger and point to the crisis as the outcome of Dr. Jagan's supposed Marxism and connections with the Communist bloc. But, looking one step further back, these connections were themselves the results of Western distrust and concerted pressure—the latter mainly from American policy, which is now openly opposed to Dr. Jagan's Government.[2] The rifts caused by the February riots were evident a few months later, at the constitutional conference held in October 1962. The prospect of independence had vanished. The three parties came to London with radically opposed programmes. The

1. *Report of the Commission of Enquiry into the Disturbances in British Guiana in February 1962* (Colonial No. 354, H.M.S.O., October 1962).
2. See Appendix E, which describes later events through late 1964.

P.P.P. demanded immediate independence and a voting age of eighteen; but the P.N.C. and the U.F. wanted new elections and proportional representation. No one would compromise. At the end of the conference, Mr. Sandys stated that, unless some agreement could be reached, the British Government might have to impose a settlement.[1] Under the circumstances, this could lead to civil war on a largely racial basis. Although the political loyalties of the Guianese are not just racially motivated, racialism can be used by minority forces. If Dr. Jagan and Mr. Burnham have both recognized this, perhaps they will form the coalition which seems to be the only answer to Guiana's problems—a coalition based, on both sides, on genuine neutrality and the avoidance of fixed ideologies, either from East or West. Only this can really fulfil the promise of 1953 on a non-totalitarian basis.[2]

1. *British Guiana Independence Conference, 1962* (Command 1870, H.M.S.O., 1962).
2. Subsequent political developments through late 1964 are described in Appendix E. In view of these later events, such a coalition no longer seems remotely possible unless there are at least partial changes in party leadership.

APPENDIX B

The Indian Background

(i) *The Guiana Tribes before and during the European Conquest of the New World*

Father Gumilla, the Spanish missionary and historian, had an unusual explanation of the origin of the Indian tribes of South America:

'The Indians are the children of Ham, the second son of Noah, and are descended from him just as we are descended from Japhet, through Tubal, founder and populator of Spain. . . . Owing to their ships being borne along by the fury of the winds, they crossed from Cape Verde to the most outlying point in all South America, which is in Brazil'. . . .[1]

What further proof was required, he asked, of the Spanish right to the New World? Modern ethnologists are less decisive. Although they usually accept the theory that some of the tribes have an Asian background, the migrations would be so far back that they remain an hypothesis.

The movements of the various tribal groups are known only for the period just before the European conquest of the New World, which dates from Columbus's first voyage in 1492. Archaeology, Indian traditions and surviving details of language and culture give a fairly complete picture for the Guiana area. This, for ethnological purposes, includes the Antilles and the Bahamas, and stretches from the Orinoco in the west to the Rio Negro and the Amazon in the south. During the historical period its two largest ethnic groups—each one having a common language—have been the Arawakan- and Cariban-speaking tribes.[2] The former seem to have reached Guiana from somewhere south of the Orinoco, in about A.D. 900, with the Caribs following close behind them. They brought with them the Tropical Forest culture which is still characteristic of all the Guiana Indians. This displaced the Marginal culture of the previous inhabitants, who had no pottery or agriculture.

1. *Historia Natural de las Naciónes del Orinoco.*
2. These categories are confusing. Each group contains several tribes, which speak dialects of the group tongue. The Caribs are simply the leading tribe of the Cariban-speaking group, and the Arawaks of the Arawakan.

Guiana's only modern descendants of these earlier tribes are the Warraus, who have since been absorbed by the later culture.

Guiana was once thought to have been the source of the Tropical Forest pattern, but this theory has been dismissed by the discovery of the Arawaks' and Caribs' arrival from the south at this fairly late date. Some of them settled in Guiana, splitting into the present-day tribes; but most of the Arawaks moved on to the Antilles, via Trinidad, with the Caribs attacking them from the rear. Here they encountered the Ciboney, a more primitive, cave-dwelling people, who had probably come from Florida and were now pushed back towards the north-west. This wave of expansion was at its height when the first Europeans arrived, in the 1490's. As little was written about Guiana until a century later, the Indians' history at this stage can only be followed in the islands.

The Ciboney were already a dying race, confined to the extremities of the Bahamas, Cuba and Hispaniola (now divided into Haiti and the Dominican Republic). The Arawaks controlled the Greater Antilles, from Jamaica to Puerto Rico. Their culture was more highly developed, including large villages and the worship of effigies known as zemis. Modern archaeologists have distinguished five island Arawak groups— the Igneri, Taino, sub-Taino, Ciguayo and Lucayo. The Caribs were still close behind them, in the Lesser Antilles, and were just beginning to attack Puerto Rico. They were a more aggressive people, who ate their male Arawak captives and took the women as wives—hence the early tales of a tribe with a different language for the men and women, which was thought to be their means of concealing military secrets.

The Arawaks whom Columbus met, on first landing in the Bahamas, gave him a friendly welcome:

'At daybreak great multitudes of men came to the shore, of fine shapes, very handsome; their hair not curled, but straight, and coarse like horse-hair, and all with foreheads and heads much broader than any people I have hitherto seen. Their eyes were very large and beautiful; they were not black, but the colour of the inhabitants of the Canaries. They were straight-limbed without exception, and not with prominent bellies, but handsomely shaped. They came to the ship in canoes made of a single trunk of a tree . . . loaded with balls of cotton, parrots, javelins and other things too numerous to mention; these they exchanged for whatever we chose to give them.'[1]

But farther south, the Arawaks warned him, lay the dreaded Caniba, or Caribs:

1. Christopher Columbus, *Journal of the First Voyage to America, 1492* (edited by Van Wyck Brooks, Jarrolds, London, 1925).

'who are regarded by their neighbours as exceedingly ferocious; they feed upon human flesh. These people have many sorts of canoes, with which they make incursions upon all the isles of India (the West Indies), robbing and plundering wherever they go. Their difference from the others consists in their wearing long hair like that of the women, and in using bows and arrows of cane. . . . Their women exercise none of the common occupations of their sex, but manage the bow and dart, as we are told of the ancients. . . .'[1]

It was not until his second voyage that Columbus met the Caribs, who lived up to their reputation by driving him back from Santa Cruz with a volley of poisoned arrows. Their hostility and location gave them a longer lease of life than the island Arawaks, whom the Spaniards used as forced labour, under the system of repartimiento, in the gold mines and plantations. In Hispaniola alone, during the first thirty years of the sixteenth century, the Arawak population dropped from roughly five thousand to five hundred. In 1586 Drake reported that there was not an Indian left in the island. The same thing happened in Puerto Rico, Jamaica and the Bahamas. The only survivors were in Cuba, where they eventually intermarried with the Spaniards and African slaves. Otherwise the island Arawaks, who probably numbered half a million, were exterminated in less than a century.

The Spaniards were afraid of the Caribs, who consumed their only envoys, a handful of Dominican friars—from a sense of honour rather than taste, as they found the Spaniards gristly compared to the tender Frenchman, according to De Rochefort, another contemporary historian. It was not until the seventeenth century that the British and French started fighting over the Lesser Antilles. Everywhere the Caribs were slaughtered, after a fierce resistance; in 1650, when Grenada fell to the French, they leapt off the cliffs into the sea, rather than surrender. By the end of the eighteenth century, they too had vanished from the islands, except in Dominica, Trinidad and St. Vincent. There are still a few survivors, especially in Dominica, where a trace of their Carib spirit lives on in their fame as smugglers.

Little was heard of Guiana's Indians until the seventeenth century, when their numbers were increased by refugees from the islands. Here they fared rather differently. The forest provided them with a refuge, while the Dutch and British were weaker and less oppressive than the Spaniards. But although they escaped extermination, their numbers declined steadily through contact with Europeans. The precise extent is hard to gauge, as early estimates were vague. Both Keymis, in the

1. Ibid.

1590's and a Major Scott, in the 1660's, put them at over two hundred thousand, but this seems exaggerated. They probably never amounted to more than roughly a third of this number. Their fortunes can best be indicated by a survey of all the tribes reported within the boundaries of what is now British Guiana since about 1600. They fall into three groups—the Warrau-, Arawakan- and Cariban-speaking—and nineteen separate tribes. Two of these have almost died out, while five more are completely extinct and three have been driven beyond the borders. Although their numbers are now increasing, they have clearly been more than halved during the last three centuries:

Linguistic Groups	Extinct	Almost Extinct	Surviving outside Br. Guiana	Surviving in Br. Guiana
Warrau-speaking	—	—	—	*Warrau*
Arawak-an-speaking	*Amariba* (Takutu River. Extinct mid 19th C.) *Atorai* (Takutu and Rupununi Rivers. Extensive 18th C. Extinct early 20th C.)	*Maopityan* (Mapuera River. Almost extinct 1950's. Possibly more in Brazil) *Taruma* (Upper Essequibo. Extensive mid 19th C. Almost extinct 1950's.)	—	*Arawak* *Wapisiana*
Cariban-speaking	*Attaraya* (Mazaruni River early 19th C. Not heard of again) *Paraviyana* (Rio Branco and Takutu River early 19th C. Extinct early 20th C.) *Pianocoto* (Upper Corentyne River mid 19th C. Not heard of again)	—	*Maiongkong* (Extensive in Upper Mazaruni River mid 19th C. Surviving in Venezuela) *Serekong* (As Maiongkong) *Yao* (Reported in Moruca 1590's. Surviving in Brazil)	*Akawaio* *Arecuna* *Carib* *Macusi* *Patamona* *Wai-Wai*
TOTAL	5	2	3	9

During the two centuries of Dutch occupation the Indians played an important part in Guiana's affairs. Their hatred of the Spaniards made them amenable to the Dutch settlers, who, for mainly strategic reasons, encouraged their dependence. They had frequent dealings with the Arawaks and Caribs and, to a lesser extent, with the Warraus and the Akawaio. The various tribes were still very different in personality. The passive, friendly Arawaks were the settlers' main source of trade, while the Caribs were regarded as aristocrats, 'the most numerous, brave, warlike and industrious of all the known tribes inhabiting Guiana'.[1] The Warraus were more reserved, still swamp-dwellers and rarely seen; the Akawaio seemed unpredictable, except in their enmity to the Caribs, only visiting the coast on brief trading expeditions.

Dutch policy was conciliatory. The Indians, especially the Caribs, were used to maintain the precarious balance between the planters and slaves. The Articled Letters of the Dutch West India Company, for example, stipulated that its employees should offer no harm to the Indians. Any offence was severely punished, and the planters could only obtain Indian slaves from the more remote tribes. Even these were heavily taxed, and in 1793 Indian slavery was totally abolished. During van's Gravesande's time, contact was maintained through a system of post-holders, stationed at different points in the interior. There were regular distributions of rum and presents for the caiques, or chiefs, at a cost of ten thousand florins a year. Despite his policy of keeping them at bay by playing them off against each other, van's Gravesande encouraged them to bring their quarrels before the Dutch courts. He often reported that his house was full of Indian chiefs who had come to visit him. Sometimes they settled on the plantations, where they worked as hunters or fishermen, usually in return for rum. Few of them stayed for long, but in other respects Dutch policy paid good dividends. At first it brought a commercial profit, through the dyes, timber, cotton and hammocks which the Indians brought to the trading posts. But by the end of the seventeenth century, this had taken second place to their more notorious rôle— that of slave-hunters against the Africans who had escaped from the estates.

The racial feeling which this provoked is now almost forgotten. It seems surprising that the Indians, who usually died of grief when enslaved, should have had so little sympathy for the Africans' freedom.

1. E. Bancroft, *Essay on the Natural History of Guiana* (1769).

But persecution was of little account to a people who had always fought, both amongst themselves and with others, for their self-preservation. The Europeans' example and policy bred their hostility to the slaves. Van's Gravesande speaks of promoting this feeling, 'which, if well and reasonably stimulated, cannot fail to be of much use and service in the future of the colonies'.[1] From the Dutch point of view, it certainly succeeded. Farther east, in Surinam, where there was no such policy, the African slaves escaped in thousands, and their descendants still survive as an independent people; but, to this day, there are few 'bush-negroes' in the interior of British Guiana. By the middle of the eighteenth century this system was highly organized. The Carib chiefs agreed to hunt down all runaway slaves, exterminate refugee settlements and come to the planters' aid whenever revolts occurred. Frequent allocations were made for rewards and expeditions, the standard price for a captured slave being ten axe-heads. More or less regular Indian contingents were stationed just behind the plantations under their recognized chiefs. Between them, they could summon some five thousand men at a few days notice. The Arawaks and Akawaio also took part occasionally, though much less often than the Caribs; but for the Indians' help, the Berbice slave revolt of 1763 might have been the end of the colonies.

Administration grew more complex towards the end of the Dutch phase. The post-holders earned a salary of one thousand two hundred guilders (one hundred pounds) per annum, and their duties were now specified. They were to attach Indians to the posts, settle quarrels among them, prevent them from being exploited by traders, distribute annual gifts and hand out enough rum to placate them. When the British acquired Guiana, they adapted this system wholesale and maintained it while slavery lasted. In 1809, for example, a hundred thousand florins were spent on a bush expedition, a fifth of which was paid to the Indians. Pinckard, a military doctor, has left a description of one of these forays, written in 1796. They were usually led by European officers, whom the Indians naturally despised for their clumsiness in the forest:

'But for the assistance given by the Indians, the brigands would probably never have been subdued; perhaps not found. The expertness of these men in such a pursuit is peculiar, and beyond all that could be imagined by those who live in a crowded city. They not only hear sounds in the woods, which are imperceptible to others, but judge, with surprising accuracy, of the distance and direction from whence they proceed . . . with such guides, the corps moved in confidence and was

1. Laurens Storm van's Gravesande, *Despatches* (see Selected Bibliography).

conducted with safety. Seven encampments of the brigands were discovered and completely routed; some of which had existed during fifteen years, concealed in the profoundest gloom of the forest.'[1]

Payments to the Indians continued; as late as 1823, the Caribs came down the Essequibo in their war-canoes, to quell the emancipation disturbances, with their women fighting beside them. William Hilhouse, who was Indian Quartermaster during the 1820's, considered this policy essential. But he also admitted, at candid moments, that it was destroying the Indians—over a quarter of them had abandoned their own way of life in favour of an uneasy dependence on rewards and presents from the post-holders. Rum, which was the major weapon in British diplomacy, was killing them off in hundreds. When, after emancipation, the system was no longer required, the damage was already done. Those who had been in touch with the coast no longer had the capacity to revert to their former independence. Only a new and enlightened policy could have provided for them.

Hilhouse now spoke openly about the effects of the past. The Indians had been physically and morally degraded by being made to depend on presents and organized killing. Their self-sufficiency had collapsed and the Dutch had fostered tribal hatred by allowing them to enslave each other. The post-holders were exploiting them, while those who settled near the plantations were simply taught to lie, steal, work as prostitutes and finally drink themselves to death. The Government had used them in the same way. He cited a batch of three hundred and fifty Indians brought down to Georgetown in 1823, as a security force; in the space of ten years over half of them had died through patronized alcoholism. Deprived of their former livelihood, the surviving Caribs were fleeing up country—partly for fear of the ex-slaves and also to search for a new market for the Indian slave trade, over in Brazil. Hilhouse demanded a new policy. A constructive mission system was needed, with a practical emphasis; instead of rum and European goods the Indians should be given agricultural tools.

These suggestions were highly enlightened, and in 1838 Governor Light promised to help. 'We have used these people as auxiliaries,' he said, 'and they were useful and faithful; we gave them presents, often misapplied, too often baneful. . . . We owe them a debt; let us endeavour to repay it, in a way beneficial to a fallen race.'[2]

This statement was important in setting a precedent for later policy, which was based, for over a century, on pious, condescending promises

1. Dr. G. Pinckard, *Letters from Guiana 1796-7* (see Selected Bibliography).
2. Cited by J. Rodway, *The Indian policy of the Dutch* (Timehri, 1896).

that were never fulfilled. The reality was very different. The Government had used the Indians, almost destroying them in the process, while they were still a vital part of the status quo. They were much too independent to work as ill-paid labourers, and now that slavery was over, there was no further use for them. As a result they were simply ignored. The post-holder system was abolished. Indian welfare became a minor part of the job of a single local official, the Commissioner for Lands and Mines, who frequently left them unmentioned in his official reports. 'Since when', wrote Rodway, in 1893, 'the Indians have been left alone, except for the missions'.[1]

(iii) 1830–1910. The Expansion of Missionary Influence

The Dutch had prohibited missions in Indian territory, apart from the short-lived Moravian posts on the Corentyne and the Berbice. But during most of the British period, they were the Indians' main link with coastal Guiana. The first Anglican station was founded in 1829, at Bartica, on the Essequibo. It was soon followed by others on most of the big rivers, while the Catholics established themselves in the Moruca. The remotest mission was the Rev. Youd's, at Pirara, in the Rupununi; but after this had been suppressed by the Brazilians,[2] the interior tribes remained untouched until after the turn of the century.

These early missions affected roughly a third of the Indians. They had few of the qualities which Hilhouse had advocated. Even from the missionaries' own accounts, it appears that their first effect on the Indians was to make them thoroughly ashamed of their way of life. The Anglican priest Bernau expressed the views of most of his colleagues when he described the Indians as a people who 'in their natural state, differ little from the brute creation'.[3] They set about changing this natural state as quickly as possible. Their early influence was superficial and they often found their missions deserted after a brief absence. Their diaries also indicate that their methods were not always laudable; religious threats and material influence were two of their main weapons. Bernau, for example, relates with ingenuous pride how he burnt an Indian's hand to warn him of the nature of hell-fire. His victim was promptly converted and died soon afterwards, assured of heavenly bliss. But clothes and food were their main attractions, and the Indians' self-sufficiency,

1. J. Rodway, op. cit., (see Selected Bibliography).
2. See Chapter 8, page 170.
3. Rev. J. H. Bernau, *Missionary Labours in British Guiana* (see Selected Bibliography).

already seriously diminished, was weakened even further. The missionaries rarely understood the social and economic significance of the Indians' various customs, which they suppressed indiscriminately. Their marriage systems and rituals died out, and their agriculture and hunting skill were seriously affected. Hilhouse found an example of this as early as 1837, when he travelled up the Cuyuni, and found the Indians starving for want of their usual cassava. They told him that they had grown very little because the missionaries disapproved of their using it for paiwari. When Hilhouse reproached them for their improvidence, they answered that they had been assured that God would provide for them. Even at the end of the century, this situation had scarcely changed. Describing the Potaro River Indians in 1896, a passing traveller wrote: 'As far as my observations lead me, the only benefit the Indian has yet derived from the effort to Christianize him is that he has learnt to steal, indulge in strong drink and wear ill-fitting clothes.'[1]

These sudden changes of custom weakened the Indians' resistance. They were frequently decimated by the European diseases brought in mainly through the missions. Smallpox, measles, chickenpox, cholera and finally 'flu swept through them regularly, destroying whole villages. 'They have so decreased in numbers', wrote Bernau of the Caribs in 1847, 'that it would be difficult now to collect a hundred of them together in the country below the rapids, where twenty years ago they mustered a thousand fighting men'.[2] The surveys of the Corentyne are typical of this period. In 1831 there were seven hundred and fifty-two Indians in the lower reaches; seven years later they had dropped to five hundred and seventy-five, and by 1866 to two hundred and forty-five. By the end of the century their total numbers can hardly have been more than twelve thousand. It was fairly widely assumed that they would soon be extinct.

Although the early missionaries were often devoted men, their zeal apparently blinded them to the human effects of their work. But they did help to exclude rum and predatory traders from their districts, while the changes taking place elsewhere were often much more harmful. Many of the Indians were drifting down to the coast, or into employment as log-cutters. When he travelled up the Corentyne, in 1836, Robert Schomburgk reported that exploitation was already rife. There was no attempt to protect the Indians, who were usually paid in rum, if at all. Though often remarked on by travellers, this plight remained unchanged. The gold rushes in the north were almost a death-blow to the

1. C. A. Lloyd, *On the Potaro* (Timehri, 1896).
2. Rev. J. H. Bernau, op. cit.

Caribs, again through rum and epidemics; and farther south, in the Rupununi, the Macusi and Wapisiana were soon being driven off their land by the cattle-ranchers. By the end of the nineteenth century, there were only four tribes in the remote interior—the Wai-Wai, Arecuna, Akawaio and Patamona—which were still undisturbed.

(iv) *1910–63. Official Policy and the Problem of Integration*

Meanwhile the missionaries' work had relieved the Government's slender conscience. Indian affairs were still no more than the part-time concern of the Commissioner for Lands and Mines. Administration was negligible, and a vague protective ordinance had very little effect, for want of anyone to enforce it. Only in 1910 did the Government even profess any interest, by extending its provisions; but they contained no policy, emphasizing protection, rather than planned integration or vocational training. Like the seclusion imposed by the missionaries, this simply retarded the Indians. The tone of the ordinance was implicit in the way in which it was summarized by the 1910 Colonial Report: 'By its provisions it is hoped to protect the Aboriginal Indians of the colony, who intellectually are little better than children.'[1] The writer seems not to have realized that any criticism of the Indians was also a criticism of those who had ruled them for over a century. Almost every clause in the ordinance showed the same imperception. Reservations were established which only Indians could enter, but the land was Crown Property and the Indians had no title to it, so that they could be dispossessed at a moment's notice. The Governor-in-Council could detain any Indian, or remove him from one district to another. He could also forbid any customs which he thought unsuitable. Local officials, described as 'Protectors', could 'take possession of, retain, sell or dispose of any property of an Aboriginal Indian';[2] they could also commandeer his wages and spend them as they thought fit. The other clauses were all protective, if slightly less repressive; but in reality they were still ineffective, because of the lack of administration. Basically the impasse remained. The Government ignored the problem of whether anything positive could be done about the Indians' transition.

During the next thirty years, sparse missionary influence reached every tribe except for the Wai-Wai. The decline of the previous century

1. *British Guiana, Annual Report, 1910* (H.M.S.O., 1911).
2. *British Guiana, Ordinance No. 22 of 1910* (An Ordinance to Provide for the Better Protection of the Aboriginal Indians of the Colony).

ended with the Indians' numbers remaining level at about fourteen thousand. Thanks to the ordinance, casual employment was higher and exploitation slightly less. The Indian problem was not unnoticed. In 1914, for example, the Attorney-General remarked 'that he did not think that their [the Government's] record in regard to the Indians of the Colony was one of which they had reason to be proud. They had systematically ignored them.'[1] Despite his rebuke, they continued to do so. Apart from a few statistics, which indicated that their death-rate was still the highest in the colony, the Indians were completely unmentioned in the Colonial Reports from 1911 to 1938. This was in spite of constructive opinions, such as that of the Reverend James Williams, an Anglican priest in the Rupununi, who pointed out the Macusis' land problems and the Indians' need for land titles and more progressive treatment.

It was not until after the Second World War that the problem was reconsidered. A Welfare Officer was appointed to conduct a survey of Indian affairs. P. S. Peberdy's report embodied the only far-reaching suggestions ever offered on Indian policy. He stated that the Indians' contacts with the coast had led to their steady decline, while current views on their situation ranged 'from the neglectful to the over-sentimental'.[2] He recognized that integration was inevitable; 'protection' simply retarded the Indians and had been used as a screen for neglect. His proposals were revolutionary. Had they been put into force, they might well have transformed the Indians' future. They included a new administrative system, based on local Superintendents, with Indian assistants, village councils and a central tribal committee. All 'undesirable religious bodies', i.e. the small unorthodox sects which imposed harmful religious taboos, would be excluded from Indian districts. The reservations on the coast would be gradually opened up, once they were no longer needed for protective ends. Peberdy's major proposal entailed three large Indian districts—in the North-West, the Mazaruni and the Rupununi—as centres for intensive development, to bring the Indians to the point where they could be treated as ordinary citizens. He suggested a co-operative framework for the production of timber, balata and mineral products; cattle would also be reared by the Indians in the Rupununi, where radical reforms would take place. The R.D.C. and the private ranchers would lose their monopoly of the land in favour of new systems of tenure which no longer excluded the Macusi and Wapisiana.[3]

1. *Daily Argosy*, Georgetown, February 28th, 1914.
2. P. S. Peberdy, *Report on a Survey of Amerindian affairs in the Remote Interior of British Guiana* (British Guiana Government, 1948).
3. See Chapter 8, p. 183.

It was soon clear that the Government was not going to prejudice vested interests. Booker Bros, for example, held a legal monopoly of the balata business and shares in the R.D.C., whose control of the land was described as fatal to the Indians. Even the private ranchers were consulted as to the wisdom of the new plans! They were followed, later in 1948, by another report[1] which watered them down beyond recognition. It acknowledged the need for integration through local councils, development schemes and the planned reduction of the reservations; but the Rupununi projects were dropped. The Macusi were now to be moved to the Karasabai reservation, whilst the Wapisiana would receive their eight hundred square miles of grazing land in the south—an optimistic reckoning of their minimum needs at the time. The Governor supported these changes and the programme was finally approved in its revised form.

The British administration of Indian affairs continued for another thirteen years, until August 1961. But during this time the new proposals were hardly implemented. One large new reservation was formed in the Mazaruni, but the rest were unchanged. The others proposed were not established, while the old ones remained as before, confirming the Indians' suspicion of the coast and making the prospect of integration even more remote. The 'undesirable religious bodies' were never removed. There were only half-hearted attempts to market Indian products on the basis suggested by Mr. Peberdy. Even in their revised form, the Rupununi projects failed. The Macusi declined to leave their homes for the sake of vague promises, while the Wapisiana grazing scheme was delayed and then drastically cut down, despite the rapid increase in their numbers.[2]

But meanwhile there were some improvements. Their numbers leapt up through medical aid, partly from five Indian medical rangers, including Nash Atkinson.[3] The revised Indian ordinance (No. 22 of 1951) hardly differed from the previous one; but a new Interior Department was founded, to deal with Indian affairs, and by 1961, it had some twelve officers in the field. Their work was mainly administrative, but development schemes were introduced, although their success was limited. Several local councils were established, and most of the Indians were now within reach of denominational primary schools. Training courses were also held, but, for want of planning and suitable subjects, they were poorly attended.

1. H. G. Gregory-Smith, *Report by the Commissioner of the Interior, British Guiana* (British Guiana Government, 1948).
2. See Chapter 8, p. 183.
3. See Chapter 9, p. 192.

There were two related reasons for this general lack of success. The first was a shortage of funds and staff, caused by top level indifference about a small minority who had no political weight or economic potential. The per capita expenditure on Indian development, for example, from 1954 to 1961, was approximately a twentieth of that spent on the coastal population. Secondly, in planning and execution, the level of contact with the Indians was far too impersonal—partly because of the lack of staff, which placed administration and development in the same hands.

The Indians' suspicion of the other Guianese, bred by every stage of the past, was maintained by the reservations, which were never opened as planned; the retention of the Interior Department under direct British control completed their isolation. Their reactions are evident in their conservative alignment with the largely European U.F. party. The result is a wide gap, social, economic and cultural, between the Indians and the coastal society, which must somehow be reduced within the next few years. This is now a Guianese problem. Its major economic aspects clearly require trained attention, but otherwise the solution could lie in the formation of a team of young Guianese to work in Indian communities.[1] Any realistic programme will have to consider several practical factors— close consultation with the Indians themselves; the distinction of administration and development; planned economic progress, mainly agricultural, to fit in with coastal markets; a new school syllabus to foster this, allowing for traditional skills and environment;[2] and the gradual reduction of the reservations in favour of standard land tenure, perhaps on a communal basis under the control of local councils. The Indians' identity is bound to weaken, but their numbers are mounting. An enlightened Guianese policy could easily bring them to the stage where they need no longer be treated as a 'problem people'.

1. See Chapter II, p. 237.
2. The Guianese Education Department has already suggested this to head-teachers in Indian districts.

APPENDIX C

The Sources and Original Versions of the Hallelujah Songs and Prayer Quoted in Translation in Chapter 6

All the Hallelujah songs are composed in the traditional Indian style. Each one consists simply of two short lines, which are constantly repeated, with occasional variations in words and rhythm. The first one which I have quoted is said to be the work of Abel, the earliest Akawaio prophet. It is also sung by the Patamona, under the guidance of Henry of Kaibarupai, who explained its origin to me:

> 'Urli u yape tane
> Evil is coming but
>
> Weboolimado Hallelujah.
> We are praying (for) Hallelujah.'

The second is quoted by Dr. Butt (see Selected Bibliography). It is still sung by the Akawaio, who claim to have acquired it from the Macusi, to whom it was given by Bichiwung, the original Hallelujah prophet:

> 'Inungelon gobodobong Gado
> Earth Maker God
>
> U yonobok mang,
> Is coming,
>
> Uraianda gobodobong Gado
> Mist Maker God
>
> U yonobok mang.
> Is coming.'

The extract from the prayer is an improvisation by Henry, on a traditional theme. This is also repeated continually, but as it has no set rhythm, it allows more variations than the songs.

> 'Musakane maimu, Hallelujah unpawung, melundule
> Raise up (my) voice, Hallelujah (in my) heart, strength
>
> Aibilibing mulage ulibage, sililidule, wakundage
> Father (and) wealth give (me), today, give (me)
>
> wakobe ikiali-bona, uyeni-bona, pana-bona, iwung-bona.'
> goodness on my food, on my eyes, on my ears, in my heart.'

The third song, which is in Patamona, is of a much later date. It belongs, psychologically, to the final stage of Hallelujah, and is said by both Henry and Daniell of Kaibarupai to have been composed by Benjamin, the latter's father:

> 'Pada wela terope,
> My place turn to be,
>
> Uwi yapong tabichi-co.
> Father bench touch.'

i.e.
> 'Take me up to Heaven, Father,
> Let me touch my bench there.'

APPENDIX D

Millennial cults similar to Hallelujah

The significance of Hallelujah lies in its close connection with other cults of this kind. They amount to the primitive world's reaction to European culture and political power—the reaction being, at its simplest, to share the culture and escape the power.

In the Pacific islands, for instance, there has been a series of movements known as cargo cults. The Melanesian and Papuan inhabitants were anxious both to explain and share their white rulers' wealth and behaviour. Their explanation was fairly natural—the white man's God provided his wealth, sending it in the form of cargoes, in ships and aeroplanes; his otherwise inexplicable antics—flag-poles, wirelesses, cricket clubs, etc—were his means of praying to this God. The white man monopolized his wealth as a means of gaining power. The islanders felt that they were being excluded; if they imitated the white man's magic, they would gain their rightful share. Cults developed everywhere, predicting days of freedom and riches, which would be sent as cargoes. The white man's magic was adopted, with make-believe wirelesses and cricket clubs. Jetties, airstrips and platforms were built, on which the cargoes would arrive. In terms of the islanders' own way of thought, these beliefs were a rational solution. But most of the cults died out when the prophecies failed to come true. Others were suppressed by colonial governments, German, French, Dutch and British.

A sense of European oppression created many similar movements among the North American Indians. Like Hallelujah most of these were based on traditional shamanism. Eventually they became militant, providing an inspiration for the Indians' resistance to European expansion. Many of the Indian outbreaks, depicted by Westerns and history books merely as painted savagery, had this deep spiritual content. They were often based on a partnership between a spiritual and a military leader. Pontiac, Tecumtha and subsequent chieftains were all inspired in this way, by prophets foretelling a millennium of renewed wealth and freedom. The most famous of these movements was the final Ghost Dance cult, which swept through the Sioux in 1890. Deprived of their hunting grounds and their staple diet of buffaloes, they adopted the vision of the prophet Wovoka, who predicted the return of the buffaloes and the destruction of the whites. Their leader, the great Chief Sitting Bull, added the concept of Ghost shirts, which would make the Sioux immune to bullets. But the movement was crippled when he was shot. It ended with the shelling of the Sioux camp in the so-called battle—in fact a massacre, mainly of Sioux women and children—at Wounded Knee Creek.

Some of these cults were passive and others militant; but in terms of their background history, ideology and rituals, they are strikingly similar. They all arose soon after their followers first came into contact with Europeans. The same feelings are expressed in their songs and mythology—a sense of lost freedom and poverty, and a need for tribal regeneration, which is foretold in a prophet's vision. They are not mere resistance cults. They suggest, to different degrees, an urge to adopt the white man's culture, sometimes as a means of expelling him.

But each of them was bound to fail, for two related reasons—the prophet's original misconception and the European's misunderstanding. This pattern always recurs. Awacaipu, Bichiwung, the cargo cult leaders and even Sitting Bull, with his ghost shirts, all misconstrued the nature of something which they learnt from Europeans; hence the failure of their prophecies. But European imperception is often the decisive factor; this is the case with Hallelujah, whose missionary opponents refuse to recognize the psychological force behind it. Although the cult is dying out, this imperception is still significant, as it is bound to leave the Indians with a lasting sense of coercion.

Ironically enough, the spiritual feeling is usually much deeper on the primitive side—though less ironically, perhaps when one considers that the conflict often matches a sense of superiority against one of grief. This is reflected in two songs connected with the Ghost Dance cult. First an American military ballad, describing the 'battle' of Wounded Knee Creek:

'The Red Skins left their Agency, the soldiers left their Post,
  All on the strength of an Indian tale, about Messiah's Ghost,
  Got up by Savage chieftains, to lead their tribes astray,
  But Uncle Sam wouldn't have it so, for he ain't built that way.' (etc.)

273

And then a final Ghost Dance Song, reflecting the despair of the Sioux:

'For the fires grow cold and the dances fail,
And the songs in their echoes die,
And what have we left, but the graves beneath,
And, above, the waiting sky.'

These are much the same emotions as those which gave birth to Hallelujah and other related cults. On which side, one wonders, are the 'savage chieftains'? The question is not irrelevant—the conflict is still going on today.

APPENDIX E

Postscript: Guianese Politics through late 1964

Since the failure of the 1962 constitutional conference, the rifts in Guianese politics have deepened. Subsequent talks between Dr. Jagan and Mr. Burnham failed to produce any mutually agreeable basis for a coalition. In March 1963 the two opposition parties had a further opportunity to challenge the P.P.P.'s position when Dr. Jagan introduced his controversial Labour Relations Bill, designed to enable the Government to decide which unions should be recognized by employers. Both sides had a strong case; although the Bill looked like a threat to genuine trade unionism, Dr. Jagan quite rightly argued that several unions had been used for political ends in recent attempts to bring down the Government by non-parliamentary means. Demonstrations against the Bill developed into a general strike; when the opposition parties joined in, violence returned to the streets of Georgetown. The clashes became dangerously racial, victimizing mainly East Indians. It was over three months before the strike was fully settled. The unions secured a promise that the Bill would not be reintroduced; but, thanks to the import of oil and flour from Cuba, which helped to tide over the crisis, the opposition parties were thwarted in their attempts to bring down Dr. Jagan.

Meanwhile the American Government had come into the open in its attempts to intervene in Guianese affairs. Throughout the strike, the unions had been receiving advice and aid, to the tune of eighty thousand dollars a week, from American sources. At the end of June, Mr. Dean Rusk, in conference with Lord Home and Mr. Duncan Sandys, urged the American view that the constitution should be suspended in favour of a reversion to direct colonial rule.[1] This plea contrasts strangely with the American Government's professed principle of independence for colonial territories; it was apparently based on the assumption that several years' suspension of democratic processes would enable Anglo-

1. *London Times*, June 29th, 1963.

275

American investment to win away Dr. Jagan's following. Although it clearly had its effect, Mr. Sandys was understandably reluctant to discuss it. When the question was raised in the House of Commons by Miss Jennie Lee, he replied—and this was less than three weeks after his conference with Mr. Dean Rusk—'I do not understand what I'm supposed to warn the Americans on.'[1] It is significant, however, that he made no attempt to deny the fact of American pressure on British policy towards Dr. Jagan's Government.

When I met Dr. Jagan in London in September, he described his apprehension at the political and racial tension which is being intensified, as Miss Jennie Lee pointed out, by American policy. He sees it as a factor which has influenced Guianese politics since the suspension of the Constitution in 1953; this, he feels, was largely a part of the wave of American pressure which also resulted in the overthrow of the Arbenz Government in Guatemala in 1954. Since then it has increased, with financial support for the activities of the U.F. and, more recently, of the P.N.C.

When the constitutional conference was reconvened in October, the deadlock continued. In view of this, the three leaders suggested that Mr. Sandys should impose an 'Independence Constitution'. His answer was a plan which delays independence indefinitely and provides for new elections under proportional representation. This was a complete concession to the demands of the U.F.—i.e. to some sixteen per cent of Guiana's most conservative elements. While the P.N.C. also welcomed proportional representation, Mr. Burnham expressed disgust at the delaying of independence. Dr. Jagan described it as the 'dastardly and unprincipled decision' of a British Government 'subservient to American wishes'. Mr. D'Aguiar was naturally delighted, and it is fair to assume that the American Government, for want of a direct suspension, shared his reactions.

It is difficult to discern whether the Sandys decision was 'unprincipled' or merely naïve in its neglect of the available alternatives. Their extent makes it look like an elaborate substitute for the American proposal for a direct removal of the Government. Dr. Jagan made several suggestions —coalition with the P.N.C., backed by an Ombudsman of Commonwealth or U.N. members, or else a constitution modelled on that of Trinidad, whose structure safeguards minority rights and national neutrality. But these possibilities were ignored. Furthermore, proportional representation was imposed without a Guianese referendum; also the Sandys plan—perhaps in view of the possibility of Dr. Jagan's

1. Ibid., July 17th, 1963.

276

winning an election even under the new constitution—offers no guarantee as to the date of independence.

The new plan claims to be an attempt to solve the mounting racial tension of the past few years. This makes it worthwhile analysing, firstly, whether Guianese politics are fundamentally, or only incidentally, racial; and, secondly, whether proportional representation is likely to solve racial problems. Until quite recently, Guiana was remarkable for its lack of race-consciousness. As in Trinidad, the separatism of East Indians and Africans is derived from their historical backgrounds, which have simply diffused them onto different social strata. Rapid economic growth is creating a class structure which has already begun to blur the social distinctions between them. The root of the recent trouble in Guiana lies in the fact that the African population is concentrated in Georgetown, next to the middle class and business interests which are militantly opposed to the P.P.P.'s socialist programme. It is only since they have come into politics, in the form of the U.F., that racial tension has really existed. Trinidad confirms this conclusion; there, although the two main parties tend to represent East Indian and African interests respectively, there is no third force to exploit this, so that racial feeling is rare. The danger of the Guianese situation is that, although the career of the U.F. is likely to be short-lived, racial tension, once created, may perpetuate itself.

This was evident in 1964, when the very prospect of proportional representation helped to usher in an unprecedented state of violence. Early in February the sugar-workers' Guiana Agricultural Workers' Union, unrecognized by the T.U.C. but supported by the P.P.P., went on strike on the sugar estates. Just as the earlier general strike was supported by the opposition, this one was probably encouraged by the P.P.P. as a means of delaying the elections. Violence swept through the country, with bombings, murder and arson commonplace. There was talk of a coalition, but Mr. D'Aguiar refused to co-operate, while Mr. Burnham demanded a degree of power which the P.P.P. would never concede. The pattern of violence was one of reprisal on a strictly racial basis. Dozens of people were murdered, hundreds wounded and thousands evacuated from communities where racialism had never before existed. The Governor declared a state of emergency which only ended several months later, with the arrest of a number of politicians and an amnesty promised in return for the surrender of weapons.

Meanwhile effective government had ceased and the elections were delayed until December. These events were far more than a mere renewal of past crises. They were a point of no return. Racialism has now become a widespread reality. Its development is a pitiful illustration of the impotence of a small country exposed by its economic weakness to cold war exploitations. Guiana's original nationalism, that of 1953, was unacceptable to the British, who quashed it by suspending the government, thereby opening the way for an internal power struggle. This split was intensified in 1961 by the West's refusal of loans and disguised support of the opposition, which now included the U.F. The resulting stalemate reinforced the division of Guiana into two socio-economic blocks which also happened to be racial. When violence developed, this racial pattern soon gave it a racial motivation. Meanwhile three men were struggling for power. Dr. Jagan refused to relinquish it, since, for him, it still represented Guiana's only possible future, while Mr. Burnham and Mr. D'Aguiar both valued their personal interests above the prospect of national unity. This made Guiana a playground for the U.S. State Department and the Communist bloc alike; Cuban-trained saboteurs contributed to the recent violence, but so did the Central Intelligence Agency. Guiana has been all but destroyed by their respective interests.

Elections are now scheduled for December, but the only possible advantage of the new system—the prospect of a forced coalition—has vanished in the recent troubles. Despite the development of a few splinter groups, the stalemate will almost certainly be renewed. The P.P.P. will gain the largest number of seats but lack a working majority, while their opponents have nothing positive in common. The present leaders are so identified with the current rifts in the country that the only hope for the future is a complete change of leadership and the growth of a new, multi-racial party, perhaps under Commonwealth or United Nations trusteeship. Only this, it seems, could now eliminate racialism and the political bias of the rival unions. Historians may then conclude that Dr. Jagan lost an impossible battle, while Mr. Burnham abrogated a political responsibility which Mr. D'Aguiar never possessed. But unless there is some new realignment, Guiana has two alternatives— continuing colonial rule or a racial civil war which could make Cyprus look like a Sunday-school outing.

SELECTED BIBLIOGRAPHY

(Most of the material on British Guiana is scattered and of little but documentary value. I have listed only the publications which are of more general interest)

Bernau, Rev. J. H., *Missionary Labours in British Guiana* (London, 1847)

Brett, Rev. W. H., *The Indian Tribes of Guiana* (London, 1868)

Brown, C. B., *Canoe and Camp Life in British Guiana* (London, 1876)

Butt, Dr. A. J., 'The Birth of a Religion' (*Journal of the Royal Anthropological Institute*, Vol. 90, Part 1, 1960)

Clements, Sir C., *A Constitutional History of British Guiana* (Macmillan, London, 1937)

Evans, C., and Meggars, B. J., *Archaeological Investigations in British Guiana* (Smithsonian Institute, Bureau of American Ethnology, Bulletin No. 177, Washington, 1960)

Gravesande, L. S. van's, *The Rise of British Guiana* (2 vols. Despatches, 1742–72. Hakluyt Society, London, 1911)

Guppy, N., *Wai-Wai* (Murray, London, 1958)

Im Thurn, Sir E. F., *Among the Indians of Guiana* (Kegan Paul, Trench and Co., London, 1883)

Jagan, Dr. C. B., *Bitter Sugar* (Georgetown, undated); *Forbidden Freedom* (Lawrence and Wishart, London, 1954)

Keymis, L., *The Second Voyage to Guiana, 1596* (Reprinted from original edition in *A Selection of the Principal Voyages of the British Nation*, Vol. x, Hakluyt Society, Glasgow, 1903–4)

Naipaul, V. S., *The Middle Passage* (André Deutsch, London, 1962)

Pinckard, Dr. G., *Letters from Guiana, 1796–7* (Daily Chronicle Ltd., Georgetown, 1942)

Raleigh, Sir W., *The Discoverie of the Large and Bewtiful Empyre of Guiana* (Reprinted from 1596 edition, Argonaut Press Ltd., London, 1928)

Rodway, J., *History of British Guiana, 1688–1893* (3 vols. Georgetown, 1891–4)

Roth, W. E., *The Animism and Folklore of the Guiana Indians* (Smithsonian Institute, 30th Annual Report of the Bureau of American Ethnology, 1908–9); *The Arts, Crafts and Customs of the Guiana Indians.* (Smithsonian Institute, 38th Annual Report of the Bureau of American Ethnology, 1916–17)

Schomburgk, Richard, *Travels in British Guiana, 1840–44* (2 vols., translated from the German by W. E. Roth, Daily Chronicle Ltd., Georgetown, 1922)

Smith, R. T., *British Guiana* (Oxford University Press, London, 1962)

Steward, J. H. (Editor), *Handbook of South American Indians* (6 vols., Smithsonian Institute, Bureau of American Ethnology, Bulletin No. 143, 1946–50)

Swan, M., *British Guiana: the Land of Six Peoples* (H.M.S.O., London, 1957); *The Marches of El Dorado* (Jonathan Cape, London, 1958–)

Timehri, Journal of the Royal Agricultural and Commercial Society of British Guiana (Georgetown, 1882–)

Trollope, A., *The West Indies and the Spanish Main* (London, 1867)

Waterton, C., *Wanderings in South America* (Sturgis and Walton, New York, 1909)

Index and Glossary

ABBREVIATIONS

f.	footnote	R.	river
G.	Guianese (Guiana)	T.	tribe
I (s).	Indian (s)	UF	United Force
PNC	People's National Congress	V.	village
PPP	People's Progressive Party		

Burnham, Forbes, leader of PNC, 28, 38, 251, 252, 253, 254, 255, 275, 276, 277. *See also* PNC.

Bushmen of Australia, 237

Butt, Dr. Audrey: research on Hallelujah cult, 73, 129 f.

CAMOUDI (anaconda): rôle in I. mythology. *See* Legends and myths of Is.

Campbell, Stephen, I. member of Legislative Council, 39, 195, 211.

Cane-juice (I. drink brewed from sugar cane). *See* Drinks of Is.

Cannibalism. *See* Carib T.

Cargo cults, 272

Carib T., 18, 44, 45, 56, 57, 58–9, 170, 182, 217, 219–20, 242–3, 258–9, 261

Cash employment of Is.: balata-bleeding, 153 f., 193, 198 and f.; conflicts with I. traditions, 198; exploitation, 64–5, 81, 265; log-cutting, 63–4; need for locally, 221

Cassack (Akawaio term for cassiri). *See* Drinks of Is.

Cassava-bread (staple diet of Is., also known as manioc or yuca): method of processing, etc., 51–2

Cassiri (sweet type of cassava beer). *See* Drinks of Is.

Cassiri-bina (tattoo marks to aid brewing of cassiri). *See* Charms of Is.

Cassou, Mr., Commissioner of Interior, 97, 204, 205–6, 209–10, 213–15, 217–19, 220 f.

Catholic missionaries among Is.: Fr. Banham, S.J., 147–8; conservative influence, 223; policy, 148

Cattle-ranching in Rupununi: effect on Is., 171, 173, 202; history of, 170–1; open ranch system, 165; prevents land reform, 183, 199

Charity, 207, 208–9

Charms used by Is.: against illness, 130; blowing, 125–6; cassiri-bina, 80, 110; for hunting, 123–4, love, 145, revenge, 105

Chinese: character, 39; culture and social stratification, 248; nos., 247 f.; political affiliations, 28

Ciboney Is., 258

Columbus, Christopher: description of Caribs and Arawaks, 258–9 and f.

Constitutional development of G: in 19th C., 245; 1927 Constit., 250; 1947 elections, 250; 1953 Constit., 251 and f., suspension of, 251–2 and f., Robertson Commission on, 253 and f.; 1957 elections, 253; internal self-government, 27, 253; elections of 1961, 254; constit. conference, 1962, 255–6 and f.; prospects of coalition, 256; constit. conference, 1963, 276; Sandys plan for proportional representation, 276

Co-operative societies among Is.: logging C., 65; Moruca Producers' C., 215–16

Corentyne R., 18, 41–5, 230, 241

Corial (I. canoe), 41, 112

Crafts of Is.: basket work—animal figure designs, *see* end-papers; decline of, 55, 233; hammock-making, 54; tibisiri baskets, 54

Cuba: relations with G., 39, 205, 254, 275

DEMERARA, original name of G., 19, 241

Demerara R., 206

Diamonds, 249; D.-rushes, 73, 75, 99; effect on Is., 73; porknockers, 72 f., 75, 142, 159, 161–2

Drinks of Is.: cane-juice, 49; cassiri (cassack, parakari), 52, 76, 98, 107, 120, 151, 161; paiwari, 20, 52, 233, 234–5. *See also* Charms of Is.

Drougher (bearer), 102

Dummett, Jack, 172, 184–8, 220, 238

Dutch Guina (Surinam), 18, 19, 54

Dutch in G., 44 f., 242–5. *See also* Is., Dutch policy towards.

Dutch West India Co., 242

Dyaks, 237

EAST Indians: character, 38, 206, 207; cultural change, 37; culture and social stratification, 247; expansion into interior, 44; family ties, 36; indentured immigration, 246; nos., 247 f.; political affiliations, 27, 253; use of term, 17 f.; villages, 38. *See also* Race relations.

Economic development: of G., 249–50; of Is.—low expenditure on, 269; neglected, 172; requisites for, 200, 238; self-help schemes, 66 f.; training courses,

284

in 19th C. and effects, 264–5; on Wai-Wai, 21; seclusion, 76; suppression of Hallelujah, see Hallelujah cult, of kinship systems and housing methods, 84, of piai-men, 70. See also Anglican Missionaries; Catholic Missionaries; Pilgrim Holiness sect; Seventh Day Adventists; Unevangelized Fields Mission.

Moka-Moka V., 98, 171, 173–84, 188

Moravian Church, 44

Moruca R. District, 19, 210–28

Moruca R. Is. (Spanish Arawaks), 163, 166, 192, 203, 204, 208, 209, 210–28, 230, 238

Music and dances of Is.: decline of, 70, 196, 212; palishara dance, 196; tugoit dance, 108. See also Hallelujah, dances and songs.

Myths of Is. See Legends and myths of Is.

NAIPAUL, V. S., 21 and f.

Names of Is.: acquisition of English names, 123; original names, 123

Nappi development scheme, 172, 184–8

New Amsterdam, 35, 230

North-West District, 204, 207–8

OREALLA V., 18, 19, 44–71, 230–7

Orinduik, 97, 99, 100–3, 140, 142

Orinoco R., 210

Oriyu (water spirit). See Legends and myths of Is.

PAIWARI (bitter type of cassava beer). See Drinks of Is.

Pakaraima Mts., 74, 99, 140, 142, 157–66, 167

Papuans, 237, 272

Parakari (Macusi type of cassiri). See Drinks of Is.

Paramakatoi V., 148, 149–55, 237

Patamona T., 98, 100, 106–31, 134–9, 144–7, 149–55, 156–7, 158, 164

Peberdy Report on I. development, 267 and f., 268

People's National Congress (PNC): alleged American aid, 276; composition, 28; demands at constitutional conference, 1962, 256; formation, 38; in opposition, 253; possibility of coalition, 256, 277. See also Burnham, Forbes.

People's Progressive Party (PPP), 26; composition, 27; demands at constitutional conference, 1962, 256; formation, 251; split in, 38, 253; victory in elections, 1953, 251, 1957, 253, 1961, 27, 254. See also Jagan, Dr. Cheddi.

Philipai V., 82–3, 94–5

Piai-man (I. shaman or witch-doctor): connection with Hallelujah cult, 70; function and methods, 69–70, 234; suppression by missionaries, 70

Pilgrim Holiness sect: at Paramakatoi V., 150–4; at Philipai V., 83; suppression of I. customs, 83, 95, 148, 152, and economic consequences, 152–3

Pinckard, Dr. G., 262–3 and f.

Pirana, 114

Political involvement of Is.: apprehension, 138, 180, 199, 216, 221, 224, 225–6; exploitation, 21, 62; with UF, 39, 62, 66–7, 180–1, 269. See also Campbell, Stephen.

Pomeroon R., 208, 209, 228, 242

Population figures, 247 f. See also Is., total numbers.

Porknockers (gold and diamond seekers). See Diamonds; Gold.

Portuguese: at Charity, 208–9; character, 39; nos., 247 f.; political affiliations, 28; social stratification, 248

Potaro R., 99–100

Primary Education amongst Is.: at Moka-Moka V., 174, Orealla V., 60, Sand Creek V., 201, Santa Rosa Mission, 223; conflicts with I. traditions, 52, and need for special syllabus, 60–1, 175, 269 and f.; I. teachers, 166, 174, 195, 200–1; secularization of schools, 223

Progressive Youth Organization, 222

Proportional Representation: demanded by opposition, 256; granted under Sandys plan, 276–7

QUEBANA V., 217, 219

RACE relations: Africans and East Indians, 23, 38, in politics, 253, 275, 276, 277; assimilation, 247, 248; I. separatism and causes, 181–3, 248–9

Raleigh, Sir Walter, 57 and f., 169, 241

285